THE SONGLINES

ALSO BY BRUCE CHATWIN

In Patagonia
The Viceroy of Ouidah
On the Black Hill

BRUCE CHATWIN

THE SONGLINES

ELISABETH SIFTON BOOKS
VIKING

ELISABETH SIFTON BOOKS · VIKING
Viking Penguin Inc.
40 West 23rd Street,
New York, New York 10010, U.S.A.

First American Edition
Published in 1987

A signed first edition of this book
has been privately printed by The Franklin Library.

LIBRARY OF CONGRESS CATALOGING IN PUBLICATION DATA
Chatwin, Bruce, 1942–
The songlines.
1. Australia—Description and travel—1981–
2. Chatwin, Bruce, 1942–   —Journeys—Australia.
3. Australia—Social life and customs.   4. Australian
aborigines—Social life and customs.   I. Title.
DU105.2.C43   1987   919.4'0463   86-40512
ISBN 0-670-80605-6

Printed in the United States of America by
Arcata Graphics, Fairfield, Pennsylvania
Set in Sabon

THE SONGLINES

I

IN ALICE SPRINGS – a grid of scorching streets where men in long white socks were forever getting in and out of Land Cruisers – I met a Russian who was mapping the sacred sites of the Aboriginals.

His name was Arkady Volchok. He was an Australian citizen. He was thirty-three years old.

His father, Ivan Volchok, was a Cossack from a village near Rostov-on-Don, who, in 1942, was arrested and sent with a trainload of other *Ostarbeiter* to work in a German factory. One night, somewhere in the Ukraine, he jumped from the cattle-car into a field of sunflowers. Soldiers in grey uniforms hunted him up and down the long lines of sunflowers, but he gave them the slip. Somewhere else, lost between murdering armies, he met a girl from Kiev and married her. Together they drifted to a forgetful Adelaide suburb, where he rigged up a vodka still and fathered three sturdy sons.

The youngest of these was Arkady.

Nothing in Arkady's temperament predisposed him to live in the hugger-mugger of Anglo-Saxon suburbia or take a conventional job. He had a flattish face and a gentle smile, and he moved through the bright Australian spaces with the ease of his footloose forbears.

His hair was thick and straight, the colour of straw. His lips had cracked in the heat. He did not have the drawn-in lips of so many white Australians in the Outback; nor did he swallow his words. He rolled his r's in a very Russian way. Only when you came up close did you realise how big his bones were.

He had married, he told me, and had a daughter of six. Yet, preferring solitude to domestic chaos, he no longer lived with his wife. He had few possessions apart from a harpsichord and a shelf of books.

He was a tireless bushwalker. He thought nothing of setting out, with a water-flask and a few bites of food, for a hundred-mile walk along the Ranges. Then he would come home, out of the heat and light, and draw the curtains, and play the music of Buxtehude and Bach on the harpsichord. Their orderly progressions, he said, conformed to the contours of the Central Australian landscape.

Neither of Arkady's parents had ever read a book in English. He delighted them by winning a first-class honours degree, in history and philosophy, at Adelaide University. He made them sad when he went to work as a school-teacher, on an Aboriginal settlement in Walbiri country to the north of Alice Springs.

He liked the Aboriginals. He liked their grit and tenacity, and their artful ways of dealing with the white man. He had learnt, or half-learnt, a couple of their languages and had come away astonished by their intellectual vigour, their feats of memory and their capacity and will to survive. They were not, he insisted, a dying race – although they did need help, now and then, to get the government and mining companies off their backs.

It was during his time as a school-teacher that Arkady learned of the labyrinth of invisible pathways which meander all over Australia and are known to Europeans as 'Dreaming-tracks' or 'Songlines'; to the Aboriginals as the 'Footprints of the Ancestors' or the 'Way of the Law'.

Aboriginal Creation myths tell of the legendary totemic beings who had wandered over the continent in the Dreamtime, singing out the name of everything that crossed their path – birds, animals, plants, rocks, waterholes – and so singing the world into existence.

Arkady was so struck by the beauty of this concept that he began to take notes of everything he saw or heard, not for publication, but to satisfy his own curiosity. At first, the Walbiri Elders mistrusted him, and their answers to his questions were evasive. With time, once he had won their confidence, they invited him to witness their most secret ceremonies and encouraged him to learn their songs.

One year, an anthropologist from Canberra came to study Walbiri systems of land tenure: an envious academic who resented Arkady's friendship with the song-men, pumped him for information and promptly betrayed a secret he had promised to keep. Disgusted by the row that followed, the 'Russian' threw in his job and went abroad.

He saw the Buddhist temples of Java, sat with saddhus on the ghats of Benares, smoked hashish in Kabul and worked on a kibbutz. On the Acropolis in Athens there was a dusting of snow and only one other tourist: a Greek girl from Sydney.

They travelled through Italy, and slept together, and in Paris they agreed to get married.

Having been brought up in a country where there was 'nothing', Arkady had longed all his life to see the monuments of Western civilisation. He was in love. It was springtime. Europe should have been wonderful. It left him, to his disappointment, feeling flat.

Often, in Australia, he had had to defend the Aboriginals from people who dismissed them as drunken and incompetent savages; yet there were times, in the flyblown squalor of a Walbiri camp, when he suspected they might be right and that his vocation to help the blacks was either wilful self-indulgence or a waste of time.

Now, in a Europe of mindless materialism, his 'old men' seemed wiser and more thoughtful than ever. He went to a Qantas office and bought two tickets home. He was married, six weeks later in Sydney, and took his wife to live in Alice Springs.

She said she longed to live in the Centre. She said she loved it when she got there. After a single summer, in a tin-roofed house that heated like a furnace, they began to drift apart.

The Land Rights Act gave Aboriginal 'owners' the title to their country, providing it lay untenanted; and the job Arkady invented for himself was to interpret 'tribal law' into the language of the Law of The Crown.

No one knew better that the 'idyllic' days of hunting and gathering were over – if, indeed, they were ever that idyllic. What could be done for Aboriginals was to preserve their most essential liberty: the liberty to remain poor, or, as he phrased it more tactfully, the space in which to be poor if they wished to be poor.

Now that he lived alone he liked to spend most of his time 'out bush'. When he did come to town, he worked from a disused newspaper shop-floor where rolls of old newsprint still

(3)

clogged the presses and his sequences of aerial photos had spread, like a game of dominoes, over the shabby white walls.

One sequence showed a three-hundred-mile strip of country running roughly due north. This was the suggested route of a new Alice to Darwin railway.

The line, he told me, was going to be the last long stretch of track to be laid in Australia; and its chief engineer, a railway-man of the old school, had announced that it must also be the best.

The engineer was close to retiring age and concerned for his posthumous reputation. He was especially concerned to avoid the kind of rumpus that broke out whenever a mining company moved its machinery into Aboriginal land. So, promising not to destroy a single one of their sacred sites, he had asked their representatives to supply him with a survey.

Arkady's job was to identify the 'traditional landowners'; to drive them over their old hunting grounds, even if these now belonged to a cattle company; and to get them to reveal which rock or soak or ghost-gum was the work of a Dreamtime hero.

He had already mapped the 150-mile stretch from Alice to Middle Bore Station. He had a hundred and fifty to go.

'I warned the engineer he was being a bit rash,' he said. 'But that's the way he wanted it.'

'Why rash?' I asked.

'Well, if you look at it *their* way,' he grinned, 'the whole of bloody Australia's a sacred site.'

'Explain,' I said.

He was on the point of explaining when an Aboriginal girl came in with a stack of papers. She was a secretary, a pliant brown girl in a brown knitted dress. She smiled and said, 'Hi, Ark!' but her smile fell away at the sight of a stranger.

Arkady lowered his voice. He had warned me earlier how Aboriginals hate to hear white men discussing their 'business'.

'This is a Pom,' he said to the secretary. 'A Pom by the name of Bruce.'

The girl giggled, diffidently, dumped the papers on the desk, and dashed for the door.

'Let's go and get a coffee,' he said.

So we went to a coffee-shop on Todd Street.

2

IN MY CHILDHOOD I never heard the word 'Australia' without calling to mind the fumes of the eucalyptus inhaler and an incessant red country populated by sheep.

My father loved to tell, and we to hear, the story of the Australian sheep-millionaire who strolled into a Rolls-Royce showroom in London; scorned all the smaller models; chose an enormous limousine with a plate-glass panel between the chauffeur and passengers, and added, cockily, as he counted out the cash, 'That'll stop the sheep from breathing down my neck.'

I also knew, from my great-aunt Ruth, that Australia was the country of the Upside-downers. A hole, bored straight through the earth from England, would burst out under their feet.

'Why don't they fall off?' I asked.

'Gravity,' she whispered.

She had in her library a book about the continent, and I would gaze in wonder at pictures of the koala and kookaburra, the platypus and Tasmanian bush-devil, Old Man Kangaroo and Yellow Dog Dingo, and Sydney Harbour Bridge.

But the picture I liked best showed an Aboriginal family on the move. They were lean, angular people and they went about naked. Their skin was very black, not the glitterblack of negroes but matt black, as if the sun had sucked away all possibility of reflection. The man had a long forked beard and carried a spear or two, and a spear-thrower. The woman carried a dilly-bag and a baby at her breast. A small boy strolled beside her – I identified myself with him.

I remember the fantastic homelessness of my first five years. My father was in the Navy, at sea. My mother and I would shuttle back and forth, on the railways of wartime England, on visits to family and friends.

All the frenzied agitation of the times communicated itself to me: the hiss of steam on a fogbound station; the double clu-unk of carriage doors closing; the drone of aircraft, the searchlights, the sirens; the sound of a mouth-organ along a platform of sleeping soldiers.

Home, if we had one, was a solid black suitcase called the Rev-Robe, in which there was a corner for my clothes and my Mickey Mouse gas-mask. I knew that, once the bombs began to fall, I could curl up inside the Rev-Robe, and be safe.

Sometimes, I would stay for months with my two great-aunts, in their terrace house behind the church in Stratford-on-Avon. They were old maids.

Aunt Katie was a painter and had travelled. In Paris she had been to a very louche party at the studio of Mr Kees van Dongen. On Capri she had seen the bowler hat of a Mr Ulyanov that used to bob along the Piccola Marina.

Aunt Ruth had travelled only once in her life, to Flanders, to lay a wreath on a loved one's grave. She had a simple, trusting nature. Her cheeks were pale rose-pink and she could blush as sweetly and innocently as a young girl. She was very deaf, and I would have to yell into her deaf-aid, which looked like a portable radio. At her bedside she kept a photograph of her favourite nephew, my father, gazing calmly from under the patent peak of his naval officer's cap.

The men on my father's side of the family were either solid and sedentary citizens—lawyers, architects, antiquaries—or horizon-struck wanderers who had scattered their bones in every corner of the earth: Cousin Charlie in Patagonia; Uncle Victor in a Yukon gold camp; Uncle Robert in an oriental port; Uncle Desmond, of the long fair hair, who vanished without trace in Paris; Uncle Walter who died, chanting the suras of the Glorious Koran, in a hospital for holy men in Cairo.

Sometimes, I overheard my aunts discussing these blighted destinies; and Aunt Ruth would hug me, as if to forestall my following in their footsteps. Yet, from the way she lingered over such words as 'Xanadu' or 'Samarkand' or the 'wine-dark sea', I think she also felt the trouble of the 'wanderer in her soul'.

The house was full of cumbersome furniture inherited from the days of lofty ceilings and servants. In the drawing-room, there were William Morris curtains, a piano, a cabinet of porcelain and a canvas of cockle-pickers by Aunt Katie's friend A. E. Russell.

My own most treasured possession, at the time, was the conch shell called Mona, which my father had brought from the West Indies. I would ram my face against her sheeny pink vulva and listen to the sound of the surf.

One day, after Aunt Katie had shown me a print of Botticelli's *Birth of Venus*, I prayed and prayed that a beautiful blonde young lady would suddenly spew forth from Mona.

Aunt Ruth never scolded me except once, one evening in May 1944, when I pissed in the bathwater. I must be one of the last children anywhere to be menaced by the spectre of Bonaparte. 'If you ever do that again,' she cried, 'Boney will get you.'

I knew what Boney looked like from his porcelain statuette in the cabinet: black boots, white breeches, gilded buttons and a black bicorn hat. But the drawing Aunt Ruth drew for me – a version of one drawn for her, as a child, by her father's friend Lawrence Alma-Tadema – showed the furry bicorn only on a pair of spindly legs.

That night, and for weeks to come, I dreamed of meeting Boney on the pavement outside the vicarage. His two halves would open like a bivalve. Inside, there were rows of black fangs and a mass of wiry blue-black hair – into which I fell, and woke up screaming.

On Fridays, Aunt Ruth and I would walk to the parish church to make it ready for Sunday service. She would polish the brasses, sweep the choir stalls, replace the frontal and arrange fresh flowers on the altar – while I clambered into the pulpit or held imaginary conversations with Mr Shakespeare.

Mr Shakespeare would peer from his funerary monument on the north side of the chancel. He was a bald man, with upturned moustaches. His left hand rested on a scroll of paper, and his right hand held a quill.

I appointed myself the guardian and guide of his tomb, and charged G.I.s threepence a tour. The first lines of verse I learned by heart were the four lines engraved on his slab:

> Good frend, for Jesus sake, forbeare
> To digge the dust encloased here
> Bleste be ye man yt spares thes stones
> And curst be he yt moves my bones.

Long afterwards, in Hungary, where I had gone to study the archaeology of nomads, I had the luck to witness the opening of a Hunnish 'princess's' grave. The girl lay on her back, on a bed of black soil, her brittle bones covered with a shower of gold plaques, while across her breast, with wings outspread, lay the skeleton of a golden eagle.

One of the excavators called to some peasant women who were haymaking in the field nearby. They dropped their rakes and clustered round the gravemouth, crossing themselves fumble-handedly, as if to say, 'Leave her. Leave her with her lover. Leave her alone with Zeus.'

'Curst be he . . . ' I seemed to hear Mr Shakespeare calling, and for the first time began to wonder if archaeology itself were not cursed.

Whenever the afternoon was fine in Stratford, Aunt Ruth and I – with her cocker-spaniel, Amber, straining at his leash – would go on what she said was Mr Shakespeare's favourite walk. We would set off from College Street, past the grain silo, past the foaming mill-race, across the Avon by footbridge, and follow the path to Weir Brake.

This was a hazel wood on a slope that tumbled into the river. In springtime, primroses and bluebells flowered there. In summer it was a tangle of nettles, brambles and purple loosestrife, with the muddy water eddying below.

My aunt assured me this was the spot where Mr Shakespeare came to 'tryst' with a young lady. It was the very bank whereon the wild thyme blew. But she never explained what a tryst was, and, no matter how hard I searched, there were neither thyme nor oxlips, although I did find a few nodding violets.

Much later, when I *had* read Mr Shakespeare's plays and *did* know what a tryst was, it struck me that Weir Brake was far too muddy and prickly for Titania and Bottom to settle on, but an excellent spot for Ophelia to take the plunge.

Aunt Ruth loved reading Shakespeare aloud and, on days when the grass was dry, I would dangle my legs over the riverbank and listen to her reciting, 'If music be the food of love . . . ,' 'The quality of mercy is not strained . . . ,' or 'Full fathom five thy father lies.'

'Full fathom five . . . ' upset me terribly because my father was still at sea. I had another recurring dream: that his ship had sunk; that I grew gills and a fishy tail, swam down to join him on the ocean floor, and saw the pearls that had been his bright blue eyes.

A year or two later, as a change from Mr Shakespeare, my aunt would bring an anthology of verse especially chosen for travellers, called *The Open Road*. It had a green buckram binding and a flight of gilded swallows on the cover.

I loved watching swallows. When they arrived in spring, I knew my lungs would soon be free of green phlegm. In autumn, when they sat chattering on the telegraph wires, I could almost count the days until the eucalyptus inhaler.

Inside *The Open Road* there were black and white end-papers in the style of Aubrey Beardsley which showed a bright path twisting through pine woods. One by one, we went through every poem in the book.

We arose and went to Innisfree. We saw the caverns measureless to man. We wandered lonely as a cloud. We tasted all the summer's pride, wept for Lycidas, stood in tears among the alien corn, and listened to the strident, beckoning music of Walt Whitman:

> O Public Road . . .
> You express me better than I can express myself
> You shall be more to me than my poem.

One day, Aunt Ruth told me our surname had once been 'Chettewynde', which meant 'the winding path' in Anglo-Saxon; and the suggestion took root in my head that poetry, my own name and the road were, all three, mysteriously connected.

As for bedtime stories, my favourite was the tale of the coyote pup in Ernest Thompson Seton's *Lives of the Hunted*.

Coyotito was the runt of a litter whose mother had been shot by the cowboy, Wolver Jake. Her brothers and sisters had been knocked on the head and her own life spared to give sport to Jake's bull-terrier and greyhounds. Her picture, in chains, showed the saddest little dog-person I ever saw. Yet Coyotito grew up smart and, one morning, after shamming dead, she bolted for the wild: there to teach a new generation of coyotes the art of avoiding men.

I cannot now piece together the train of associations that led me to connect Coyotito's bid for freedom with the Australian Aboriginals' 'Walkabout'. Nor, for that matter, where I first heard the expression 'Walkabout'. Yet somehow I picked up an image of those 'tame' Blackfellows who, one day, would be working happily on a cattle-station: the next, without a word of warning and *for no good reason*, would up sticks and vanish into the blue.

They would step from their work-clothes, and leave: for weeks and months and even years, trekking half-way across the continent if only to meet a man, then trekking back as if nothing had happened.

I tried to picture their employer's face the moment he found them gone.

He would be a Scot perhaps: a big man with blotchy skin and a mouthful of obscenities. I imagined him breakfasting on steak and eggs – in the days of food-rationing, we knew that *all* Australians ate a pound of steak for breakfast. Then he would march into the blinding sunlight – all Australian sunlight was blinding – and shout for his 'boys'.

Nothing.

He would shout again. Not a sound but the mocking laugh of a kookaburra. He would scan the horizon. Nothing but gum trees. He would stalk through the cattle-yards. Nothing there either. Then, outside their shacks, he'd find their shirts and hats and boots sticking up through their trousers . . .

3

ARKADY ORDERED a couple of cappuccinos in the coffee-shop. We took them to a table by the window and he began to talk.

I was dazzled by the speed of his mind, although at times I felt he sounded like a man on a public platform, and that much of what he said had been said before.

The Aboriginals had an earthbound philosophy. The earth gave life to a man; gave him his food, language and intelligence; and the earth took him back when he died. A man's 'own country', even an empty stretch of spinifex, was itself a sacred ikon that must remain unscarred.

'Unscarred, you mean, by roads or mines or railways?'

'To wound the earth', he answered earnestly, 'is to wound yourself, and if others wound the earth, they are wounding you. The land should be left untouched: as it was in the Dreamtime when the Ancestors sang the world into existence.'

'Rilke', I said, 'had a similar intuition. He also said song was existence.'

'I know,' said Arkady, resting his chin on his hands. '"Third Sonnet to Orpheus."'

The Aboriginals, he went on, were a people who trod lightly over the earth; and the less they took from the earth, the less they had to give in return. They had never understood why the missionaries forbade their innocent sacrifices. They slaughtered no victims, animal or human. Instead, when they wished to thank the earth for its gifts, they would simply slit a vein in their forearms and let their own blood spatter the ground.

'Not a heavy price to pay,' he said. 'The wars of the twentieth century are the price for having taken too much.'

'I see,' I nodded doubtfully, 'but could we get back to the Songlines?'

'We could.'

My reason for coming to Australia was to try to learn for myself, and not from other men's books, what a Songline was – and how it worked. Obviously, I was not going to get to the heart of the matter, nor would I want to. I had asked a friend in Adelaide if she knew of an expert. She gave me Arkady's phone number.

'Do you mind if I use my notebook?' I asked.

'Go ahead.'

I pulled from my pocket a black, oilcloth-covered notebook, its pages held in place with an elastic band.

'Nice notebook,' he said.

'I used to get them in Paris,' I said. 'But now they don't make them any more.'

'Paris?' he repeated, raising an eyebrow as if he'd never heard anything so pretentious.

Then he winked and went on talking.

To get to grips with the concept of the Dreamtime, he said, you had to understand it as an Aboriginal equivalent of the first two chapters of Genesis – with one significant difference.

In Genesis, God first created the 'living things' and then fashioned Father Adam from clay. Here in Australia, the Ancestors created themselves from clay, hundreds and thousands of them, one for each totemic species.

'So when an Aboriginal tells you, "I have a Wallaby Dreaming," he means, "My totem is Wallaby. I am a member of the Wallaby Clan."'

'So a Dreaming is a clan emblem? A badge to distinguish "us" from "them"? "Our country" from "their country"?'

'Much more than that,' he said.

Every Wallaby Man believed he was descended from a universal Wallaby Father, who was the ancestor of all other Wallaby Men and of all living wallabies. Wallabies, therefore, were his brothers. To kill one for food was both fratricide and cannibalism.

'Yet,' I persisted, 'the man was no more wallaby than the British are lions, the Russians bears, or the Americans bald eagles?'

'Any species', he said 'can be a Dreaming. A virus can be a Dreaming. You can have a chickenpox Dreaming, a rain Dreaming, a desert-orange Dreaming, a lice Dreaming. In the Kimberleys they've now got a money Dreaming.'

'And the Welsh have leeks, the Scots thistles and Daphne was changed into a laurel.'

'Same old story,' he said.

He went on to explain how each totemic ancestor, while travelling through the country, was thought to have scattered a trail of words and musical notes along the line of his footprints, and how these Dreaming-tracks lay over the land as 'ways' of communication between the most far-flung tribes.

'A song', he said, 'was both map and direction-finder. Providing you knew the song, you could always find your way across country.'

'And would a man on "Walkabout" always be travelling down one of the Songlines?'

'In the old days, yes,' he agreed. 'Nowadays, they go by train or car.'

'Suppose the man strayed from his Songline?'

'He was trespassing. He might get speared for it.'

'But as long as he stuck to the track, he'd always find people who shared his Dreaming? Who were, in fact, his brothers?'

'Yes.'

'From whom he could expect hospitality?'

'And vice versa.'

'So song is a kind of passport and meal-ticket?'

'Again, it's more complicated.'

In theory, at least, the whole of Australia could be read as a musical score. There was hardly a rock or creek in the country that could not or had not been sung. One should perhaps visualise the Songlines as a spaghetti of Iliads and Odysseys, writhing this way and that, in which every 'episode' was readable in terms of geology.

'By episode', I asked, 'you mean "sacred site"?'

'I do.'

'The kind of site you're surveying for the railway?'

'Put it this way,' he said. 'Anywhere in the bush you can point to some feature of the landscape and ask the Aboriginal with you, "What's the story there?" or "Who's that?" The chances are he'll answer "Kangaroo" or "Budgerigar" or "Jew Lizard", depending on which Ancestor walked that way.'

'And the distance between two such sites can be measured as a stretch of song?'

(13)

'That', said Arkady, 'is the cause of all my troubles with the railway people.'

It was one thing to persuade a surveyor that a heap of boulders were the eggs of the Rainbow Snake, or a lump of reddish sandstone was the liver of a speared kangaroo. It was something else to convince him that a featureless stretch of gravel was the musical equivalent of Beethoven's Opus 111.

By singing the world into existence, he said, the Ancestors had been poets in the original sense of *poesis*, meaning 'creation'. No Aboriginal could conceive that the created world was in any way imperfect. His religious life had a single aim: to keep the land the way it was and should be. The man who went 'Walkabout' was making a ritual journey. He trod in the footprints of his Ancestor. He sang the Ancestor's stanzas without changing a word or note – and so recreated the Creation.

'Sometimes,' said Arkady, 'I'll be driving my "old men" through the desert, and we'll come to a ridge of sandhills, and suddenly they'll all start singing. "What are you mob singing?" I'll ask, and they'll say, "Singing up the country, boss. Makes the country come up quicker."'

Aboriginals could not believe the country existed until they could see and sing it – just as, in the Dreamtime, the country had not existed until the Ancestors sang it.

'So the land', I said, 'must first exist as a concept in the mind? Then it must be sung? Only then can it be said to exist?'

'True.'

'In other words, "to exist" is "to be perceived"?'

'Yes.'

'Sounds suspiciously like Bishop Berkeley's Refutation of Matter.'

'Or Pure Mind Buddhism,' said Arkady, 'which also sees the world as an illusion.'

'Then I suppose these three hundred miles of steel, slicing through innumerable songs, are bound to upset your "old men's" mental balance?'

'Yes and no,' he said. 'They're very tough, emotionally, and very pragmatic. Besides, they've seen far worse than a railway.'

Aboriginals believed that all the 'living things' had been made in secret beneath the earth's crust, as well as all the white man's gear – his aeroplanes, his guns, his Toyota Land Cruisers – and every invention that will ever be invented; slumbering below the surface, waiting their turn to be called.

'Perhaps,' I suggested, 'they could sing the railway back into the created world of God?'

'You bet,' said Arkady.

4

IT WAS AFTER FIVE. The evening light was raking down the street and through the window we could see a party of black boys, in chequered shirts and cowboy hats, walking jerkily under the poincianas in the direction of the pub.

The waitress was clearing up the leftovers. Arkady asked for more coffee but already she had turned the machine off. He looked at his empty cup, and frowned.

Then he looked up and asked, abruptly, 'What's your interest in all this? What do you want here?'

'I came here to test an idea,' I said.

'A big idea?'

'Probably a very obvious idea. But one I have to get out of my system.'

'And?'

His sudden shift of mood made me nervous. I began to explain how I had once tried, unsuccessfully, to write a book about nomads.

'Pastoral nomads?'

'No,' I said. 'Nomads. "Nomos" is Greek for "pasture". A nomad moves from pasture to pasture. A pastoral nomad is a pleonasm.'

'Point taken,' said Arkady. 'Go on. Why nomads?'

When I was in my twenties, I said, I had a job as an 'expert' on modern painting with a well-known firm of art auctioneers. We had sale-rooms in London and New York. I was one of the bright boys. People said I had a great career, if only I would play my cards right. One morning, I woke up blind.

During the course of the day, the sight returned to the left eye, but the right one stayed sluggish and clouded. The eye specialist who examined me said there was nothing wrong organically, and diagnosed the nature of the trouble.

'You've been looking too closely at pictures,' he said. 'Why don't you swap them for some long horizons?'

'Why not?' I said.

'Where would you like to go?'

'Africa.'

The chairman of the company said he was sure there was something the matter with my eyes, yet couldn't think why I had to go to Africa.

I went to Africa, to the Sudan. My eyes had recovered by the time I reached the airport.

I sailed down the Dongola Reach in a trading felucca. I went to the 'Ethiopians', which was a euphemism for brothel. I had a narrow escape from a rabid dog. At an understaffed clinic, I acted the role of anaesthetist for a Caesarean birth. I next joined up with a geologist who was surveying for minerals in the Red Sea Hills.

This was nomad country – the nomads being the Beja: Kipling's 'fuzzy-wuzzies', who didn't give a damn: for the Pharaohs of Egypt or the British cavalry at Omdurman.

The men were tall and lean, and wore sand-coloured cottons folded in an X across the chest. With shields of elephant hide and 'Crusader' swords dangling from their belts, they would come into the villages to trade their meat for grain. They looked down on the villagers as though they were some other animal.

In the early light of dawn, as the vultures flexed their wings along the rooftops, the geologist and I would watch the men at their daily grooming.

They anointed each other's hair with scented goat's grease and then teased it out in corkscrew curls, making a buttery parasol which, instead of a turban, prevented their brains from going soft. By evening, when the grease had melted, the curls bounced back to form a solid pillow.

Our camel-man was a joker called Mahmoud, whose mop of hair was even wider than the others. He began by stealing the geological hammer. Then he left his knife for us to steal. Then, with hoots of laughter, we swapped them back and, in this way, we became great friends.

When the geologist went back to Khartoum, Mahmoud took me off into the desert to look for rock-paintings.

(17)

The country to the east of Derudeb was bleached and sere, and there were long grey cliffs and dom palms growing in the wadis. The plains were spotted with flat-topped acacias, leafless at this season, with long white thorns like icicles and a dusting of yellow flowers. At night, lying awake under the stars, the cities of the West seemed sad and alien – and the pretensions of the 'art world' idiotic. Yet here I had a sense of homecoming.

Mahmoud instructed me in the art of reading footprints in the sand: gazelles, jackals, foxes, women. We tracked and sighted a herd of wild asses. One night, we heard the cough of a leopard close by. One morning, he lopped off the head of a puff-adder which had curled up under my sleeping-bag and presented me with its body on the tip of his sword blade. I never felt safer with anyone or, at the same time, more inadequate.

We had three camels, two for riding and one for waterskins, yet usually we preferred to walk. He went barefoot; I was in boots. I never saw anything like the lightness of his step and, as he walked, he sang: a song, usually, about a girl from the Wadi Hammamat who was lovely as a green parakeet. The camels were his only property. He had no flocks and wanted none. He was immune to everything we would call 'progress'.

We found our rock-paintings: red ochre pin men scrawled on the overhang of a rock. Nearby there was a long flat boulder with a cleft up one end and its surface pocked with cup-marks. This, said Mahmoud, was the Dragon with its head cut off by Ali.

He asked me, with a wicked grin, whether I was a Believer. In two weeks I never saw him pray.

Later, when I went back to England, I found a photo of a 'fuzzy-wuzzy' carved in relief on an Egyptian tomb of the Twelfth Dynasty at Beni Hassan: a pitiful, emaciated figure, like the pictures of victims in the Sahel drought, and recognisably the same as Mahmoud.

The Pharaohs had vanished: Mahmoud and his people had lasted. I felt I had to know the secret of their timeless and irreverent vitality.

I quit my job in the 'art world' and went back to the dry places: alone, travelling light. The names of the tribes I travelled among are unimportant: Rguibat, Quashgai, Taimanni, Turkomen, Bororo, Tuareg – people whose journeys, unlike my own, had neither beginning nor end.

I slept in black tents, blue tents, skin tents, yurts of felt and windbreaks of thorns. One night, caught in a sandstorm in the Western Sahara, I understood Muhammed's dictum, 'A journey is a fragment of Hell.'

The more I read, the more convinced I became that nomads had been the crankhandle of history, if for no other reason than that the great monotheisms had, all of them, surfaced from the pastoral milieu . . .

Arkady was looking out of the window.

5

A BATTERED RED TRUCK had drawn up on the sidewalk and parked. Five black women sat huddled in the back, among a heap of bundles and jerry cans. Their frocks and headscarves were covered with dust. The driver was a hefty fellow with a beer stomach and a greasy felt hat rammed down over a tangle of hair. He leaned from the door of the cab and started shouting at the passengers. Then a gangly old man got out and pointed to an object stuck in among the bundles.

One of the women handed him a tubular thing wrapped in clear plastic. The old man took it and, as he turned round, Arkady recognised him.

'It's my old friend Stan,' he said. 'From Popanji.'

We went out on to the street and Arkady hugged Old Stan, and Stan looked anxious that either he or the thing in plastic would get crushed, and when Arkady unhugged him he really looked relieved.

I stood in the doorway, watching.

The old man had clouded red eyes and a dirty yellow shirt, and his beard and hairy chest resembled smoke.

'So what you got there, Stan?' asked Arkady.

'Painting,' Stan said, smiling sheepishly.

'What you going to do with him?'

'Sell him.'

Stan was a Pintupi elder. The hefty fellow was Stan's son, Albert. The family had driven into town to sell one of Stan's paintings to Mrs Lacey, the owner of the Desert Bookstore and Art Gallery.

'Come on,' Arkady jerked his thumb at the package. 'Let's have a see!'

But Old Stan turned his mouth down at the corners, tightened his fingers and mumbled, 'Have to show him first to Mrs Lacey.'

The coffee-shop was closing. The girl had piled the chairs on the tables and was vacuuming the carpet. We paid the bill and walked out. Albert leaned against the truck and talked to the ladies. We walked along the sidewalk to the bookstore.

The Pintupi were the last 'wild tribe' to be brought in out of the Western Desert and introduced to white civilisation. Until the late 1950s, they had continued to hunt and forage, naked in the sandhills, as they had hunted for at least ten thousand years.

They were a carefree and open-minded people, not given to the harsher initiation rites of more sedentary tribes. The men hunted kangaroo and emu. The women gathered seeds and roots and edible grubs. In winter, they sheltered behind windbreaks of spinifex; and even in the searing heat they seldom went without water. They valued a pair of strong legs above everything, and they were always laughing. The few whites who travelled among them were amazed to find their babies fat and healthy.

The government, however, took the view that Men of the Stone Age must be saved – for Christ, if need be. Besides, the Western Desert was needed for mining operations, possibly for nuclear tests. An order went out to round up the Pintupi in army trucks, and settle them on government stations. Many were sent to Popanji, a settlement to the west of Alice Springs, where they died of epidemics, squabbled with the men of other tribes, took to the bottle, and knifed each other.

Even in captivity, Pintupi mothers, like good mothers every-where, tell stories to their children about the origin of animals: *How the Echidna got its spines . . . Why the Emu cannot fly . . . Why the Crow is glossy black . . .* And as Kipling illustrated the *Just So Stories* with his own line drawings, so the Aboriginal mother makes drawings in the sand to illustrate the wanderings of the Dreamtime heroes.

She tells her tale in a patter of staccato bursts and, at the same time, traces the Ancestor's 'footprints' by running her first and second fingers, one after the other, in a double dotted line along the ground. She erases each scene with the palm of her hand and, finally, makes a circle with a line passing through it – something like a capital Q.

This marks the spot where the Ancestor, exhausted by the labours of Creation, has gone 'back in'.

The sand drawings done for children are but sketches or 'open versions' of *real* drawings representing the *real* Ancestors, which are only done at secret ceremonies and must only be seen by initiates. All the same, it is through the 'sketches' that the young learn to orient themselves to their land, its mythology and resources.

Some years ago, when the violence and drunkenness threatened to get out of hand, a white adviser hit on the idea of supplying the Pintupi with artists' materials and getting them to transfer their Dreamings on to canvas.

The result was an instant, Australian school of abstract painting.

Old Stan Tjakamarra had been painting for eight years. Whenever he finished a composition, he would bring it to the Desert Bookstore and Mrs Lacey would deduct the cost of his materials and pay him a lump sum in cash.

6

I LIKED ENID LACEY. I had already spent a couple of hours in the Bookstore. She certainly knew how to sell books. She had read almost every book about Central Australia and tried to stock every title in print. In the room which served as an art gallery, she had two easy chairs for customers. 'Read as much as you like,' she'd say. 'No obligation!' – knowing damn well, of course, that once you sat in that chair, you couldn't go away without buying.

She was an Old Territorian in her late sixties. Her nose and chin were excessively pointed: her hair was auburn, from the bottle. She wore two pairs of spectacles on chains and a pair of opal bracelets around her sun-withered wrists. 'Opals', she said to me, 'have brought *me* nothing but luck.'

Her father had been manager of a cattle station near Tennant Creek. She had lived with Aboriginals all her life. She would stand for no nonsense, and secretly adored them.

She had known all the older generation of Australian anthropologists and didn't think much of the new ones: the 'jargon-mongers', as she called them. The truth was that, though she tried to keep abreast of the latest theories, though she battled with the books of Lévi-Strauss, she never made much headway. For all that, when Aboriginal affairs were up for discussion, she would assume her best pontifical manner, changing pronouns from 'I' to 'We', not the royal 'We' but 'We' meaning the 'body of scientific opinion'.

She had been among the first to see the merit of Pintupi painting.

Being a shrewd businesswoman, she knew when to give credit to an artist, when to withhold it and to refuse payment altogether if the artist seemed set on a blinder. So when if one of her 'boys' turned up, doddery on his feet, at closing time – which, at the Frazer Arms, was opening time – she'd click her tongue and say, 'Dearie me! I can't find the key to the cash-box. You'll have to come back in the morning.' And when, next morning, the artist came back, grateful not to have drunk away his earnings, she'd waggle her finger grimly, and say, 'You're going home? Now? Aren't you?' 'Yes, mam!' he'd say, and she'd add a little extra for the wife and kids.

Mrs Lacey paid far less for paintings than galleries in Sydney or Melbourne, but then she charged far less for paintings and the paintings always sold.

Sometimes, a white welfare worker would accuse her of 'ripping off' the artists: but money from Sydney or Melbourne had a way of getting siphoned off into Aboriginal co-operatives, whereas Mrs Lacey paid cash, on the nail. Her 'boys' knew a deal when they saw one and kept coming back to the Bookstore.

We followed Stan inside.

'You're late, silly!' Mrs Lacey adjusted her spectacles.

He was edging towards her desk, between two customers and the bookshelf.

'I said to come Tuesday,' she said. 'I had the man in from Adelaide yesterday. Now we'll have to wait another month.'

The customers were a couple of American tourists, who were deciding which of two colour-plate books to buy. The man had a tanned and freckled face and wore blue Bermudas and a yellow sports shirt. The woman was blonde, nice-looking but a little drawn, and dressed in a red batik smock printed with Aboriginal motifs. The books were *Australian Dreaming* and *Tales of the Dreamtime.*

Old Stan laid the package on Mrs Lacey's desk. His head swayed to and fro as he muttered some excuse. His musty smell filled the room.

'Idiot!' Mrs Lacey raised the pitch of her voice. 'I've told you a thousand times. The man from Adelaide doesn't want Gideon's paintings. He wants yours.'

Arkady and I kept our distance, at the back, by the shelves of Aboriginal studies. The Americans had perked up, and were listening.

'I know there's no accounting for taste,' Mrs Lacey continued.

'He says you're the best painter at Popanji. He's a big collector. He should know.'

'Is that so?' asked the American man.

'It is,' said Mrs Lacey. 'I can sell anything Mr Tjakamarra sets his hand to.'

'Could we see?' asked the American woman. 'Please?'

'I couldn't say,' Mrs Lacey replied. 'You'll have to ask the artist.'

'Could we?'

'*Can* they?'

Stan trembled, hunched his shoulders, and covered his face with his hands.

'You can,' said Mrs Lacey, smiling sweetly and snipping at the plastic with her scissors.

Stan withdrew the fingers from his face and, taking hold of one edge of the canvas, helped Mrs Lacey unroll it.

The painting was about four foot by three and had a background of pointillist dots in varying shades of ochre. In the centre there was a big blue circle with several smaller circles scattered around it. Each circle had a scarlet rim around the perimeter and, connecting them, was a maze of wiggly, flamingo-pink lines that looked a bit like intestines.

Mrs Lacey switched to her second pair of glasses and said, 'What you got here, Stan?'

'Honey-ant,' he whispered in a hoarse voice.

'The honey-ant', she turned to the Americans, 'is one of the totems at Popanji. This painting's a honey-ant Dreaming.'

'I think it's beautiful,' said the American woman, thoughtfully.

'Like it's an ordinary ant?' asked the American man. 'Like a termite ant?'

'No, no,' said Mrs Lacey. 'A honey-ant's something very special. Honey-ants feed on mulga sap. Mulga, that's a tree we have here in the desert. The ants grow honey-sacks on their rear ends. They look like clear plastic bubbles.'

'Is that so?' the man said.

'I've eaten them,' said Mrs Lacey. 'Delicious!'

'Yes,' sighed the American woman. She had fixed her gaze on the painting. 'In its own way, it is truly beautiful!'

'But I can't see any ants in this painting,' the man said. 'You mean it's like . . . like it's a painting of an ant's nest? Like those pink tubes are passages?'

'No,' Mrs Lacey looked a little discouraged. 'The painting shows the journey of the Honey-ant Ancestor.'

'Like it's a route-map?' he grinned. 'Yeah, I thought it looked like a route-map.'

'Exactly,' said Mrs Lacey.

The American wife, meanwhile, was opening and closing her eyes to see what impression the painting would make on her when, finally, she kept them open.

'Beautiful,' she repeated.

'Now, sir!' the man addressed himself to Stan. 'Do you eat these honey-ants yourself?'

Stan nodded.

'No! No!' the wife shrilled. 'I told you this morning. You do *not* eat your own totem! You could be killed for eating your Ancestor!'

'Dearest, this gentleman says he does eat honey-ants. Is that correct, sir?'

Stan continued to nod.

'I'm confused,' said the woman in an exasperated tone. 'You mean that Honey-ant is not your Dreaming?'

Stan shook his head.

'Then what *is* your Dreaming?'

The old man quivered like a schoolboy forced to betray a secret, and managed to wheeze the word 'Emu'.

'Oh, I am *so* confused,' the woman bit her lip in disappointment.

She liked this soft-mouthed old man in his yellow shirt. She liked to think of the honey-ants dreaming their way across the desert with the bright sun shining on their honey-sacks. She had loved the painting. She wanted to own it, to have him sign it, and now she'd have to think again.

'Do you think', she mouthed her words slowly and carefully, 'that if we deposited the money with Mrs – ?'

'Lacey,' said Mrs Lacey.

' . . . that you could paint us an Emu Dreaming and send it . . . have Mrs Lacey send it to us in the United States?'

'No,' Mrs Lacey interrupted. 'He could not. No artist paints his own Dreaming. It's too powerful. It might kill him.'

'Now I am *totally* confused,' the woman wrung her hands. 'You mean he can't paint his own Dreaming but he can paint somebody else's?'

'I get it,' said the husband, brightening. 'Like he can't eat emus but he can eat honey-ants?'

'You've got it,' Mrs Lacey said. 'Mr Tjakamarra cannot paint an Emu Dreaming because an emu is his paternal totem and it would be sacrilege to do so. He can paint honey-ant because that is the totem of his mother's brother's son. That's right, isn't it, Stan? Gideon's Dreaming is honey-ant?'

Stan blinked and said, 'Right!'

'Gideon', she continued, 'is Stan's ritual manager. They both tell each other what they can and cannot paint.'

'I think I understand,' said the American woman, doubtfully. But she still looked quite bewildered and took time to compose her next thought.

'You said that this Mr Gideon is an artist too?'

'He is,' Mrs Lacey agreed.

'And he paints Emu Dreamings?'

'He does.'

'Goodee!' the woman laughed, unexpectedly, and clapped her hands. 'We could buy one of each and hang them as a pair.'

'Now, dearest,' said the husband in an effort to calm her. 'First, we have to ascertain if this honey-ant painting is for sale. And if so, how much?'

Mrs Lacey fluttered her eyelashes and said, archly, 'I couldn't say. You'll have to ask the artist.'

Stan rolled the whites of his eyes to the ceiling and rustled his lips. Obviously, he was thinking of a price – the price he'd get from Mrs Lacey – and doubling it. Obviously he and Mrs Lacey had been through this rigmarole before. He then lowered his head and said, 'Four hundred fifty.'

'Australian dollars,' Mrs Lacey chipped in. 'Of course, I'll have to charge my commission. Ten per cent! That's only fair. And I'll have to add twenty for the paint and canvas.'

'Per cent?'

'Dollars.'

'Fair enough,' said the man, looking rather relieved.

'It *is* beautiful,' the woman said.

'Are you happy now?' he asked her in a soothing voice.

'I am,' she said. 'I am *so* happy.'

'Can I pay American Express?' he asked.

'Surely,' said Mrs Lacey. 'As long as you don't mind paying *their* commission.'

'Fair enough,' the man gulped. 'But now I want to know what's going on. In the painting, I mean.'

Arkady and I crept up behind the Americans and watched Old Stan point his bony finger at the large blue circle on the canvas.

It was the Eternal Home, he explained, of the Honey-ant Ancestor at Tátátá. And suddenly it was as though we could see the row on row of honey-ants, their bodies striped and gleaming, bursting with nectar in their cells beneath the roots of the mulga tree. We saw the ring of flame-red earth around the entrance to their nest, and the routes of their migration as they spread to other places.

'The circles', Mrs Lacey added helpfully, 'are honey-ant ceremonial centres. The "tubes", as you call them, are Dreaming-tracks.'

The American man was captivated. 'And can we go and look for these Dreaming-tracks? Out there, I mean? Like at Ayer's Rock? Some place like that?'

'They can,' she said. '*You* can't.'

'You mean they're invisible?'

'To you. Not to them.'

'Then where are they?'

'Everywhere,' she said. 'For all I know there's a Dreaming-track running right through the middle of my shop.'

'Spooky,' the wife giggled.

'And only *they* can see it?'

'Or sing it,' Mrs Lacey said. 'You can't have a track without a song.'

'And these tracks run every place?' the man asked. 'All over Australia?'

'Yes,' said Mrs Lacey, sighing with satisfaction at having found a catchy phrase. 'The song and the land are one.'

'Amazing!' he said.

The American woman had pulled out her handkerchief and was dabbing the corners of her eyes. I thought for one moment she was going to kiss Old Stan. She knew the painting was a thing done for white men, but he had given her a glimpse of something rare and strange, and for that she was very grateful.

Mrs Lacey readjusted her spectacles to fill out the American Express form. Arkady waved goodbye to Stan and we heard the triumphant *rrumpff* of the machine as we went out on to the street.

'What a woman!' I said.

'Some nerve,' said Arkady. 'Come on. Let's go and get a drink.'

7

I WAS WEARING rubber thongs and, since saloon bars all over Alice posted notices reading 'No Thongs' – with a view to discouraging Abos – we went to the public bar of the Frazer Arms.

Alice is not a very cheerful town either by day or night. Old-timers can remember Todd Street in the days of horses and hitching posts. It has since become a dreary, americanised strip of travel agents, souvenir shops and soda fountains. One shop was selling stuffed koala-bear dolls and t-shirts with 'Alice Springs' written in flies. In the newsagent's, they were selling copies of a book called *Red over White*. Its author, a former Marxist, insisted that the Aboriginal Land Rights Movement was a 'front' for Soviet expansion in Australia.

'Which makes me', said Arkady, 'one of the leading suspects.'

Outside the pub, there was an off-licence and the boys we saw earlier were lurching round it. In the middle of the street a battered eucalyptus reared its trunk up through the asphalt.

'Sacred tree,' he said. 'Sacred to the Caterpillar Dreaming and a dangerous traffic hazard.'

Inside, the public bar was noisy and crowded with blacks and whites. The seven-foot barman was supposed to be the best bouncer in town. There were puddles of beer on the linoleum, wine-red curtains in the windows, and a disorder of fibreglass chairs.

An obese, bearded Aboriginal sat scratching the bites on his belly, and had set a buttock on each of two bar-stools. An angular woman sat beside him. There was a beermat stuck into her purple knitted cap. Her eyes were closed and she was giggling hysterically.

'The gang's all here,' said Arkady.

'Who?'

'My mates from the Pintupi Council. Come on. Let me introduce you to the Chairman.'

We bought our beers and threaded through the drinkers to where the Chairman, in a booming voice, was haranguing a knot of admirers. He was a huge, very dark-skinned man, in jeans, a black leather jacket, black leather hat and a studded knuckle-duster round his wrist. He extended a smile full of teeth, locked my hand in a fraternal handshake, and said, 'Man!'

I said, 'Man!' back and watched the pink tip of my thumb poking up out of his fist.

'Man!' he said.

'Man!' I said.

'Man!' he said.

I said nothing. I felt that if I said 'Man!' a third time, we'd go on saying 'Man!' indefinitely.

I looked away. The pressure of his grip decreased and, in the end, I got my crushed hand free.

The Chairman went on telling the story he'd interrupted for my benefit: about his habit of shooting the padlocks off cattle-station gates. His listeners found this very amusing.

I then tried talking to an urban activist, up here on a visit from Sydney. Or rather, since he averted his face, I found myself talking to the Aboriginal flag dangling as an earring from his left lobe.

To begin with, I got no reaction other than the odd wobble of the flag. Then the face swivelled round and started speaking, 'Are you English?'

'Yes.'

'Why don't you go back home?'

He spoke slowly, in clipped syllables.

'I just arrived,' I said.

'I mean all of you.'

'All of who?'

'White men,' he said.

The whites had stolen his country, he said. Their presence in Australia was illegal. His people had never ceded one square inch of territory. They had never signed a treaty. All Europeans should go back where they came from.

'What about the Lebanese?' I asked.

(31)

'They must go back to Lebanon.'

'I see,' I said, but the interview had come to an end, and the face swivelled back to its previous position.

I next caught the eye of an attractive fair-haired woman and winked. She winked back and we both sidled round the edge of the group.

'Having a hard time with the Leader?' she whispered.

'No,' I said. 'Instructive.'

Her name was Marian. She had driven into town only half an hour earlier, from Walbiri country, where she was working on a women's land claim.

She had level blue eyes and looked very innocent and happy in a skimpy, flower-printed dress. There were crescents of red dirt under her fingernails and the dust had given a smooth bronze-like sheen to her skin. Her breasts were firm and her arms were solid and cylindrical. She had slashed the sleeves of the dress to allow the air to circulate freely under her armpits.

She and Arkady had been teachers at the same school in the bush. From the way she kept glancing at his blond thatch, shining in a spotlight, I guessed they must once have been lovers.

He was wearing a sky-blue shirt and baggy fatigue pants.

'How long have you known Ark?' she asked.

'All of two days,' I said.

I mentioned the name of the girl we both knew in Adelaide. She lowered her eyelids and blushed.

'He's a bit of a saint,' she said.

'I know it,' I said. 'A Russian saint.'

I could have gone on talking to Marian, were it not for a grating voice at my left elbow. 'And what brings you to the Territory?'

I looked round to see a wiry, prickle-mouthed white in his thirties. His pumped-up biceps and sleeveless grey sweatshirt announced him as a Gym Bore.

'Looking round,' I said.

'Anything special?'

'I want to find out about the Aboriginal Songlines.'

'How long are you staying?'

'Couple of months, maybe.'

'Are you attached to any body?'

'My own.'

'And what makes you think you can show up from Merrie Old England and clean up on sacred knowledge?'

'I don't want to clean up on sacred knowledge. I want to know how a Songline works.'

'You're a writer?'

'Of sorts.'

'Published?'

'Yes.'

'Science fiction?'

'I hate science fiction.'

'Look,' said the Gym Bore, 'you're wasting your time, mate. I've lived ten years in the Territory. I know these Elders. *They* are not going to tell *you* anything.'

His glass was empty. The one way to discourage this conversation was to buy the man a drink.

'No thanks,' he lifted his chin. 'I'm all right.'

I winked again at Marian, who was trying to suppress a fit of giggles. The other glasses were empty, so I offered to pay for a round. I went to the bar and gave orders for 'schooners' and 'middies'. I ordered for the Gym Bore, whether he liked it or not.

Arkady came over to help me with the glasses. 'I say!' he grinned. 'You *are* having fun.'

I paid and we carried them over.

'Say when you want to get out of here,' he whispered. 'We can go over to my place.'

'Ready when you are.'

The Gym Bore winced as he took the glass, and said, 'Thank you, mate.'

The Chairman took his without a word.

We drank up. Arkady kissed Marian on the lips and said, 'See you later.' The Gym Bore put his hand in mine and said, 'See you around, mate.'

We went outside.

'Who was that?' I asked.

'Bad news,' said Arkady.

The town was quiet in the dusk. An orange rim smouldered along the line of the MacDonnell Ranges.

'How did you like the Frazer Arms?' he asked.

'I liked it,' I said. 'It was friendly.'

It was friendlier, anyway, than the pub in Katherine.

8

I HAD HAD TO CHANGE buses in Katherine, on my way down to Alice from the Kimberleys.

It was lunchtime. The pub was full of truckies and construction workers, drinking beer and eating pasties. Most of them were wearing the standard uniform of the Outback male: desert boots, 'navvy' singlets to show off their tattoos, yellow hard-hats and 'stubbies', which are green, tight-fitting, zipless shorts. And the first thing you saw, pushing past the frosted glass door, was a continuous row of hairy red legs and bottle-green buttocks.

Katherine is a stopover for tourists who come to see its famous Gorge. The Gorge was designated a National Park, but some Land Rights lawyers found a flaw in the legal documents and were claiming it back for the blacks. There was a lot of ill-feeling in the town.

I went to the men's room and, in the passage, a black whore pressed her nipples against my shirt and said, 'You want me, darling?'

'No.'

In the time I took to piss, she had already attached herself to a stringy little man on a bar-stool. He had bulging veins on his forearm, and a Park Warden's badge on his shirt.

'Nah!' he sneered. 'Yer dirty Gin! You couldn't excite me. I got me missus. But if you sat on the bar here, and spread your legs apart, I'd probably stick a bottle up yer.'

I took my drink and went to the far end of the room. I got talking to a Spaniard. He was short, bald and sweaty, and his voice was high-pitched and hysterical. He was the town baker. A few feet away from us, two Aboriginals were starting, very slowly, to fight.

The older Aboriginal had a crinkled forehead and a crimson

shirt open to the navel. The other was a scrawny boy in skin-tight orange pants. The man was drunker than the boy, and could scarcely stand. He supported himself by propping his elbows on his stool. The boy was shrieking blue murder and frothing from the sides of his mouth.

The baker dug me in the ribs. 'I come from Salamanca,' he screeched. 'Is like a bullfight, no?'

Someone else shouted, 'The Boongs are fighting,' although they weren't fighting – yet. But the drinkers, jeering and cheering, began shifting down the bar to get a look.

Gently, almost with a caress, the Aboriginal man tipped the boy's glass from his hand, and it fell and shattered on the floor. The boy stooped, picked up the broken base and held it like a dagger in his palm.

The truckie on the next stool poured out the contents of his own glass, smashed its rim against the lip of the counter, and shoved it in the older man's hand. 'Go on,' he said, encouragingly. 'Give it 'im.'

The boy lunged forward with his glass, but the man parried him with a flick of the wrist. Both had drawn blood.

'Olé!' shouted the Spanish baker, his face contorted into a grimace. 'Olé! Olé! Olé!'

The bouncer vaulted over the bar and dragged the two Aboriginals outside on to the sidewalk, across the tarmac, to an island in the highway where they lay, side by side, bleeding beneath the pink oleanders while the road-trains from Darwin rumbled by.

I walked away but the Spaniard followed me.

'They are best friends,' he said. 'No?'

9

I was hoping for an early night, but Arkady had asked me to a barbecue with some friends on the far side of town. We had an hour or more to kill. We bought a bottle of chilled white wine from the off-licence.

Arkady lived in a rented studio apartment above a row of lock-up garages, in the lot behind the supermarket. The metal rail of the stairway was still hot from the sun. The air-conditioner was on and, as he unlocked the door, a cool draught blew in our faces. There was a note shoved through on to the mat. He switched on the light, and read.

'Not before time,' he mumbled.

'What's that?' I asked.

He explained how one of the Kaititj elders, an old man called Alan Nakumurra, had been holding up the survey for the last four weeks. He was the last male survivor of his clan and 'traditional owner' of the country north of Middle Bore Station. The railway surveyors had been champing to peg out this particular stretch of track. Arkady had put them off till Alan could be found.

'Where did he go?'

'Where do you think?' he laughed. 'He went Walkabout.'

'What happened to the others?'

'Which others?'

'The others of his clan.'

'Shot,' said Arkady. 'By police patrols in the twenties.'

The room was neat and white. There was a juice-extractor on the bar of the kitchenette and a basket of oranges beside it. Some Indonesian cloths and cushions were strewn over a mattress on the floor. Pages of sheet music, of *The Well-tempered Clavier*, lay open on top of the harpsichord.

Arkady uncorked the bottle, poured two glasses, and, while I glanced at the contents of his bookshelf, he put through a call to his boss.

He talked business for a minute or two and then said there was this Pom in town who wanted to go 'out bush' with the survey team . . . No, not a journalist . . . Yes, as Poms went, relatively harmless . . . No, not a photographer . . . No, not interested in watching rituals . . . No, not tomorrow . . . the day after . . .

There was a pause. You could almost hear the man thinking on the far end of the line. Then Arkady smiled and gave a 'thumbs up' sign.

'You're on,' he said, and replaced the receiver.

He next called the truck-hire company to have a vehicle for Wednesday morning. 'Make it a Land Cruiser,' he said. 'We might get rain.'

On the bookshelf there were Russian classics, books on the Pre-Socratics and a number of Aboriginal studies. Among the latter were two of my favourites: Theodore Strehlow's *Aranda Traditions* and *Songs of Central Australia*.

Arkady opened a tin of cashew nuts and we both sat, cross-legged on the mattress.

'Nazdorovye!' He raised his glass.

'Nazdorovye!' We clinked glasses.

He unfolded his legs once more, pulled a photo album from the shelf and started turning the pages.

The first pictures were all colour snapshots, mostly of himself, the record of any young Australian on his first trip overseas: Arkady on a beach in Bali; Arkady at Kibbutz Hulda; Arkady beside the temple at Sounion; Arkady with his wife-to-be in Venice, with pigeons; Arkady back in Alice with the wife and baby.

He then flipped to the back of the album, to a faded black-and-white picture: of a youngish couple, on a ship's deck, with a lifeboat in the background. 'Mum and Dad,' he said. 'May '47 when the ship docked at Aden.'

I leaned forward to get a close look. The man was short, with a flat, powerful body, solid black eyebrows and slanting cheekbones. A wedge of dark hair showed in the neck of his shirt. His baggy trousers were cinched in at the waist and looked several sizes too big.

The woman was taller and shapely, in a simple smock dress, and had pale hair tied up in braids. Her plump arm bulged over the stanchion rail. They screwed up their faces to the sunlight.

Lower down the same page, there was a second photo of the man: shrunken and grey now, standing beside a wicket fence, in a garden of cabbages that could only be Russian cabbages. Beside him, forming a group, were a round peasant woman and two young bruisers in karakul hats and boots.

'That's my auntie,' said Arkady. 'And those are my Cossack cousins.'

The karakul hats took me back to a stifling summer afternoon in Kiev and the memory of a squadron of Cossack cavalry exercising down a cobbled street: glossy black horses; scarlet capes, high hats worn at an angle; and the sour, resentful faces of the crowd.

The date was August 1968, a month before the invasion of Czechoslovakia. All through that summer there had been rumours of unrest in the Ukraine.

Arkady refilled the glasses and we went on talking of Cossacks: of 'Kazakh' and 'Cossack'; the Cossack as mercenary and Cossack as rebel; of Yermak the Cossack and the conquest of Siberia; of Pugachev and Stenka Razin; Makhno and Budenny's Red Cavalry. I happened to touch on Von Pannwitz's Cossack Brigade, which fought for the Germans against the Soviet Army.

'Funny you should mention Von Pannwitz,' he said.

In 1945, his parents had found themselves in Austria, in the British-occupied zone. It was a time when the Allies were sending Soviet refugees, traitors or otherwise, back home to the mercy of Stalin. His father was interrogated by a British intelligence major, who accused him, in faultless Ukranian, of fighting for Von Pannwitz. After a week of intermittent interviews, he succeeded in convincing the man that the accusation was unjust.

They were moved on to Germany, where they were billeted in what had been an officers' club, below the Eagle's Nest at Berchtesgaden. They applied for emigration papers, to the United States and Canada: Argentina, they were told, was a better bet for people of doubtful status. At last, after a year of anxious waiting, there came news of jobs in Australia, and passages for the ones who signed.

They took the chance, gladly. All they wanted was to get away from a murderous Europe – from the cold, mud, hunger and lost families – and come to a sunny country where everyone ate.

They sailed from Trieste on a converted hospital ship. Every married couple was segregated on the voyage and could only meet in daylight on deck. After landing at Adelaide, they were interned in a camp of Nissen huts, where men in khaki barked orders in English. Sometimes, they thought they were back in Europe.

I had noticed, earlier, something fierce in Arkady's obsession with Australian Railways. Now, he explained himself.

The job assigned to Ivan Volchok was to work as a maintenance man on the Transcontinental line, in the middle of the Nullarbor Plain. There, between the stations of Xanthus and Kitchener, without wife or children, driven crazy by the sun and the diet of bully-beef and billy-tea, he laboured at the work of replacing sleepers.

One day they brought him back to Adelaide on a stretcher. The doctors said, 'Heat exhaustion,' and the railway paid no proper compensation. Another doctor said, 'You've got a dicky heart.' He never worked again.

Luckily, Arkady's mother was a capable and determined woman, who, starting with a street stall, built up a prosperous fruit and vegetable business. She bought a house in an eastern suburb. She read Russian novels to herself, Russian folktales to Arkasha and his brothers, and took them on Sundays to Orthodox Mass.

Her husband had none of her resources. He had once been all muscle and rebellion. With age, he would shuffle round the shop, get in everyone's way, get drunk on his home-made hooch, and gloomily brood on the past.

He would mumble incoherently about a pear tree in his mother's garden and of some amulet he had hidden in the fork. Trees, he said, were half-dead in Australia. In Russia there were real trees, which shed their leaves and came alive again. One evening, Arkady's brother Petró found him hacking down their Norfolk Island Pine. They knew, then, that things were seriously wrong.

Through the Soviet Embassy in Canberra, they got permission for him and Petró to go back and visit his village, Gornyatskiye. He saw his sister, the old samovar, wheatfields, birches and a sluggish river. The pear tree had been cut down, long ago, for firewood.

In the cemetery he cleared the burdock from his parents' grave and sat listening to the squeak of the rusty weathervane. After dark, they all sang, his nephews taking turns to play the family bandura. The day before their departure, the KGB took him to Rostov for questioning. They went over and over his dossier, and asked a lot of tricky questions, about the war.

'Dad', said Arkady, 'was happier to see Vienna this time than the last.'

This had happened seven years ago. Now, once again, he was yearning to go back to Russia. He now talked of nothing but the grave at Gornyatskiye. They knew he wanted to die there, and they didn't know how to arrange it.

'Even as a Westerner', I said, 'I know how he must feel. Whenever I've been to Russia, I can't wait to get away. Then I can't wait to go back.'

'You like Russia?'

'The Russians are a wonderful people.'

'I know that,' he answered sharply. 'Why?'

'Hard to say,' I said. 'I like to think of Russia as a land of miracles. Just as you fear the worst, something wonderful always happens.'

'Such as?'

'Small things, mostly. Humble things. Humility in Russia is endless.'

'I believe you,' he said. 'Come on. We'd better get going.'

10

IT WAS A BRIGHT, moonlit night. Only in the moonlight was it safe to take a short cut through the Todd. The Aboriginals had the habit of sleeping off their liquor in the river-bed. In the pitch dark, you ran the risk of running into one of them, who might or might not be dangerously drunk.

The trunks of the ghost-gums were shining white: several trees had been uprooted by another year's flood. Across the river we could see the Casino and the headlights of cars driving up to it. The sand was loose and grainy, and we went in over our ankles. On the far bank a tousled figure rose up from the bushes, mumbled 'Fuckers!' and sank back with a thud and crack of branches.

'Harmlessly drunk!' said Arkady.

He led the way past the Casino along a street of newly built houses. They had solar heaters clamped to their roofs and camper-trucks parked in the driveways. At the far end of the street, set aslant to the others, was an old, ramshackle pioneer house with a wide veranda and fly-screens. From the garden came the smell of frangipani and sizzling meat fat.

A grey-bearded man called Bill, shirtless and pouring with sweat, was grilling steaks and sausages over a charcoal brazier.

'Hello there, Ark!' he waved a fork in the air.

'Hello, Bill,' said Arkady. 'This is Bruce.'

'Pleased to meet you, Bruce,' Bill said, hastily. 'Help yourselves to food.'

Bill's blonde wife, Janet, sat behind a trestle table serving salad. She had a broken arm in plaster. On the table were various bottles of wine, and a plastic tub full of ice and canned beers.

The night bugs were whirling around a couple of hurricane lamps.

The guests moved about the garden with their food on paper plates, or sat laughing on the ground in groups, or sat in serious conversation on camping chairs. They were nurses, teachers, lawyers, linguists, architects. All of them, I would guess, worked in one way or other with or for the Aboriginals. They were young and had wonderful legs.

There was only one Aboriginal present: a lanky man in white shorts with a beard that fanned out below his naval. A half-blood girl was hanging on his arm. Her hair was tied tightly in a lilac headscarf. He allowed her to do all the talking.

She spoke in a querulous voice: of how the Alice Town Council proposed to put a ban on public drinking. 'And where would our people drink,' she asked, 'if they're not allowed to drink in public?'

I then saw the Gym Bore making a bee-line across the garden. He had changed into a Land Rights t-shirt and electric-green boxer shorts. He was, it had to be said, good-looking in a sourish way. His name was Kidder. The shrill, upward note on which he ended his sentences gave each of his statements, however dogmatic, a tentative and questionable bias. He would have made an excellent policeman.

'As I was saying in the pub,' he said, 'the days of that kind of research are over.'

'What kind of research?'

'Aboriginals are sick and tired of being snooped at like they were animals in a zoo. They've called a halt.'

'Who's called the halt?'

'They have,' he said. 'And their community advisers.'

'Of which you are one?'

'I am,' he agreed, modestly.

'Does that mean I can't talk to an Aboriginal without first asking your permission?'

He jutted his chin, lowered his lids and looked sideways.'Do you wish', he asked, 'to be initiated?'

He added that, if I did so wish, I'd be obliged to submit to circumcision if I hadn't been circumcised, then to subincision, which, as I doubtless knew, was to have your urethra peeled back like a banana skin and flayed with a stone knife.

'Thank you,' I said. 'I'll pass.'

'In which case', said Kidder, 'you've no right poking your nose into business that doesn't concern you.'

'Have you been initiated?'

'I . . . er . . . I . . .'

'I asked, have *you* been initiated?'

He ran his fingers through his hair and resumed a more civil tone.

'I think I should acquaint you', he said, 'with certain policy decisions.'

'Tell me.'

Kidder, expanding to his theme, said that sacred knowledge was the cultural property of the Aboriginal people. All such knowledge which had got into the hands of white men had been acquired either by fraud or by force. It was now going to be de-programmed.

'Knowledge is knowledge,' I said. 'It's not that easy to dispose of.'

He did not agree.

To 'de-programme' sacred knowledge, he said, meant examining archives for unpublished material on Aboriginals; you then returned the relevant pages to the rightful 'owners'. It meant transferring copyright from the author of a book to the people it described; returning photographs to the photographed (or their descendants); recording tapes to the recorded, and so forth.

I heard him out, gasping with disbelief.

'And who', I asked, 'will decide who these "owners" are?'

'We have ways of researching that kind of information.'

'Your ways or their ways?'

He did not reply. Instead, changing the subject, he asked if I knew what a tjuringa was.

'I do,' I said.

'What is a tjuringa?'

'A sacred board,' I said. 'An Aboriginal's "holy of holies". Or, if you like, his "soul".'

A tjuringa is usually an oval-ended plaque, carved from stone or mulga wood, and covered with patterns which represent the wanderings of its owner's Dreamtime Ancestor. In Aboriginal law, no uninitiated person was *ever* allowed to look on one.

'Have you seen a tjuringa?' Kidder asked.

(43)

'I have.'

'Where?'

'In the British Museum.'

'Did you realise you were acting illegally?'

'I never heard anything so silly.'

Kidder folded his arms and squeezed his empty beer can; *clu . . . unk*! His chest was heaving up and down like a pouter pigeon's. 'People have been speared for less,' he said.

Arkady, I was relieved to see, was coming across the lawn. He had a pile of coleslaw on his plate and a dribble of mayonnaise down his chin.

'I knew you two should get together,' he grinned. 'Pair of talking heads!'

Kidder drew his lips into a tight smile. He was an attractive commodity to women. An intense, dark-headed girl had been hovering round for some minutes. She was obviously dying to talk to him. She grabbed her chance. I grabbed mine: to get away and get some food.

'You owe me an explanation,' I said to Arkady. '*Who* is Kidder?'

'Rich boy from Sydney.'

'I mean *what* is he to the Land Rights movement?'

'Nothing and nobody. He's got a plane, that's all. Flies about taking messages. Makes him feel important.'

'Air lout,' I said.

'He's a nice guy,' said Arkady. 'So they tell me.'

I got some more salad and we went to join Marian. She was sitting on a rug and talking to a barrister. She had put on a dress more faded and tattered than the last, with a pattern of Japanese chrysanthemums. Rags suited her. Rags were her style. Anything other than rags might have made her look dowdy.

She gave me either cheek to kiss and said she was glad I was coming.

'Where to?'

'Middle Bore,' she said. 'You *are* coming, I hope?'

'You too?'

'Me too,' she glanced across at Arkady and crinkled up her eyes. 'I'm the Grand Duke's sidekick.'

She told me how Aboriginal women have song cycles of their own and, therefore, different sites to be protected. Few people had realised this until recently: the reason being that the women were that much tighter with their secrets than the men.

'Anyway, it's nice you're coming,' she smiled. 'It'll be fun.'

She introduced me to the barrister, 'Bruce, this is Hughie.'

'How do you do?' I said.

He acknowledged my greeting with a slow inclination of the head.

He had a pale, oval face and a clipped and pernickety way of enunciating his syllables; and with his freckles, his steel-framed glasses, and the tuft of mousy hair sticking up on the back of his head, he really did look like the brightest boy in school. When the lamplight caught his features, you could tell he was lined and tired.

He yawned. 'Couldn't we find a chair, my dear? I can't stand another minute and I do *hate* sitting on the ground. Don't you?'

I found a couple of chairs and we sat down. Arkady and Marian, meanwhile, had gone off to discuss arrangements for the trip.

The barrister had been in court all day, defending a black kid on a homicide charge. He would be all day in court tomorrow. He was a New Zealander. He had gone to public school in England and had been called to the Bar in London.

We talked about the Lawson case, which had been tried in the Alice court. Lawson was a truckie, who, when apparently drunk, had been refused a drink by the lady proprietor of an Outback motel. He had gone out into the glare of noon, unhitched his trailer, and, twenty minutes later, had driven the truck through the bar at 35 m.p.h., killing five drinkers and wounding twenty.

After the incident, Lawson went missing in the bush and, when found, said he could not recall a thing.

'Do you believe that?' I asked.

'Believe it? Of course, I believe it! Mr Lawson's a very nice and truthful person, and his company kept him dreadfully overworked. The trouble with his defence is that he wasn't drunk, he was drugged.'

'What on?'

'Amphetamines, poor thing! Hadn't slept a wink for five days. All these truckies *feed* on amphetamines! Pop them in their mouths like sweeties! One, two, three, four, five and *Whooeee* . . . ! they're away. No wonder he was a little blotto!'

'Did that come out in court?'

'The five days, yes, the amphetamines, no.'

'Why ever not?'

'Unmentionable! Amphetamines and the trucking business? *Un*-mentionable! Imagine if there had to be an inquiry. Amphetamines are this country's answer to distance. Without them, the place'd seize up.'

'It's a weird country,' I said.

'It is.'

'Weirder than America.'

'Much!' he agreed. 'America's *young*! Young, innocent and cruel. But this country's old. Old rock! That's the difference! Old, weary and wise. Absorbent too! No matter what you pour on to it, it all gets sucked away.'

He waved his thin white arm at the healthy, suntanned people on the lawn. 'Look at them!' he said. 'They *think* they're young. But they're not, you know. They're *old*. Born old!'

'Not Arkady,' I objected. 'Arkady doesn't strike me as old.'

'Ark's the exception,' he said. 'I think Ark must have dropped from Heaven. But the rest of them are old,' he continued. 'Have you ever noticed the eyelids of young people in this country? They're the eyelids of the old. You wake them up and they look like startled fauns – for a bit! Then they go back to being old.'

'Perhaps it's the light?' I suggested. 'The glare of Australia that makes one long for the dark.'

'Ark tells me you've got all sorts of interesting theories about this and that. I'd like to hear them one day, but tonight I'm tired.'

'So am I.'

'Not, of course, that I haven't a few pet theories of my own. I suppose that's why I'm here.'

'I was wondering that.'

'What?'

'What you were doing here.'

'I ask myself, my dear. Every time I brush my teeth, I ask the same question. But what would I do in London? Prissy little dinners? Pretty little flat? No. No. Wouldn't suit me at all.'

'But why here?'

'I love it here,' he said thoughtfully. 'The abstraction, you understand me?'

'I think so.'

'Suitable for marsupials, but never meant for man. The land, I mean. Makes people do the most peculiar things. Did you hear the story of the German girl and the bicycle?'

'No.'

'*Very* interesting case! Nice, healthy German girl. Hires a bike from a shop on Todd Street. Buys a lock from a shop on Court Street. Rides out of town along the Larapinta Drive and gets as far as Ormiston Gorge. She drags the bike through the Gorge, which, as you know if you've ever been there, is a superhuman feat. Then, in the middle of absolutely nowhere, she locks her leg to the frame, chucks away the key, and lies down to grill in the sun. The sun-bathing impulse gone haywire! Picked clean, she was! Picked!'

'Nasty!'

'No,' he shook his head. 'Reconciled! Dissolved! That's all part of my little theory about Australia. But I *won't* bore you with it now, because I'm really so dreadfully tired and I should be in bed.'

'So should I,' I said and stood up.

'Sit *down*!' he said. 'Why must you Poms always be in such a hurry?'

He sipped his wine. We sat in silence for a minute or two, and then he said, dreamily, 'Yes, it's a lovely place to be lost in. Being lost in Australia gives you a lovely feeling of security.'

He jumped to his feet. 'And now,' he said, 'I simply *must* go! It's been very nice talking to you and I'm sure we shall talk again. Good night!'

He walked away towards the garden gate, nodding his head and saying 'Goodnight!' to everyone he passed.

I rejoined Arkady and Marian.

'What did you make of Hughie?' he asked.

'What an odd fish!'

'Bloody good barrister,' he said. 'Has the court in stitches.'

'I'll be off now,' I said. 'Don't move. I'll look in at the office tomorrow.'

'You're not going yet,' he said. 'There's someone I want you to meet.'

'Who's that?'

'Dan Flynn.' He pointed towards the bearded Aboriginal.

'*The* Father Flynn?'

'Himself,' he said. 'You know the story?'

'I do,' I said.

'How?'

'Heard it from an Irishman called Father Terence.'

'Never heard of him.'

'You wouldn't have,' I said. 'He's a hermit. He told me to look Flynn up.'

Arkady threw back his head and laughed.

'Everyone wants to look up Father Dan,' he said. 'Until they get the brush-off. If he likes you, you'll learn a lot. If he doesn't . . . you'll know it.'

'Yes,' I said. 'I did hear he was difficult.'

I I

SELDOM IN ITS missionary endeavours can the Catholic Church in Australia have suffered from so difficult a case as that of Father Flynn.

He was a foundling, dumped by an unknown mother at the store of an Irishman at Fitzroy Crossing. At the age of six, he was sent to the Benedictine Mission at Cygnet Bay, where he refused to play with other black children, learned to serve at Mass, and had the habit of asking questions, about dogma, in a soft reverential brogue. One day, he reeled off pat the name of every Pope, from St Peter to Pius XII. The Fathers saw this as proof of his craving for Christ.

They taught him Latin and encouraged him to take Holy Orders. He was taken in hand by the Mission's oldest inhabitant, an apparently harmless crank, Father Herzog, who had trained as an ethnographer and taught him the rudiments of comparative religion.

Flynn was ordained in 1969. He went to Rome. He walked with fellow seminarians in the Alban Hills. He had an audience with the Holy Father, which lasted approximately one and a quarter minutes. On his return to Australia, the Order decided he should be the first Aboriginal to take charge of a mission on his own.

The place they chose was Roe River, in the Kimberleys. And to equip himself for the task, Flynn was sent to learn from two old-timers, Fathers Subiros and Villaverde, at another Benedictine outpost: Boongaree.

Father Subiros – I was later to meet him in the monastery of his retirement – was a sweet-tempered man: short, fat, Catalan and bookish. Father Villaverde was a leathery Extremeñan, from Trujillo. Together for fifty years, they had suffered flood, famine, disease, mutiny, a Japanese bombardment, and many other onslaughts of the Devil.

Boongaree was an hour's walk from the coast. Roe River, on the other hand, lay a hundred and fifty miles upcountry and could be cut off by the 'wets' for three months or more. Neither was a mission in the usual sense but cattle-stations, which the Order had picked up for a song in 1946 and were intended as refuge areas for tribes whose lands had been taken by the pastoralists. They had proved to be a very sound investment.

Coming as he did from the birthplace of the Pizarros, Father Villaverde felt obliged to cast himself in the role of Conquistador. He said it was useless to try and impress the heathen with acts of love, when all they understood was force. He forbade them to hunt or even to garden. The only hope for their economic salvation was to foster an addiction to horseflesh.

He would snatch small boys from their mothers and set them on a bucking saddle. Nothing gave him greater joy than to charge through the bush at the head of his troop of young daredevils. On Saturday afternoons, he would preside over a sports meeting, with sprinting, wrestling, spear-throwing and boomerang-throwing – and in each event he took part himself. A natural athlete – although in his seventies – he rejoiced at the chance of showing off his superior, European physique. The blacks, who knew how to humour him, would hold back their strength, allow him to win, crown him with a victor's wreath, and carry him shoulder-high to his quarters.

He banned from the Mission all anthropologists, journalists and other snoopers. He prohibited 'traditional' ceremonies. Above all, with a kind of priestly envy, he resented his lads going off to look for wives. Once they got away, to Broome or Fitzroy Crossing, they picked up foul language, foul diseases and a taste for drink. So, having done everything to prevent them going, he did everything to prevent them coming back.

The blacks believed he was deliberately trying to run down their numbers.

I never went to either mission: by the time I got to Australia, they'd been closed for seven years. I only know of these goings-on from Father Terence, who, when Flynn arrived at Boongaree, was living a mile or so from the compound, in a hut of leaves and branches.

Father Villaverde hated Flynn on sight and put him through every kind of ordeal. He made him wade up to his neck in floodwater, castrate bullocks and scrub the latrines. He accused him of eyeing the Spanish nursing sisters at Mass, whereas it was they – poor village girls sent out in batches from a convent near Badajoz – who had, of course, been eyeing him.

One day, as the Spaniards were conducting a Texan cattle-king over the mission, the Texan's wife insisted on photographing a white-bearded elder, who sat cross-legged and unbuttoned in the dust. The old man was furious. He spat a neat gob of phlegm, which landed at the lady's feet. But she, rising to the occasion, apologised, ripped the film from her camera and, bending forward with the air of Lady Bountiful, asked, 'Is there anything I can send you from America?'

'You can,' he snapped. 'Four Toyota Land Cruisers!'

Father Villaverde was very shocked. To this authentic *caballero*, the internal combustion engine was an anathema. Someone must have been stirring up trouble. His suspicions fell on Father Flynn.

A month or so later, he intercepted a letter from the Department of Aboriginal Affairs in Canberra, thanking the Boongaree Council for their request for a Land Cruiser: the matter would receive consideration.

'And what', shrieked Father Villaverde, 'is the Boongaree Council?'

Flynn folded his arms; waited for the tirade to blow over, and said, 'We are.'

From that day on, there was open war.

At the next Saturday's sports meeting, just as Father Villaverde had hurled his winning throw, Flynn, in a white soutane, strode out from behind the Chapel carrying a spear which had been rubbed with red ochre. He beckoned the spectators to clear a space and, with an apparently effortless flick, sent the weapon soaring into the air.

The length of the throw was over twice that of the Spaniard – who took to his bed in rage.

I forget the name of the three tribes camped around the mission. Father Terence scribbled them on a scrap of paper, but I lost it. The point to remember is that Tribe A was the friend and ally of

Tribe B, and both were blood-enemies of the men of Tribe C – who, outflanked and deprived of their source of women, were in danger of dying out.

The three camps lay equidistant from the Mission buildings: each tribe facing the direction of its former homeland. Fights would break out only after a period of taunts and accusations of sorcery. Yet, by tacit agreement, neither of the allies would gang up on their common enemy. All three recognised the Mission itself as neutral ground.

Father Villaverde preferred to condone these periodic bouts of bloodletting: as long as the savages persisted in their ignorance of the Gospel, they were bound to go on fighting. Besides, the role of peacemaker suited his vanity. At the sound of screams, he would rush to the scene, stride through the clashing spears and, with the gesture of Christ calming the waters, say, 'Stop!' – and the warriors would shamble off home.

The leading lawman of Tribe C had the unforgettable name of Cheekybugger Tabagee. An expert tracker in his youth, he had guided prospecting expeditions through the Kimberleys. He now hated every white man and, in thirty years, had not addressed one word to the Spaniards.

Cheekybugger was built on a colossal scale: but he was old, arthritic and covered with the scabs of a skin disease. His legs were useless. He would sit in the half-shade of his humpy and let the dogs lick his sores.

He knew he was dying and it enraged him. One by one, he had watched the young men go, or go to pieces. Soon there would be no one: either to sing the songs or to give blood for ceremonies.

In Aboriginal belief, an unsung land is a dead land: since, if the songs are forgotten, the land itself will die. To allow that to happen was the worst of all possible crimes, and it was with this bitter thought that Cheekybugger decided to pass his songs to the enemy – thereby committing his people to perpetual peace, which, of course, was a far, far graver decision than conniving at perpetual war.

He sent for Flynn and asked him to act as mediator.

Flynn went from camp to camp, argued, exhorted and finally arrived at a formula. The snag was one of protocol.

Cheekybugger had begun the negotiations: in Law, it was he who must deliver the songs in person. The question was how.

(52)

He couldn't walk. He would not be carried. He scoffed at the offer of a horse. In the end it was Flynn who hit on the solution: by borrowing a wheelbarrow from the Malay cook who worked the kitchen-garden.

The procession set off between two and three of a blistering blue afternoon, when the cockatoos were silent and the Spaniards snoring through their siesta. Cheekybugger went ahead in the wheelbarrow, pushed by his eldest son. Across his knee, wrapped in newspaper, lay his tjuringa, which he now proposed to lend to the enemy. The others followed in single file.

At some point beyond the Chapel, two men – from Tribes A and B – stepped from the bushes and escorted the party to the place of 'business'.

Flynn lagged behind, his eyes half-closed, with the air of a man in a trance. He brushed past Father Terence without a flicker of recognition.

'I could see he was "off",' Father Terence told me. 'And I could see we were in for trouble. But it was all very moving. For the first time in my life I had a vision of peace on earth.'

Around sunset, one of the nursing sisters took a short cut through the bush and heard the drone of voices and the *tak* . . . *tak* . . . of boomerangs being clacked together. She hurried to tell Father Villaverde.

He rushed out to break up the meeting. Flynn walked out from behind a tree and warned him to stay away.

After the fight, people said that Flynn had simply clamped his hands around his attacker's wrists and held them. This, however, did not prevent Father Villaverde from writing letter after letter to his superiors, claiming unprovoked assault and demanding that this acolyte of Satan be drummed from the body of the Church.

Father Subiros advised him not to send them. Already, Aboriginal pressure groups were lobbying for an end to the missions. Flynn had not taken part in a heathenish rite: he had only acted as peacemaker. What if the press got wind of the affair? What if it came out that two elderly Spaniards had been stirring up tribal warfare?

Father Villaverde gave in, against his better judgment; and in October 1976, two months before the 'wets', Flynn left to take charge of Roe River. The previous incumbent refused to meet him and left for Europe on sabbatical. The rains came – and there was silence.

Sometime during Lent, the Catholic Bishop of the Kimberleys radioed Boongaree to confirm or deny a rumour that Flynn had 'gone native' – to which Father Villaverde answered, 'He *is* native!'

On the first day fit for flying, the Bishop flew the Benedictine to Roe River in his Cessna, where they inspected the damage 'like two conservative politicians at the scene of a terrorist bomb'.

The Chapel was in disarray. Buildings had been burnt for firewood. The stock-pens were empty and there were charred beef-bones everywhere. Father Villaverde said, 'Our work in Australia is at an end.'

Flynn then overplayed his hand. He believed the Land Rights movement was advancing faster than it was. He counted on the assurance of certain left-wingers that missions all over the country would be handed over to the blacks. He refused to compromise. Father Villaverde trumped him.

The affair had touched the Church at its most brittle point: the financial. It was not generally known that both Boongaree and Roe River had been financed with capital raised originally in Spain. A bank in Madrid held the title deeds as collateral. To forestall any attempt at confiscation, both missions were sold, secretly, to an American businessman and absorbed into the assets of a multinational corporation.

The press campaigned for their return. The Americans threatened to close an unprofitable smelter, north of Perth, with a loss of 500 jobs. The unions intervened. The campaign subsided. The Aboriginals were dispersed, and Dan Flynn – as he styled himself – went to live with a girl in Broome.

Her name was Goldie. In her ancestry were Malay, Koipanger, Japanese, Scot and Aboriginal. Her father had been a pearler and she was a dentist. Before moving into her apartment, Flynn wrote a letter, in faultless Latin, requesting Holy Father to release him from his vows.

The couple moved to Alice Springs and were active in Aboriginal politics.

12

THE EX-BENEDICTINE was holding court to half a dozen people in the darker part of the garden. The moonlight shone on his brow-ridges: his face and beard were swallowed up in the darkness. His girlfriend sat at his feet. From time to time, she would stretch her lovely long neck across his thigh and he would reach out a finger and tickle her.

He was, there was no denying it, difficult. When Arkady crouched beside the chair and explained what I wanted, I heard Flynn mutter, 'Christ, not another!'

I had to wait a full five minutes before he deigned to turn his head in my direction. Then he asked in a flat, ironic voice, 'Is there anything I can do to help you?'

'There is,' I said, nervously. 'I'm interested in the Songlines.'

'Are you?'

His presence was so daunting that whatever one said was sure to sound silly. I tried to interest him in various theories on the evolutionary origins of language.

'There are linguists', I said, 'who believe the first language was in song.'

He looked away and stroked his beard.

I then tried another tack and described how gipsies communicate over colossal distances by singing secret verses down the telephone.

'Do they?'

Before being initiated, I went on, a young gipsy boy had to memorise the songs of his clan, the names of his kin, as well as hundreds and hundreds of international phone numbers.

'Gipsies', I said, 'are probably the best phone-tappers in the world.'

'I cannot see', said Flynn, 'what gipsies have to do with our people.'

'Because gipsies', I said, 'also see themselves as hunters. The world is their hunting ground. Settlers are "sitting-game". The gipsy word for "settler" is the same as the word for "meat".'

Flynn turned to face me.

'You know what our people call the white man?' he asked.

'Meat,' I suggested.

'And you know what they call a welfare cheque?'

'Also meat.'

'Bring a chair,' he said. 'I want to talk to you.'

I fetched the chair I had been sitting on and sat down beside him.

'Sorry I was a bit sharp,' he said. 'You should see the nutters I have to deal with. What are you drinking?'

'I'll have a beer,' I said.

'Four more beers,' Flynn called to a boy in an orange shirt.

The boy went eagerly to get them.

Flynn leaned forward and whispered something in Goldie's ear. She smiled and he talked.

White men, he began, made the common mistake of assuming that, because the Aboriginals were wanderers, they could have no system of land tenure. This was nonsense. Aboriginals, it was true, could not imagine territory as a block of land hemmed in by frontiers: but rather as an interlocking network of 'lines' or 'ways through'.

'All our words for "country"', he said, 'are the same as the words for "line".'

For this there was one simple explanation. Most of Outback Australia was arid scrub or desert where rainfall was always patchy and where one year of plenty might be followed by seven years of lean. To move in such landscape was survival: to stay in the same place suicide. The definition of a man's 'own country' was 'the place in which I do not have to ask'. Yet to feel 'at home' in that country depended on being able to leave it. Everyone hoped to have at least four 'ways out', along which he could travel in a crisis. Every tribe – like it or not – had to cultivate relations with its neighbour.

'So if A had fruits,' said Flynn, 'and B had duck and C had an ochre quarry, there were formal rules for exchanging these commodities, and formal routes along which to trade.'

What the whites used to call the 'Walkabout' was, in practice, a kind of bush-telegraph-cum-stock-exchange, spreading messages between peoples who never saw each other, who might be unaware of the other's existence.

'This trade', he said, 'was not trade as you Europeans know it. Not the business of buying and selling for profit! Our people's trade was always symmetrical.'

Aboriginals, in general, had the idea that all 'goods' were potentially malign and would work against their possessors unless they were forever in motion. The 'goods' did not have to be edible, or useful. People liked nothing better than to barter useless things – or things they could supply for themselves: feathers, sacred objects, belts of human hair.

'I know,' I interrupted. 'Some people traded their umbilical cords.'

'I see you've done your reading.'

'Trade goods', he continued, should be seen rather as the bargaining counters of a gigantic game, in which the whole continent was the gaming board and all its inhabitants players. 'Goods' were tokens of intent: to trade again, meet again, fix frontiers, intermarry, sing, dance, share resources and share ideas.

A shell might travel from hand to hand, from the Timor Sea to the Bight, along 'roads' handed down since time began. These 'roads' would follow the line of unfailing waterholes. The waterholes, in turn, were ceremonial centres where men of different tribes would gather.

'For what you call corroborees?'

'*You* call them corroborees,' he said. 'We don't.'

'All right,' I nodded. 'Are you saying that a trade route always runs along a Songline?'

'The trade route *is* the Songline,' said Flynn. 'Because songs, not things, are the principal medium of exchange. Trading in "things" is the secondary consequence of trading in song.'

Before the whites came, he went on, no one in Australia was landless, since everyone inherited, as his or her private property, a stretch of the Ancestor's song and the stretch of country over which the song passed. A man's verses were his title deeds to territory. He could lend them to others. He could borrow other verses in return. The one thing he couldn't do was sell or get rid of them.

Supposing the Elders of a Carpet Snake clan decided it was time to sing their song cycle from beginning to end? Messages would be sent out, up and down the track, summoning song-owners to assemble at the Big Place. One after the other, each 'owner' would then sing his stretch of the Ancestor's footprints. Always in the correct sequence!

'To sing a verse out of order', Flynn said sombrely, 'was a crime. Usually meant the death penalty.'

'I can see that,' I said. 'It'd be the musical equivalent of an earthquake.'

'Worse,' he scowled. 'It would be to un-create the Creation.'

Wherever there was a Big Place, he continued, the chances were that the other Dreamings would converge on it. So at one of your corroborees, you might have four different totemic clans, from any number of different tribes, all of whom would swap songs, dances, sons and daughters, and grant each other 'rights of way'.

'When you've been around a bit longer,' he turned to me, 'you'll hear the expression "acquiring ritual knowledge".'

All this meant was that the man was extending his song-map. He was widening his options, exploring the world through song.

'Imagine two Blackfellows', he said, 'meeting for the first time in an Alice pub. One will try one Dreaming. The other will try another. Then something's sure to click . . . '

'And that', Arkady piped up, 'will be the beginning of a beautiful drinking friendship.'

Everyone laughed at this, except for Flynn, who went on talking.

The next point, he said, was to understand that every song cycle went leap-frogging through language barriers, regardless of tribe or frontier. A Dreaming-track might start in the north-west, near Broome; thread its way through twenty languages or more; and go on to hit the sea near Adelaide.

'And yet,' I said, 'it's still the same song.'

'Our people', Flynn said, 'say they recognise a song by its "taste" or "smell" . . . by which, of course, they mean the "tune". The tune *always* stays the same, from the opening bars to the finale.'

'Words may change,' Arkady interrupted again, 'but the melody lingers on.'

'Does that mean', I asked, 'that a young man on Walkabout could sing his way across Australia providing he could hum the right tune?'

'In theory, yes,' Flynn agreed.

Around 1900, there was the case of an Arnhemlander who had walked across the continent in search of a wife. He married on the south coast and walked the bride back home with his new-found brother-in-law. The brother-in-law then married an Arnhemland girl, and marched her off down south.

'Poor women,' I said.

'Practical application of the Incest Taboo,' said Arkady. 'If you want fresh blood, you have to walk to get it.'

'But in practice,' Flynn went on, 'the Elders would advise the young man not to travel more than two or three "stops" down the line.'

'What do you mean by "stop"?' I asked.

A 'stop', he said, was the 'handover point' where the song passed out of your ownership; where it was no longer yours to look after and no longer yours to lend. You'd sing to the end of your verses, and there lay the boundary.

'I see,' I said. 'Like an international frontier. The road signs change language, but it's still the same road.'

'More or less,' said Flynn. 'But that doesn't get the beauty of the system. Here there are no frontiers, only roads and "stops".'

Suppose you took a tribal area like that of the Central Aranda? Suppose there were six hundred Dreamings weaving in and out of it? That would mean twelve hundred 'handover points' dotted around the perimeter. Each 'stop' had been sung into position by a Dreamtime Ancestor: its place on the song-map was thus unchangeable. But since each was the work of a *different* ancestor, there was no way of linking them sideways to form a modern political frontier.

An Aboriginal family, he said, might have five full brothers, each of whom belonged to a different totemic clan, each with different allegiances inside and outside the tribe. To be sure, Aboriginals had fights and vendettas and blood-feuds – but always to redress some imbalance or sacrilege. The idea of invading their neighbour's land would never have entered their heads.

(59)

'What this boils down to', I said, hesitantly, 'is something quite similar to birdsong. Birds also sing their territorial boundaries.'

Arkady, who had been listening with his forehead on his kneecaps, looked up and shot me a glance, 'I was wondering when you'd rumble to that one.'

Flynn then wound up the conversation by outlining the issue which had vexed so many anthropologists: the question of dual paternity.

Early travellers in Australia reported that the Aboriginals made no connection between sex and conception: a proof, if proof were lacking, of their hopelessly 'primitive' mentality.

This, of course, was nonsense. A man knew very well who his father was. Yet there was, in addition, a kind of parallel paternity which tied his soul to one particular point in the landscape.

Each Ancestor, while singing his way across country, was believed to have left a trail of 'life-cells' or 'spirit-children' along the line of his footprints.

'A kind of musical sperm,' said Arkady, making everyone laugh again: even, this time, Flynn.

The song was supposed to lie over the ground in an unbroken chain of couplets: a couplet for each pair of the Ancestor's footfalls, each formed from the names he 'threw out' while walking.

'A name to the right and a name to the left?'

'Yes,' said Flynn.

What you had to visualise was an *already* pregnant woman strolling about on her daily foraging round. Suddenly, she steps on a couplet, the 'spirit-child' jumps up – through her toe-nail, up her vagina, or into an open callus on her foot – and works its way into her womb, and impregnates the foetus with song.

'The baby's first kick', he said, 'corresponds to the moment of "spirit-conception".'

The mother-to-be then marks the spot and rushes off to fetch the Elders. They then interpret the lie of the land and decide which Ancestor walked that way, and which stanzas will be the child's private property. They reserve him a 'conception site' – coinciding with the nearest landmark on the Songline. They earmark his tjuringa in the tjuringa storehouse . . .

Flynn's voice was drowned by the noise of a jet coming in low overhead.

'American,' said Marian, bitterly. 'They only fly in at night.'

The Americans have a space-tracking station at Pine Gap in the MacDonnells. Flying into Alice, you see a great white globe and a cluster of other installations. No one in Australia, not even the Prime Minister, seems to know what really goes on there. No one knows what Pine Gap is for.

'Christ, it's sinister,' Marian shuddered. 'I do wish they'd go.'

The pilot applied his airbrakes and the transport slowed up along the runway.

'They'll go,' Flynn said. 'One day they'll have to go.'

Our host and his wife had cleared up the leftovers and gone off to bed. I saw Kidder coming across the garden.

'I'd better be off now,' he addressed the company. 'Got to go and do my flight plan.'

He was flying to Ayer's Rock in the morning: on some business of the Ayer's Rock Land Claim.

'Give it my love,' said Flynn, sarcastically.

'See you around, mate,' Kidder turned to me.

'See you,' I said.

His shiny black Land Cruiser was parked in the driveway. He switched on the headlights and lit up all the people in the garden. He revved the engine loudly, and backed out into the street.

'Big White Chief him gone!' Flynn said.

'Silly fart,' said Marian.

'Don't be unkind,' Arkady contradicted her. 'He's a good bloke, underneath.'

'I never got that far.'

Flynn, meanwhile, had leaned forward over his girl and was kissing her, covering her face and neck with the black wings of his beard.

It was time to go. I thanked him. He shook my hand. I gave him Father Terence's regards.

'How is he?'

'Well,' I said.

'Still in his little hut?'

'Yes. But he says he's going to leave it.'

'Father Terence', Flynn said, 'is a good man.'

13

BACK AT THE MOTEL, I was half-asleep when there was a knock on my door.

'Bru?'

'Yes.'

'It's Bru.'

'I know.'

'Oh!'

This other Bruce had sat next to me on the bus from Katherine. He was travelling down from Darwin, where he had just broken up with his wife. He was looking for a job on a road-gang. He missed his wife badly. He had a big pot belly and was not very bright.

At Tennant Creek, he had said, 'You and me could be mates, Bru. I could teach you to drive a dozer.' Another time, with greater warmth, he said, 'You're not a whingeing Pom, Bru.' Now, long after midnight, he was outside my door calling, 'Bru?'

'What is it?'

'Want to come out and get pissed?'

'No.'

'Oh!'

'We could find some sheilas,' he said.

'That a fact?' I said. 'This time of night?'

'You're right, Bru.'

'Go to bed,' I said.

'Well, goo'night, Bru.'

'Goodnight!'

'Bru?'

'What do you want now?'

'Nothing,' he said and shuffled off, dragging his rubber thongs *shlip . . . shlip* along the corridor.

There was a sodium light on the street outside my room, and a drunk was burbling on the sidewalk. I turned to the wall and tried to sleep, but I couldn't help thinking of Flynn and his girl.

I remembered sitting with Father Terence on his empty beach and him saying, 'I hope she's soft.'

Flynn, he said, was a man of tremendous passions, 'If she's soft, he'll be all right. A hard one could lead him into trouble.'

'What kind of trouble?' I asked.

'Revolutionary trouble, or something like it. Flynn had to suffer a most un-Christian act and that alone could turn him. But not if the lady is soft . . . '

Father Terence had found his Thebaid on the shores of the Timor Sea.

He lived in a hermitage cobbled from corrugated sheet and whitewashed, and set among clumps of pandanus on a dune of floury white sand. He had guyed the walls with cables to stop the sheets from flying in a cyclone. Above the roof there was a cross, its arms lashed together from two pieces of a broken oar. He had lived here for seven years, since the closing of Boongaree.

I came up from the landward side. I could see the hut a good way off, through the trees, standing out on the dune against the sun. In the paddock below, a brat na bull was grazing. I passed an altar of coral slabs and a crucifix suspended from a branch.

The dune had drifted higher than the treetops and, climbing up the scarp, I looked back inland across a level, wooded plain. To seaward, the dunes were hummocky and speckled with sea-grass, and along the north side of the bay there was a thin line of mangrove.

Father Terence was tapping at a typewriter. I called his name. He came out in shorts, and went in, and reappeared in a dirty white soutane. He wondered what had possessed me to walk all that way in the heat.

'Here!' he said. 'Come and sit in the shade, and I'll boil up a billy for tea.'

We sat on a bench in the shade, at the back of the hut. Lying on the ground were a pair of black rubber flippers, and a snorkel and mask. He broke some dead branches, lit them, and the flames flared up under the trivet.

He was a short man, with reddish hair, what was left of it, and not too many flaky brown teeth. He wrapped the teeth in a hesitant smile. He would soon have to go to Broome, he said, to have the doctor freeze off his skin cancers.

As a boy, he told me, he had lived in the Irish Embassy in Berlin, where his father, a patriot, worked in secret to destroy the British Empire: the temper of this man drove his son to a life of prayer. He had come to Australia in the 1960s: to join a new Cistercian house in Victoria.

He typed every evening at this hour: letters mostly, to friends all over the world. He had a long correspondence with a Zen Buddhist monk in Japan. Then he would read, then light the lamp, and read on into the night. He had been reading Durkheim's *Elementary Forms of Religious Life*, which another friend had sent him from England.

'Madness,' he gasped. 'Elementary forms indeed! How *can* religion have an elementary form? Was this fellow a Marxist or something?'

He was working on a book of his own. It would be a 'manual of poverty'. He hadn't yet decided on a title.

Today, he said, more than ever before, men had to learn to live without things. Things filled men with fear: the more things they had, the more they had to fear. Things had a way of riveting themselves on to the soul and then telling the soul what to do.

He poured the tea into two red enamel mugs. It was dark and scalding. We sat a minute or two until he suddenly broke the silence: 'Isn't it wonderful? To live in this wonderful twentieth century? For the first time in history, you don't need to own a thing.'

He did, it was true, have a few possessions in his hut, but soon he was going to leave them. He was going away. He had grown too fond of his little hut, and it pained him.

'There is a time for quiet,' he said, 'and a time for noise. Now I would welcome some noise.'

For seven years, the Desert Fathers had been his spiritual guides: to be lost in the desert was to find one's way to God. But he was less concerned, now, for his own salvation than for the needs of people. He was going to work for derelicts in Sydney.

'I believe something similar about the desert,' I said. Man was born in the desert, in Africa. By returning to the desert he rediscovers himself.

Father Terence clicked his tongue and sighed, 'Dear, oh dear! I can see you're an evolutionist.'

When I told him of my visit to Fathers Subiros and Villaverde, he sighed again and, in a very strong Irish accent, said, 'Those two! *Quite* a pair!' I asked about Flynn. He paused before making a measured reply.

'Flynn has to be some kind of genius,' he said. 'He's got what you'd call a virgin intellect. He can learn anything. His grasp of theology is very fine, but I don't think he was ever a Believer. He could never take the leap into faith. Didn't have the imagination for it, and that did make him dangerous in a way. He got hold of one or two quite dangerous ideas.'

'Such as?'

'Syncretism,' said Father Terence. 'The visit to Rome was a mistake.'

It was in Rome that Flynn began to hate being patronised by his white superiors and to resent the beliefs of his people being mocked. By the time he got to Boongaree, he was already thinking for himself.

The Church, he used to say to Father Terence, was wrong to picture Aboriginals as being stranded in some dreadful limbo: their condition, rather, resembled that of Adam before the Fall. He liked to compare the 'Footprints of the Ancestor' with Our Lord's saying 'I am the Way.'

'So what was I to do?' Father Terence asked me. 'Hold my tongue? Or tell him what I thought? No. I had to tell him that, to my mind, the mental world of the Aboriginals was so confused, so heartless and cruel. With what could one lessen their sufferings if not the Christian message? How else to stop the killing? The name of one of their places in the Kimberleys means "*Kill them all!*" and "*Kill them all!*" is one of those sacred sites they think so much of these days! No! No! No! These poor dark children have only two alternatives: the word of Christ, or the police!'

No one would deny, he went on, that in their concept of the Dreamtime, the Aboriginals had felt the first glimmerings of the life eternal – which was to say that man was naturally religious.

But to confuse their 'primitive' magic with the word of Christ, that was confusion indeed.

The black men were not at fault. For thousands of years, they'd been cut off from the mainstream of humanity. How could they have felt the Great Awakening that swept the Old World in the centuries before Christ? What did they know of the Tao? Or the Buddha? The teachings of the Upanishads? Or the logos of Heraclitus? Nothing! How could they? But what they could do, even now, was to take the leap into faith. They could follow the steps of the Three Wise Men and adore the helpless Babe of Bethlehem.

'And there', said Father Terence, 'I think I lost him. He never understood the story of the stable.'

It was cooler now, and we shifted to the front of the hut. A line of thunderheads, like a procession of aerial icebergs, stood out to sea. The milky blue rollers flopped ashore, and there were flights of terns, skimming low over the bay, piercing the sound of the surf with thin metallic cries. There was no wind.

Father Terence talked about computers and genetic engineering. I asked him if he ever longed for Ireland.

'Never!' he raised both arms to the horizon. 'Here I could never lose it.'

Nailed above the door of the hut was a plank of driftwood on which he had carved two lines in 'gaelic' lettering:

Foxes have holes, birds of the air have nests
But the Son of Man had no place to lay his head

The Lord, he said, had spent forty days and forty nights in the wilderness, building neither house nor cell, but sheltering in the side of a well.

'Come,' he beckoned me. 'Let me show you something.'

He led the way over middens of pinkish shells: the spoilheaps of the tribe who once lived here. After about 200 yards, he stopped beside a cream-coloured rock with a fountain of clear water bubbling up under it. He lifted his soutane and splashed about in the water, like a little boy paddling.

'Isn't water in the desert a lovely thing,' he called. 'I've called the name of this place Meribah.'

On our way back to the hut, a wallaby poked its head round the pandanus, and hopped towards him.

'My brother the wallaby,' he smiled.

He went inside for a couple of crusts. The wallaby took them from his hand, and nuzzled its head against his thigh. He stroked it behind the ears.

I said it was time for me to go. He offered to walk me along the beach.

I took off my boots, hung them by the laces round my neck and the warm sand squeezed between my toes. Crabs scuttled sideways as we came up close, and there were flocks of waders which would flutter up and settle on ahead.

What he'd miss most, he said, was the swimming. On a calm day he liked to snorkel for hours along the reef. The Customs' boat had spotted him once – and mistaken him for a floating corpse. 'And I was in birthday suit, I'm afraid.'

The fish here, he said, were so tame you could float through a shoal and touch them. He knew all their colours and all their names: the rays, wrasses, wobbegongs, the baronessa butterfly, surgeon fish, scorpion fish, rabbit fish, angel fish. Each one was a 'character' with its own individual mannerisms: they reminded him of the faces in a Dublin crowd.

Out to sea, where the coral ended, there was a deep, dark cliff where, one day, a tiger shark swam out of the gloom and circled him. He saw the eyes, the jaws and the five gill-openings, but the brute sheered off and vanished. He had swum ashore and lain on the sand, shaking with delayed shock. Next morning, as if a load were lifted from him, he knew he no longer feared death. Again, he swam along the same stretch of reef, and again the shark circled him and vanished.

'Fear not!' he gripped my hand.

The thunderheads were rolling closer. A warm wind began to blow off the waves.

'Fear not!' he called again.

I turned to wave at the two dim figures: a man in a flowing white robe and a wallaby with its tail in a question-mark.

'Fear not!' He must have said the same words in my sleep, for when I woke in the morning they were the first ones that came to me.

14

IT WAS GREY and overcast when I went downstairs for breakfast. The sun was like a white blister, and there was a smell of burning. The morning papers were full of news of the bushfires north of Adelaide. The clouds, I then realised, were smoke. I put through a call to some friends, who, so far as I could judge, were either in or near the fire zone.

'No, we're OK!' Nin's cheerful, crackly voice came down the line. 'The wind changed just in time. We did have a hair-raising night, though.'

They had watched the rim of the horizon on fire. The fire had been moving at 50 m.p.h., with nothing but state forest between them and it. The tops of the eucalyptus had been breaking off into fireballs, and flying in the gale-force winds.

'Hair-raising, I'll say,' I said.

'This is Australia,' she called back, and then the line went dead.

Outside, it was so hot and muggy that I went back to my room, switched on the air-conditioner, and spent most of the day reading Strehlow's *Songs of Central Australia*.

It was an awkward, discursive and unbelievably long book and Strehlow, by all accounts, was an awkward cuss himself. His father, Karl Strehlow, had been pastor in charge of the Lutheran Mission at Hermannsburg, to the west of Alice Springs. He was one of a handful of 'good Germans' who, by providing a secure land-base, did more than anyone to save the Central Australian Aboriginals from extinction by people of British stock. This did not make them popular. During the First World War, a press campaign broke out against this 'Teuton spies'-nest' and the 'evil effects of Germanising the natives'.

As a baby, Ted Strehlow had an Aranda wet-nurse and grew up speaking Aranda fluently. Later, as a university graduate, he returned to 'his people' and, for over thirty years, patiently recorded in notebooks, on tape and on film the songs and ceremonies of the passing order. His black friends asked him to do this so their songs should not die with them entirely.

It was not surprising, given his background, that Strehlow became an embattled personality: an autodidact who craved both solitude and recognition, a German 'idealist' out of step with the ideals of Australia.

Aranda Traditions, his earlier book, was years ahead of its time in its thesis that the intellect of the 'primitive' was in no way inferior to that of modern man. The message, though largely lost on Anglo-Saxon readers, was taken up by Claude Lévi-Strauss, who incorporated Strehlow's insights into *The Savage Mind*.

Then, in late middle age, Strehlow staked everything on a grand idea.

He wanted to show how every aspect of Aboriginal song had its counterpart in Hebrew, Ancient Greek, Old Norse or Old English: the literatures we acknowledge as our own. Having grasped the connection of song and land, he wished to strike at the roots of song itself: to find in song a key to unravelling the mystery of the human condition. It was an impossible undertaking. He got no thanks for his trouble.

When the *Songs* came out in 1971, a carping review in the *Times Literary Supplement* suggested the author should have refrained from airing his 'grand poetic theory'. The review upset Strehlow terribly. More upsetting were the attacks of the 'activists' who accused him of stealing the songs, with a view to publication, from innocent and unsuspecting Elders.

Strehlow died at his desk in 1978, a broken man. His memory was served by a dismissive biography which, when I glanced at it in the Desert Bookstore, struck me as being beneath contempt. He was, I am convinced, a highly original thinker. His books are great and lonely books.

Around five in the afternoon I dropped in on Arkady at the office.

'I've got good news for you,' he said.

A radio message had come in from Cullen, an Aboriginal out-station about 350 miles away on the West Australian border. Two clans were having a quarrel about mining royalties. They had called in Arkady to mediate.

'Like to come?' he asked.

'Sure.'

'We can get through the railway business in a couple of days. Then we'll head out west across country.'

He had already arranged my permit to visit an Aboriginal reservation. He had a long-standing date for the evening, so I called up Marian and asked if she felt like a meal.

'Can't!' she called back, breathlessly.

She'd been locking the front door when the phone rang. She was off that minute to Tennant Creek, to pick up the women for the survey.

'See you tomorrow,' I said.

'See you.'

I had supper at the Colonel Sanders on Todd Street. Under the glaring neon, a man in a sleek blue suit was delivering a sermon to some teenage potential chicken-friers, as if frying Kentucky chicken were a kind of religious observance.

I went back to my room and spent the evening with Strehlow and a bottle of 'burgundy'.

Strehlow once compared the study of Aboriginal myths to entering a 'labyrinth of countless corridors and passages', all of which were mysteriously connected in ways of baffling complexity. Reading the *Songs*, I got the impression of a man who had entered this secret world by the back door; who had had the vision of a mental construction more marvellous and intricate than anything on earth, a construction to make Man's material achievements seem like so much dross – yet which somehow evaded description.

What makes Aboriginal song so hard to appreciate is the endless accumulation of detail. Yet even a superficial reader can get a glimpse of a moral universe – as moral as the New Testament – in which the structures of kinship reach out to all living men, to all his fellow creatures, and to the rivers, the rocks and the trees.

I read on. Strehlow's transliterations from the Aranda were enough to make anyone cross-eyed. When I could read no more,

I shut the book. My eyelids felt like glasspaper. I finished the bottle of wine and went down to the bar for a brandy.

A fat man and his wife were sitting by the pool.

'A very good evening to you, sir!' he said.

'Good evening,' I said.

I ordered coffee and a double brandy at the bar, and took a second brandy back to the room. Reading Strehlow had made me want to write something. I was not drunk – yet – but had not been so nearly drunk in ages. I got out a yellow pad and began to write.

In the Beginning . . .

IN THE BEGINNING *the Earth was an infinite and murky plain, separated from the sky and from the grey salt sea and smothered in a shadowy twilight. There were neither Sun nor Moon nor Stars. Yet, far away, lived the Sky-Dwellers: youthfully indifferent beings, human in form but with the feet of emus, their golden hair glittering like spiders' webs in the sunset, ageless and unageing, having existed for ever in their green, well-watered Paradise beyond the Western Clouds.*

On the surface of the Earth, the only features were certain hollows which would, one day, be waterholes. There were no animals and no plants, yet clustered round the waterholes there were pulpy masses of matter: lumps of primordial soup – soundless, sightless, unbreathing, unawake and unsleeping – each containing the essence of life, or the possibility of becoming human.

Beneath the Earth's crust, however, the constellations glimmered, the Sun shone, the Moon waxed and waned, and all the forms of life lay sleeping: the scarlet of a desert-pea, the iridescence on a butterfly's wing, the twitching white whiskers of Old Man Kangaroo – dormant as seeds in the desert that must wait for a wandering shower.

On the morning of the First Day, the Sun felt the urge to be born. (That evening the Stars and Moon would follow.) The Sun burst through the surface, flooding the land with golden light, warming the hollows under which each Ancestor lay sleeping.

Unlike the Sky-dwellers, these Ancients had never been young. They were lame, exhausted greybeards with knotted limbs, and they had slept in isolation through the ages.

So it was, on this First Morning, that each drowsing Ancestor felt the Sun's warmth pressing on his eyelids, and felt his body giving birth to children. The Snake Man felt snakes slithering out of his navel. The Cockatoo Man felt feathers. The Witchetty Grub Man felt a wriggling, the Honey-ant a tickling, the Honeysuckle felt his leaves and flowers unfurling. The Bandicoot Man felt baby bandicoots seething from under his armpits. Every one of the 'living things', each at its own separate birthplace, reached up for the light of day.

In the bottom of their hollows (now filling up with water), the Ancients shifted one leg, then another leg. They shook their shoulders and flexed their arms. They heaved their bodies upward through the mud. Their eyelids cracked open. They saw their children at play in the sunshine.

The mud fell from their thighs, like placenta from a baby. Then, like the baby's first cry, each Ancestor opened his mouth and called out, 'I AM!' 'I am — Snake . . . Cockatoo . . . Honey-ant . . . Honeysuckle . . . And this first 'I am!', this primordial act of naming, was held, then and forever after, as the most secret and sacred couplet of the Ancestor's song.

Each of the Ancients (now basking in the sunlight) put his left foot forward and called out a second name. He put his right foot forward and called out a third name. He named the waterhole, the reedbeds, the gum trees — calling to right and left, calling all things into being and weaving their names into verses.

The Ancients sang their way all over the world. They sang the rivers and ranges, salt-pans and sand dunes. They hunted, ate, made love, danced, killed: wherever their tracks led they left a trail of music.

They wrapped the whole world in a web of song; and at last, when the Earth was sung, they felt tired. Again in their limbs they felt the frozen immobility of Ages. Some sank into the ground where they stood. Some crawled into caves. Some crept away to their 'Eternal Homes', to the ancestral waterholes that bore them.

All of them went 'back in'.

15

NEXT MORNING the cloud had cleared and, since the motel did not serve breakfast till eight, I went for a run to the Gap. The heat was already building up. The hills were brown and furrowed in the early light.

On my way out I passed the fat man floating upward in the pool. There was a scar on his stomach, as if the skeleton of a fish had been impressed on it.

'Good day to you, sir!'

'Good day,' I said.

Across the street, some Aboriginal families had parked themselves on the municipal lawn and were freshening up under the lawn-sprayer. They sat close enough to get sprayed and not too close to kill their cigarettes. Some snot-nosed children were tumbling about and were glistening wet all over.

I said hello to a bearded man who said, 'Goodonya, mate.' I nodded to his woman who said, 'Go and suck eggs!' and lowered her eyelids and laughed.

I passed the confused young bodies pumping iron in the 'Fun and Fitness Centre'; then turned right along the riverbank and stopped to read a notice by some ghost-gums:

Registered Sacred Site for the Injalka (Caterpillar) Dreaming
Entry by Vehicle Prohibited
Penalty for damage $2,000

There wasn't much to see, for a white man anyway: a broken barbed-wire fence, some crumbly stones lying this way and that, and a lot of broken bottles in the bristly grass.

I ran on and reached the Gap, but was too hot to go on running so I walked back. The fat man was still floating in the pool and his fat wife was floating beside him. Her hair was in curlers and covered with a crinkly pink cap.

I showered and packed my bag. I packed a pile of my old black notebooks. They were the notebooks for the 'nomad' book, which I had kept when I burned the manuscript. Some I hadn't looked at for at least ten years. They contained a mishmash of nearly indecipherable jottings, 'thoughts', quotations, brief encounters, travel notes, notes for stories . . . I had brought them to Australia because I planned to hole up somewhere in the desert, away from libraries and other men's work, and take a fresh look at what they contained.

Outside my room, I was stopped by a fair, mop-headed boy in patched and faded jeans. He was red in the face and seemed very agitated. He asked if I'd seen an Aboriginal kid, 'A kid with a rasta hair-do?'

'No,' I said.

'Well, if you do see him, say Graham's waiting by the van.'

'I will,' I said, and went in to breakfast.

I had finished my second cup of disgusting coffee when the other Bruce came in and dumped his hard-hat on my table. I said I was leaving town.

'Well, I won't see you, Bru,' he said morosely.

'Maybe not, Bru,' I said.

'Well, so long, Bru!'

'So long!' I shook his hand, and he went up to get his porridge.

Arkady drove up at nine in a brown Toyota Land Cruiser. On the roof-rack were four spare wheels and a row of jerry-cans for water. He wore a freshly laundered khaki shirt, from which the corporal's flashes had been removed. He smelled of soap.

'You're smart,' I said.

'It won't last,' he replied. 'Believe me, it will not last.'

I chucked my bag on to the back seat. The rear of the cab was stacked with boxes of soft drinks and 'Eskis'. An 'Eski', for 'Eskimo', is a polystyrene cool-pack without which a journey into the desert is unthinkable.

We were half-way up Todd Street when Arkady braked, nipped into the Desert Bookstore and came out with the Penguin Classics edition of Ovid's *Metamorphoses*. 'Present for you,' he said. 'Reading matter for the trip.'

We drove to the edge of town, past the 'Bed Shed' and 'Territory Wrecking' and stopped at a Lebanese butcher to pick up some meat. The butcher's son looked up as we came in, and went on sharpening his blade. For the next ten minutes we filled the 'Eskis' to bursting with sausages and slabs of steak.

'Tucker for my old men,' said Arkady.

'Seems an awful lot.'

'You just wait,' he said. 'They could eat a whole cow for supper.'

We also bought some steak for an old 'bushie' by the name of Hanlon, who lived alone beyond the Glen Armond Pub.

We drove on, past the sign to the Old Alice Telegraph Station, and then we were out in the bare, scrubby country of the Burt Plain.

The road was a straight band of tarmac and, on either side, there were strips of red dirt with paddy-melon growing over them. The melons were the size of cricket balls. They had been brought to Australia by the Afghans as fodder for their camels. Sometimes Arkady would swerve on to the melon to miss a road-train coming south. The road-trains had three trailers. They did not slow down but came up, steadily out of the heat-mirage, hogging the middle of the road.

Every few miles, we passed the gates of a cattle-station, or a wind-pump with cattle clustered round it. There were a lot of dead beasts, legs in the air, ballooned up with gas and the crows on top of them. The rains were two months late.

'Marginal country,' said Arkady.

Almost all the best pastoral leases had been bought up by foreigners: Vesteys, Bunker Hunt and the like. No wonder Territorians felt cheated!

'The country's against them,' he said. 'The politicians are against them. The multinationals are against them. The Abos are against them. Surely this country's only good for Abos?'

He described how once, while they were tracing a Songline near Mount Wedge, the owner had driven up and, waving a shotgun, hollered, 'Get off my land! Get them coons off my land!' So Arkady, who had already written the man five letters without receiving a reply, explained the provisions of the Land Rights Act, whereby 'traditional owners' were allowed to visit their sites.

(76)

This made the pastoralist hopping mad, 'There ain't no sacred sites on my land.'

'Oh yes, there are,' said one of the Aboriginals present.

'Oh no, they're not.'

'You're standing on one, mate.'

The road curved to cross a creek bed and, on the far side, Arkady pointed away to the east, to a switchback of pale brown hills. They stood up like cardboard scenery from the plain.

'You see the small hill, there?' he asked.

'Yes.'

There was a smaller, conical hill connected to the others by a low spur of rock.

'That', he said, 'was where the railway people wanted to make a cutting. It would have saved at least two miles of track.'

The hills lay on the northern edge of Aranda country: yet when Arkady sent word round the usual channels, no one wanted to claim them. He had been on the point of assuming there were no 'owners' when an Aranda mob showed up in his office . . . and said they were. He drove five of the men to the hills where they moped about miserably, their eyes bulging with fright. Again and again he asked, 'What are the songs of this place?', or, 'What's the Dreaming-story here?' They clamped their mouths and wouldn't say a word.

'I couldn't think what was up,' he said. 'So I told them about the cutting, and that really set them off. They all began blubbering, "Blackfella die! Whitefella die! All people die! End of Australia! End of world! Finish!"

'Well, obviously,' said Arkady, '*that* had to be something big. So I asked the Elder, who's shaking from head to foot, "What *have* you got down there?" And he cups his hand around my ear and whispers, "MAGGOT POWER!"'

The song that lay along the line of hills told of a Dreamtime Ancestor who failed to perform the correct ritual for controlling a bush-fly breeding cycle. Swarms of maggots overran the Burt Plain, stripping it bare of vegetation – as it is today. The Ancestor rounded up the maggots and crammed them back beneath the spur of rock where, ever since, they'd been breeding and breeding underground. The old men said that, if they cut into the hillside, there'd be a gigantic explosion. A cloud of flies would burst upwards and cover the whole earth and kill every man and animal with poison.

'The Bomb!' I suggested.

'The Bomb,' said Arkady, grimly. 'Some of my friends knew a lot about the Bomb. *After* it went off.'

Before the British H-Bomb test at Maralinga, the Army posted 'Keep Out!' signs, in English, for Aboriginals to read. Not everyone saw them or could read English.

'They went through it,' he said.

'The Cloud?'

'The Cloud.'

'How many died?'

'No one knows,' he said. 'It was all hushed up. You could try asking Jim Hanlon.'

16

AN HOUR OR SO later we passed the Glen Armond Pub, turned left off the tarmac, bumped along a dirt track, and stopped by a disused stockyard.

Nearby, behind a screen of tamarisks, there was an old, unpainted tin bungalow, grey going over into rust, with a brick chimney standing up the middle. This was Hanlon's house.

In the yard out front there were a stack of empty oil-drums and another stack of ex-Army surplus. At the back, under a squeaky wind-pump, there was a dead Chevrolet with silver-grass growing up through it. A faded poster, pasted to the front door, read 'Workers of the World Unite'.

The door scraped open six inches. Hanlon was standing behind it.

'Whatzamattawithya?' he crackled. 'Never seen a man naked before? Come on in, boys!'

For a man in his seventies, Hanlon looked in good shape. He was skinny and taut-muscled, with a short flat head and a craning neck. His hair was crew-cropped and white, and he would pat down the bristles with his hand. He had a broken nose, wore steel-framed spectacles, and spoke in a loud nasal voice.

We sat and he stood. He stared earnestly at his privates, scratched his crotch and bragged about a lady pharmacist he'd tupped in Tennant Creek.

'Not bad for seventy-three!' he looked down at himself. 'Serviceable knackers! Reasonable set of teeth! What more would an old man need?'

'Nothing,' said Arkady.

'You're right,' Hanlon smirked.

He tied a towel round his tummy and got out three bottles of beer. I noticed that his right hand was withered.

It was baking hot inside the house. The heat pressed down from the roof and our shirts were soaked with sweat. The outer room was an L-shaped corridor, with an old enamel bath up one end. Then there was a kitchen, then a group of table and chairs.

He showed us the clippings on the walls: a strike in Kalgoorlie, Lenin's skull, Uncle Joe's moustache, and pin-ups from *Playboy*. He had settled here, thirty years back, with a woman who had left him. He had sold off the land, and now lived on welfare.

On the table there was a scarlet oilcloth, and a tabby cat licking off a plate.

'Git, yer bastard!' He raised his fist and the cat flew off. 'So what are you boys up to?'

'Going up to Kaititj country,' Arkady answered. 'With Alan Nakumurra's Mob.'

'Survey, eh?'

'Yes.'

'Sacred sites, eh?'

'Yes.'

'Sacred bloody baloney! What those boys need is Organisation!'

He flipped off the beer caps, then blew his nose into his hand and smeared the snot carefully on the underside of his chair. He caught me looking at him. He looked at me.

He reminisced about his days at Kalgoorlie, as a paid-up Party member, before the Second World War.

'Ask him!' he pointed at Arkady. 'Ask the boy for my curriculum vitae!'

He pottered off into the inside room, where his bed was, and, after rummaging about among old newspapers, found a book with a dull red buckram binding. He sat down again, adjusted his spectacles and flattened his spine against the chair-back.

'And now,' he announced, pretending to open the book at random, 'now we will read the Gospel according to Our Father Marx. Forgive an old man's blasphemies! For today – what the fuck is today? Thursday ... thought so! the date is immaterial ... page 256 ... And what do we have –?'

What, then, constitutes the alienation of labour? First, the fact that labour is external to the worker, i.e. it does *not* belong to his essential being; that in his work he does *not* affirm himself but denies himself; does *not* feel content but unhappy; does *not* develop his physical and mental energy but mortifies his body and ruins his mind . . .

'Nothing like a few lines of Marx before food,' he beamed. 'For bracing the intellect and strengthening the digestion! Have you boys eaten?'

'We have,' said Arkady.

'Well, you're eating here with me.'

'No, honestly, Jim. We can't.'

'You bloody can.'

'We'd be late.'

'Late? What's late and what's early? An important philosophical question!'

'We'd be late for a lady called Marian.'

'*Not* a philosophical question!' he said. 'Who the hell's Marian?'

'Old friend of mine,' Arkady said. 'Works for the Land Council. She's gone to fetch the Kaititj women. We're meeting her at Middle Bore.'

'Marian! Maid Marian!' Hanlon smacked his lips. 'Descending to Middle Bore with her train of fair damsels. I tell you they can wait. Go and get the steaks, boy!'

'Only if it's quick, Jim,' Arkady relented. 'We've got an hour, and that's it.'

'*Give me . . . give me . . . one hour . . . one hour . . . with you . . .*'

Hanlon still possessed the relics of a passable baritone. He looked at me. 'Don't you look at me like that!' he snapped. 'I've sung in choirs.'

Arkady went out to fetch the steaks from the car.

'So you're a writer, eh?' Hanlon said to me.

'Of sorts.'

'Ever do an honest day's work in your life?'

His blue eyes were watering. His eyeballs were suspended in nets of red wires.

'Try to,' I said.

The withered hand shot forward. It was purplish and waxy. The little finger was off. He held the hand to my face, like a claw.

(81)

'Know what this is?' he taunted.

'A hand.'

'A working man's hand.'

'I've done farm-work,' I said. 'And timber-work.'

'Timber? Where?'

'Scotland.'

'What kind of timber?'

'Spruce . . . larch . . .'

'Very convincing! What kind of saw?'

'Power-saw.'

'What make, you fool?'

'Can't remember.'

'Very unconvincing,' he said. 'Doesn't sound right to me.'

Arkady pushed through the door with the steaks. There were drops of blood on the white plastic bag. Hanlon took the bag, opened it, and inhaled.

'Ah, ha! That's better!' he grinned. 'Nice red meat for a change.'

He got up, lit the gas-ring, poured fat from an old paint can and laid out three steaks in the skillet.

'Here you!' he called to me. 'You come and talk to the cook.'

The fat began to splutter and he took a spatula to stop the meat from sticking.

'So you're writing a book?'

'Trying to,' I said.

'Why don't you write your book right here? You and me could have uplifting conversations.'

'We could,' I said, hesitantly.

'Ark!' Hanlon called. 'Watch these steaks a minute, will you, boy? I'm going to show the bookie his billet. Here! You come with me!'

He dropped the towel to the floor, pulled on a pair of shorts and slipped his feet into thongs. I followed him into the sunlight. The wind had freshened and was kicking up clouds of red dust along the track. We went through the tamarisks to a creaking gum tree with a caravan underneath it.

He opened the door. There was the smell of something dead. The windows were wrapped in spiders' webs. The bedding was stained and torn. Someone had spilled tomato sauce over the table-top, and the ants were swarming over it.

(82)

'Nice little hidey-hole!' Hanlon said chirpily. 'Reasonable rent! And yer could oil the tree if the creaking gets you down.'

'Very nice,' I said.

'But not quite nice enough, eh?'

'I didn't say that.'

'But meant it,' he hissed. 'Of course, we *could* fumigate the place. Might fumigate you in the process!'

He banged the door to, and stalked off back to the house.

I hung about the yard for a while, and when I went in the steaks were done. Hanlon had fried six eggs and was ready to carve.

'Serve His Lordship first!' he said to Arkady.

He cut three hunks of bread and set a sauce bottle on the table. I waited for him to sit down. It was unbearably hot. I looked at the steak and the egg yolks.

Hanlon looked at me for what seemed a full minute and said, 'Get your fucking fangs into that steak!'

We ate without speaking.

Hanlon steadied his steak with his withered hand, and cut it into cubes with the good one. His knife had a serrated blade and a pair of curled-up prongs on the end of it.

'Who the hell does he think he is?' he turned to Arkady. 'Who asked him to poke his upper-snotty-class nose in here?'

'You did,' said Arkady.

'Did I? Well, I made a mistake.'

'I'm not upper class,' I said.

'But a touch too classy for my little luncheon party! Luncheon! That's what they call it in Pongleterre! Luncheon with the Queen! What?'

'Cut it out, Jim,' Arkady said. He was very embarrassed.

'None of it meant personally,' said Hanlon.

'That's something,' I said.

'It is,' he agreed.

'Tell him about Maralinga,' said Arkady, in an effort to turn the conversation. 'Tell him about the Cloud.'

Hanlon raised his good hand and clicked his fingers like castanets.

'The Cloud! Aye, aye, Sir! The Cloud! Her Majesty's Cloud. Sir Anthony-stuck-up-in-Eden's Cloud! Poor Sir Anthony! Wanted his Cloud so badly! So he could say to the Rooskie in

Geneva, "Look, old boy, we also have the Cloud!" Forgetting, of course, that there *are* such things as variables in climate . . . ! *Even* in Australia! Forgetting the wind *might* be blowing in the wrong direction! So he calls up Bob Menzies and says, "Bob, I want my Cloud now! Today!" "But the wind . . ." says Sir Bob. "Don't you give me wind," says Sir Anthony. "I said *now*!" So they let off the device – how I love that word "device"! – and the Cloud, instead of sailing out to sea to contaminate the fishes, sailed inland to contaminate *us*! Where they lost it! Lost the bugger over Queensland! All so Sir Anthony could have a nice cosy Cloud talk with Comrade Nikita! "Yes, Comrade, it's true. We *do*, too, have the Cloud. Not that my men over there didn't lose it for a while! Vaporised a few Abos on the way . . ."'

'That's enough,' said Arkady, firmly.

Hanlon hung his head.

'Aw, shit!' he said, and then prodded another steak cube and put it in his mouth.

No one spoke until Hanlon burped and said, 'Beg pardon!'

He pushed his plate away.

'Can't eat the bugger,' he said.

His face had turned putty colour. His hand was shaky.

'Anything the matter?' asked Arkady.

'I got a crook gut, Ark.'

'You should go to a doctor.'

'I been to the doctor. They want to cut me up, Ark.'

'I'm sorry,' I said.

'I won't let them cut me. That's right, isn't it?'

'No,' said Arkady. 'Maybe you should go.'

'Well, maybe I will,' he sniffed miserably.

At the end of another five minutes Arkady got up and laid his arm protectively around the old man's shoulders.

'Jim,' he said in a soft voice, 'I'm sorry, I'm afraid we've got to go. Can we take you anywhere?'

'No,' he said. 'I'll stay.'

We made a move to go.

'Stay a bit longer,' Hanlon said.

'No, really, we have to go.'

'I wish you boys'd stay a bit longer. We could have a good time.'

'We'll come again,' I said.

'Will you?' Hanlon held his breath. 'When?'

'Couple of days,' said Arkady. 'We'll be done by then. Then we're heading out to Cullen.'

'Sorry I flew at you,' he said to me. His lip was quivering. 'Always fly at Poms!'

'No worries,' I said.

It was hotter than ever outside, and the wind was dying. In the front paddock a wedge-tailed eagle was skimming down the line of the fence-posts. It was a lovely, gleaming, bronze-feathered bird and it sheered away when it saw us.

I tried to shake Hanlon's hand. He was holding it over his abdomen. We got into the Land Cruiser.

'You might have said thank you for the steaks,' he called out after us.

He was trying to resume his abrasive manner, but he looked scared. His cheeks were wet with tears. He turned his back. He could not bear to watch us going.

17

AT THE GATE TO Skull Creek Camp, there was a signboard announcing a fine of $2,000 for anyone bringing liquor on to an Aboriginal settlement, over which someone had scrawled in white chalk, 'Bullshit!' We had come here to pick up a Kaititj Elder called Timmy. He was a relative of Alan Nakumurra, on his mother's side, and knew the Dreamings around Middle Bore Station.

I unchained the gate and we drove towards a scatter of shiny tin roofs, half-seen through the bleached grass. On the edge of the settlement, some boys were bouncing on a trampoline and, nearby, there was a big brown windowless metal box which, Arkady said, was the clinic.

'Someone then called it the "Death Machine",' he said. 'Now no one'll ever go near it.'

We parked under a pair of ghost-gums, alongside a small whitewashed house. Songbirds were chattering in the branches. Two full-bosomed women, one in a loose green smock, lay asleep on the porch.

'Mavis,' Arkady called.

Neither of the snoring fat creatures stirred.

Beyond the gums, set down in a circle around an expanse of red dirt, were about twenty humpies: half-cylinders of corrugated sheet, open-ended like pig-shelters, with people lying or squatting in the shade.

Paper cartons and bits of sheet plastic were flying in the wind, and over the whole settlement there was a glint of glass. Glossy black crows hopped here and there, blinking their jaundice-coloured eyes and pecking at old bully-beef cans, until driven off by the dogs.

A small boy, recognising Arkady, shouted, 'Ark! Ark!' and, within seconds, we were surrounded by a mob of naked children clamouring, 'Ark! Ark! Ark!' Their fair hair looked like stubble in a field of black soil. Flies were feeding from the corners of their eyes.

Arkady held two in his arms. A third rode piggyback, and the others pawed at his legs. He patted their heads, squeezed their outstretched palms; then, opening the back of the Land Cruiser, he began distributing drinks and lollies.

One of the fat women sat up, pushed aside her tangle of hair, yawned, rubbed her eyes and said, 'S'that you, Ark?'

'Hello, Mavis!' he said. 'How's you today?'

'M'right,' she yawned again, and shook herself.

'Where's Timmy?'

''Sleep.'

'I want to take him out bush.'

'Today?'

'Now, Mavis. Now!'

Mavis heaved herself to her feet and went off lumpily to wake her husband. She needn't have bothered. Timmy had heard the kerfuffle outside and was standing in the doorway.

He was a pale, skinny, impish-looking old man with a wispy beard and one eye clouded with trachoma. He wore a brown felt hat at an angle and a red handkerchief knotted at his neck. He was so skinny he kept having to hitch up his pants. He waggled a finger at Arkady, and sniggered.

Arkady shed the children and fetched from the car a photo album, with snapshots from an earlier expedition. He then sat on the steps with Timmy and Timmy turned the pages with the furious concentration of a child absorbed in a story-book.

I sat behind them, looking on. An insistent white bitch with mastitis kept ramming her snout up my crotch.

Arkady hugged the old man and said, 'Are you coming with us today, then?'

'Got the tucker?' asked Timmy.

'Got the tucker.'

'Good.'

Mavis sat slumped alongside us. She had pulled her hair over her face again and all you saw of her was a cracked and pouting lower lip.

Arkady leaned round and said, 'Are you coming too, Mavis? We've got Topsy and Gladys from Curtis Springs.'

(87)

'Nah!' she growled, bitterly. 'I never go no place now. Sit down here all the time.'

'No holiday or nothing?'

She sniffed. 'Sometimes we go up Tennant Creek. I got people there. My mother come from that country. She come from the big bore by the creek. You know that place?'

'I think so,' Arkady said, uncertainly.

'Billy Boy Mob's country,' said Mavis, rousing herself with exhausted dignity, as though defining her right to exist. 'Right up to McCluhan Station.'

'And you won't come with us to Middle Bore?'

'Can't,' she snorted.

'What's stopping you?'

'No thongs.' She stretched out her foot and invited Arkady to inspect her split and calloused sole. 'Can't go no place without thongs. Got to get myself some thongs.'

'Have mine!' I volunteered. 'I've got a spare.'

I went to the car, undid my rucksack and pulled out my one and only pair of green rubber thongs. Mavis grabbed them from my hand as if it were *I* who had stolen them from her. She put them on, tossed her head, and shuffled off to fetch Timmy's billy and blanket. 'Goodonya, Sir Walter!' said Arkady, and grinned.

Timmy meanwhile was sucking at his carton of apple juice. He put it down, re-aligned his hat, sucked again and then said, thoughtfully, 'What about Big Tom?'

'Is he here?'

'Sure he's here.'

'Would he come?'

'Sure he'd come.'

We walked towards a shack with a lean-to trellis of paddy-melons under which Big Tom was sleeping. He was shirtless. His heaving paunch was covered with whorls of hair. His dog began to yap and he woke.

'Tom,' said Arkady, 'we're going up to Middle Bore. You want to come?'

'Sure I'll come,' he smiled.

He crawled out, reached for a brown shirt and hat, and pronounced himself ready to leave. His wife, Ruby, a spindly woman with a dizzy smile, then crawled out from her side of the shelter, covered her head with a green spotted scarf and said she, too, was ready.

I never saw two married people pack up and get going so quick.

We were a party of six now, and the smell inside the Land Cruiser was rich and strange.

On the way out, we passed a long-limbed young man with fair hair in rat-tails and a reddish beard. He was lying full-length on the dirt. He had on an orange t-shirt, washed-out red jeans, and around his neck there was a Rajneesh rosary. Four or five black women squatted round him. They appeared to be massaging his legs.

Arkady tooted the horn and waved. The man nearly managed a nod.

'Whoever's that?' I asked.

'That's Craig,' he said. 'He's married to one of the women.'

18

AT THE BURNT FLAT HOTEL, where we stopped for a tank of gasoline, a police patrolman was taking affidavits about a man found dead on the road.

The victim, he told us, had been white, in his twenties and a derelict. Motorists had been sighting him on and off along the highway, over the past three days. 'And he's a right mess now. We had to scrape him off the bitumen with a shovel. Truckie mistook him for a dead roo.'

The 'accident' had happened at five in the morning but the body – what was left of it by the road-train – had been cold for about six hours.

'Looks like somebody dumped him,' said the policeman.

He was being most officiously polite. His adam's apple worked up and down the V of his khaki shirt. It was his duty, we would understand that, to ask a few questions. Run over a coon in Alice Springs and no one'd give it a thought. But a *white* man . . . !

'So where were you boys at eleven last night?'

'The Alice,' said Arkady in a flat voice.

'Thank you very much,' the officer touched his hat brim. 'No need to trouble you further.'

All this he said, looking into the cab, without once removing his stare from our passengers. The passengers, for their part, pretended he did not exist and stared with set faces at the plain.

The policeman walked towards his air-conditioned car. Arkady rang the bell for service. He rang again. He rang a third time. Nobody came.

'Looks like we're in for a wait,' he shrugged.

'It does,' I agreed.

It was three in the afternoon and the buildings were swimming in the heat. The hotel was painted a toffee-brown and, on the corrugated roof, in bold but peeling white letters, were the words BURNT FLAT. Under the veranda there was an aviary of budgerigars and rosellas. The bunkrooms were boarded up, and a sign read, 'This business is for sale'.

The name of the proprietor was Bruce.

'Profits went down', said Arkady, 'when they took away his off-licence.'

Bruce had made a mint of money, until the change in licensing laws, selling fortified wine to Aboriginals.

We waited.

An elderly couple drove up in a camper, and when the husband pressed the service bell, the bar-room door opened and a man in shorts came out with a bull-terrier panting at its leash.

Bruce had quarter-to-three feet, red hair, flabby buttocks and oval jowls. His arms were tattooed with mermaids. He tied up the dog, which yelped at our passengers. He eyeballed Arkady and went to serve the couple with the camper.

After the man had paid, Arkady asked Bruce very civilly, 'Could we get a tank, please?'

Bruce untied the dog and waddled off the way he'd come.

'Pig,' said Arkady.

We waited.

The patrolman was watching from his car.

'They have to serve us eventually,' Arkady said. 'By law.'

Ten minutes later, the door re-opened and a woman in a blue skirt came down the steps. She had short hair, prematurely grey. She had been making pie and the pastry still clung to her fingernails.

'Don't mind Bruce,' she sighed. 'He's mad today.'

'Unusual?' Arkady smiled, and she hunched her shoulders and exhaled a long breath.

'Go on in,' he said to me, 'if you'd like to see some local colour.'

'Go on,' the woman urged, as she hung up the nozzle.

'Have we time?'

'We can make time,' he said. 'For your education.'

The woman tightened her forelip and let out an awkward laugh.

'Why don't I buy them a drink?' I suggested.

(91)

'Do that,' said Arkady. 'I'll have a beer.'

I poked my head through the window and asked what they'd have. Mavis said orange but changed her mind to orange and mango. Ruby said apple. Big Tom said grapefruit and Timmy said Coke.

'And a Violet Crumble,' he added. Violet Crumble is a chocolate-covered candy bar.

Arkady paid the woman and I followed her into the bar.

'And as you come out,' he called after me, 'look to the right of the light switch.'

Inside, some men from a road-gang were playing darts, and a station-hand, togged up in Western gear, was feeding coins into a juke-box. There were a lot of Polaroid pictures pinned to the walls: of fat people naked and a lot of long balloons. A notice read, 'Credit is like Sex. Some get it. Some don't.' A 'medieval' scroll had the caricature of a muscle-man and some 'Olde Englishe' lettering:

> Yea, though I walk through
> The Valley of the Shadow of Death
> I will fear no Evil
> For I, Bruce, am
> The Meanest son of a Bitch in the Valley.

Alongside the bottles of Southern Comfort, there was an old bottle topped with yellow liquid and labelled, 'Authentic N.T. Gin Piss.'

I waited.

I heard Bruce tell one of the drinkers he'd bought a place in Queensland where you could 'still call a Boong a Boong'.

A telegraph engineer came in dripping with sweat, and ordered a couple of beers.

'Hear you had a hit-and-run job up the road?' he said.

'Yeah!' Bruce displayed his teeth. 'More meat!'

'What'z'at?'

'I said more edible meat.'

'Edible?'

'White man.' Bruce hung out his tongue and guffawed. The engineer, I was glad to see, frowned and said nothing.

The engineer's mate then pushed through the door and sat on

a bar-stool. He was a lanky young Aboriginal half-blood, with a cheery, self-deprecating smile.

'No coons in here,' Bruce raised his voice above the noise of the dart-players. 'Did you hear me? I said, "No coons in here!"'

'I ain't a coon,' the half-blood answered. 'I just got skin problems.'

Bruce laughed. The road-gang laughed, and the half-blood clenched his teeth and went on smiling. I watched his fingers tighten around his beer can.

Bruce then said to me in a voice of forced politeness, 'You're a long ways from home. What'll it be?'

I gave the order.

'And a Violet Crumble,' I said.

'And a Violet Crumble for the English gent!'

I said nothing, and paid.

On my way out I looked to the right of the light switch and saw a bullet-hole in the wallpaper. Around it hung a gilded frame with a little brass plaque – the kind of plaque you see nailed below antlers or a stuffed fish – reading 'Mike – 1982'.

I handed round the drinks and they took them without a nod.

'So who was Mike?' I asked as we drove away.

'Is Mike,' Arkady said. 'He *was* Bruce's barman.'

It had been a similar baking summer afternoon, and four Pintupi boys, driving back from the Balgo Mission, had stopped to get gas and a drink. They were very tired and excitable and when the eldest boy saw the 'Gin Piss' bottle, he said something quite abusive. Mike refused to serve them. The boy aimed a beer glass at the bottle, and missed. Mike took Bruce's .22 rifle – which Bruce kept handy under the counter – and fired above their heads.

'That, at any rate,' said Arkady, 'is what Mike said at the trial.'

The first shot hit the kid through the base of the skull. The second shot hit the wall to the right of the light switch. A third, for good measure, went into the ceiling.

'Naturally,' Arkady continued in the same unemotional tone, 'the neighbours wished to contribute to the unfortunate barman's legal fees. They organised a gala, with a topless show from Adelaide.'

'And Mike got off?'

'Self-defence.'

'What about the witnesses?'

'Aboriginal witnesses', he said, 'are not always easy to handle. They refuse, for example, to hear the dead man called by name.'

'You mean they wouldn't testify?'

'It makes the case for the prosecution difficult.'

19

WE FORKED RIGHT at the sign for Middle Bore and headed east along a dusty road that ran parallel to a rocky escarpment. The road rose and fell through a thicket of grey-leaved bushes, and there were pale hawks perching on the fence-posts. Arkady kept swerving to avoid the deeper ruts.

Not far to the right, we passed an outcrop of weathered sandstone, with free-standing pinnacles about twenty feet high. I knew it had to be a Dreaming site. I nudged Big Tom in the ribs.

'Who's that one?' I asked.

'Him a small one,' he cricked his index finger to imitate a wriggling grub.

'Witchetty?'

He shook his head strenuously and, with the gesture of feeding a grub into his mouth, said, 'Smaller one.'

'Caterpillar?'

'Yeah!' he beamed, and nudged me back.

The road ran on towards a white house in a clump of trees with a spread of buildings beyond it. This was Middle Bore Station. There were chestnut horses grazing in a field of bone-white grass.

We veered left along a smaller track, crossed a watercourse and stopped at the gate of my second Aboriginal camp. The place had a less woebegone look than Skull Creek. There were fewer broken bottles, fewer festering dogs, and the children looked far healthier.

Although it was late in the afternoon, most of the people were still asleep. A woman sat sorting bush-tucker under a tree and, when Arkady greeted her, she looked down and stared at her toes.

We picked our way past the humpies, zigzagging through

clumps of spinifex towards the wheel-less body of a Volks-wagen van. There was a green tarpaulin stretched over the door, and a length of plastic hose dribbled into a patch of water-melon. Chained to the van was the usual sharp-muzzled hound.

'Alan?' Arkady raised his voice above the yapping.

No reply.

'Alan, are you there? . . . Christ,' he said under his breath, 'let's hope he's not gone off again.'

We waited a while longer and a long black hand appeared around the edge of the tarpaulin. This was followed, after an interval, by a wiry, silver-bearded man wearing a pale grey stetson, dirty white pants and a purple shirt printed with guitars. He was barefoot. He stepped into the sunlight, looked clean through Arkady, and majestically lowered his head.

The dog continued to bark, and he walloped it.

Arkady talked to him in Walbiri. The old man listened to what he had to say, lowered his head a second time, and retired back behind the tarpaulin.

'Reminds me of Haile Selassie,' I said as we walked away.

'But grander.'

'Much grander,' I agreed. 'He will come, won't he?'

'I think so.'

'Can he speak any English?'

'Can but won't. English isn't his favourite language.'

The Kaititj, Arkady told me, had had the misfortune to live along the route of the Overland Telegraph Line and so came early into contact with the white man. They also learned to make knives and spear-points from the glass-conductors, and, to put a stop to this practice, it was thought necessary to teach them a lesson. The Kaititj took revenge on their murderers.

Earlier in the afternoon we had passed on the roadside the grave of the telegraph operator who, in 1874, dying of a spear-thrust, succeeded in tapping out a farewell message to his wife in Adelaide. The police reprisals dragged on until the 1920s.

Alan, as a young man, had seen his father and brothers gunned down.

'And you say he's the last one left?'

'Of his clan,' he said. 'In this stretch of country.'

We were sitting back to back against the trunk of a gum tree, watching the camp come alive. Mavis and Ruby had gone visiting their women friends. Big Tom had dozed off, and Timmy sat cross-legged, smiling. The ground was parched and cracked, and a solid, undeviating stream of ants was passing within inches of my boots.

'Where the hell *is* Marian?' Arkady said, abruptly. 'Should have been here hours ago. Anyway, let's get some tea.'

I dragged some brushwood from the thicket and lit a fire while Arkady unpacked the tea things. He passed a ham roll to Timmy, who gobbled it up, asked for another and, with the air of a man accustomed to being waited on by servants, handed me his billy to fill.

The water was almost boiling when, all of a sudden, there was a tremendous hullabaloo in the camp. Women shrieked, dogs and children scuttled for cover, and we saw, hurtling towards us, a column of purplish-brown dust.

The willy-willy roared and crackled as it approached; sucked up leaves, branches, plastic, paper and scraps of metal sheet, spiralling them into the sky and then sweeping across the camp-ground and on towards the road.

A moment or two of panic – and everything was back to normal.

After a while we were joined by a middle-aged man in a sky-blue shirt. He was hatless. The stiff grey bristles on his head were the length of the bristles on his chin. His frank and smiling face reminded me of my father's. He squatted on his hams and shovelled spoonsful of sugar into his mug. Arkady talked. The man waited for him to finish and answered in a low whisper, doodling diagrams in the sand with his finger.

Then he walked away, in the direction of Alan's living van.

'Who was he?' I asked.

'The old man's nephew,' he said. 'And also his "ritual manager".'

'What did he want?'

'To check us out.'

'Did we pass?'

'I think we can expect a visit.'

'When?'

'Soon.'

'I wish I understood this business of "ritual manager".'

'It's not easy.'

The smoke from the fire blew in our faces but at least kept away the flies.

I took out my notebook and propped it on my knee.

The first step, Arkady said, was to get to grips with two more Aboriginal expressions: *kirda* and *kutungurlu*.

Old Alan was kirda: that is to say, he was the 'owner' or 'boss' of the land we were going to survey. He was responsible for its upkeep, for making sure its songs were sung and its rituals performed on time.

The man in blue, on the other hand, was Alan's kutungurlu, his 'manager' or 'helper'. He belonged to a different totemic clan and was a nephew – real or 'classificatory', that didn't matter – on Alan's mother's side of the family. The word kutungurlu itself meant 'uterine kin'.

'So the "manager"', I said, 'always has a different Dreaming to the boss?'

'He does.'

Each enjoyed reciprocal rites in each other's country, and worked as a team to maintain them. The fact that 'boss' and 'manager' were seldom men of the same age meant that ritual knowledge went ricocheting down the generations.

In the old days, Europeans believed the 'boss' was really 'boss' and the 'manager' some kind of sidekick. This, it turned out, was wishful thinking. Aboriginals themselves sometimes translated kutungurlu as 'policeman' – which gave a far more accurate idea of the relationship.

'The "boss"', said Arkady, 'can hardly make a move without his "policeman's" permission. Take the case of Alan here. The nephew tells me they're both very worried the railway's going to destroy an important Dreaming site: the eternal resting place of a Lizard Ancestor. But it's up to him, not Alan, to decide if they should come with us or not.'

The magic of the system, he added, was that responsibility for land resides ultimately, not with the 'owner', but with a member of the neighbouring clan.

'And vice versa?' I asked.

'Of course.'

'Which would make war between neighbours rather difficult?'

'Checkmated,' he said.

'It'd be like America and Russia agreeing to swap their own internal politics —'

'Ssh!' Arkady whispered. 'They're coming.'

20

THE MAN IN BLUE was coming through the spinifex at the pace of a slow march. Alan followed a step or two behind, his stetson rammed low over his forehead. His face was a mask of fury and self-control. He sat down next to Arkady, crossed his legs and laid his .22 across his knee.

Arkady unrolled the survey map, weighting the corners with stones to stop them lifting in the blasts. He pointed to various hills, roads, bores, fences—and the probable route of the railway.

Alan looked on with the composure of a general at a staff meeting. From time to time, he would stretch a questioning finger to some feature on the map, and then withdraw it.

I mistook this performance for a charade: it never dawned on me the old man could map-read. But then he splayed both first and second fingers into a V and ran them up and down the sheet, like dividers, his lips working silently, at speed. He was, as Arkady told me later, measuring off a Songline.

Alan accepted a cigarette from Big Tom and continued to smoke in silence.

A few minutes later, a ramshackle truck drove up, with two white men in front and a black stockhand hunched against the tailboard. The driver, a thin, weatherlined man with sideburns and a greasy brown hat, got out and shook hands with Arkady. He was Frank Olson, the owner of Middle Bore Station.

'And this here', he said, pointing to his younger companion, 'is my partner, Jack.'

Both men were wearing shorts and grubby sweatshirts and desert boots without laces or socks. Their legs were scabbed and pitted by thorns and insect bites. Because they looked so grim and purposeful, Arkady shifted to the defensive. He needn't have worried. All Olson wanted was to know where the railway line was going.

He squatted over the map. 'Lemme see what the buggers are up to,' he said angrily.

For the past two weeks, he told us, the bulldozers had cleared a wide swathe through the bush right up to his southern boundary fence. If they went on following the line of the watershed, they'd wreck his catchment system.

The map, however, showed the projected route curving away to the east.

'Whew!' said Olson, pushing his hat to the back of his head and wiping the perspiration with his palm. 'No one thought to tell me, of course.'

He spoke of falling beef prices, and the drought, and dead beasts everywhere. In a good year, they had twelve inches of rain. This year, so far, they'd had eight. Cut that to seven and he'd be out of business.

Arkady asked Olson's permission to camp beside one of his dams.

'Right by me!' he said, rolling an eye at Alan and winking. 'You'd better ask the Boss.'

The old man didn't move a muscle but a faint smile filtered through the waves of his beard.

Olson stood up. 'Be seeing you,' he said. 'Look in for a bite of tea tomorrow.'

'We will,' said Arkady. 'Thanks.'

The evening had settled into a golden calm when we saw a streak of dust along the line of the road. It was Marian.

She drove up at the wheel of her old grey Land-Rover, through the humpies, and parked fifty yards short of our fire. Two brawny women, Topsy and Gladys, squeezed themselves out of the cab and there were four thinner women behind. They jumped down, brushed off the dust, and flexed their arms and legs.

'You're late,' Arkady scolded her, playfully.

Her cheeks were creased with tiredness.

'You'd have been late,' she laughed.

Since leaving Alice Springs, she'd driven 300 miles; treated a boy for scorpion bite; dosed a baby for dysentery; drawn an elder's abscessed tooth; sewn up a woman who'd been beaten by her husband; sewn up the husband, who'd been beaten by the brother-in-law.

'And now', she said, 'I'm famished.'

Arkady fetched her a French roll and a mug of tea. He was worried in case she was too tired to go on. 'We can spend the night where we are,' he said.

'No, *thank* you,' she said. 'Let's get out of here.'

She had on the same skimpy flower-printed dress. She sat on the front bumper, planted her legs apart and stuffed the roll between her teeth. I tried to talk to her, but she looked straight through me, smiling the smile of a woman on women's business.

She drained the mug and handed it back to Arkady. 'Give me ten minutes,' she said. 'Then we'll go.'

She strolled off and doused herself under a hydrant in the women's section of the camp. Then she strolled back, silhouetted against the sunlight, glistening wet all over, the wet dress flattened out over her breasts and hips, and her hair hanging loose in golden snakes. It was no exaggeration to say she looked like a Piero madonna: the slight awkwardness of her movements made her that much more attractive.

A crowd of young mothers formed a ring round her. She hugged their babies, wiped the snot from their noses and the dirt off their behinds. She patted them, jogged them up and down, and handed them back.

So what was it, I wondered, about these Australian women? Why were they so strong and satisfied, and so many of the men so drained? I tried to talk to her again, but again the blank smile warned me off.

'What's up with Marian?' I asked Arkady as we packed the gear. 'I think I've done something wrong.'

'Don't worry,' he said. 'She's always that way when she's with the women.'

If the women saw her hobnobbing with a stranger, they'd think she was a blabmouth and tell nothing.

'Yes,' I said. 'That would explain it.'

'Come on, you mob,' he called the men away from the fire. 'We're off.'

21

THE LAND CRUISER bumped and lurched along a double rut of dust, the bushes brushing the underside of the chassis. Alan sat in front with Timmy, with his rifle upright between his knees. Marian followed hard after, with the ladies. We crossed a sandy gully and had to change to four-wheel drive. A black horse reared up, whinnied and galloped off.

On ahead the country was open woodland. The trees made dark stripes of shadow over the grass and the ghost-gums, at this orange hour of the evening, seemed to float above the ground, like balloons that had let down their anchors.

Alan raised his hand for Arkady to stop, whipped the .22 through the window and fired into a bush. A female kangaroo and young broke cover and leaped away in great lolloping bounds, their haunches white against the grey of the scrub.

Alan fired again, and again. Then he and the man in blue jumped out and sprinted after them.

'Giant red,' said Arkady. 'They come out for water at sunset.'

'Did he hit her?'

'Don't think so,' he said. 'No. Look, they're coming back.'

Alan's hat showed up first, above the level of the grass heads. The man in blue's shirt was ripped at the shoulder, and he was bleeding from a thorn scratch.

'Bad luck, old man,' said Arkady to Alan.

Alan re-cocked the rifle and glared from the window.

The sun was touching the treetops when we came to a wind-pump and some abandoned stock-pens. There had been a settlement here in the old days. There were heaps of rotted grey timbers and the wreck of a stockman's house. The wind-pump spurted a steady stream of water into two round galvanised tanks.

A flock of galahs sat perched around the rim of the tanks, several hundred of them, pink-crested cockatoos which flew up as we approached and wheeled overhead: the undersides of their wings were the colour of wild roses.

Everyone in the party surrounded a drinking trough, splashed the dirt from their faces, and filled their water-cans.

I made a point of avoiding Marian, but she came up from behind and pinched me on the bum.

'Getting to learn the rules, I see,' she grinned.

'Madwoman.'

The country away to the east was a flat and treeless waste entirely lacking in cover. Alan kept raising a finger to a solitary bump on the horizon. It was almost dark by the time we reached a small rocky hill, its boulders bursting with the white plumes of spinifex in flower, and a black fuzz of leafless mallee bush.

The hill, said Arkady, was the Lizard Ancestor's resting place.

The party split into two camps, each within earshot of the other. The men settled themselves and their swags in a circle, and began talking in hushed voices. While Arkady unpacked, I went off to hack some firewood.

I had lit the fire, using bark and grass for tinder, when we heard the sound of pandemonium from the women's camp. Everyone was shrieking and howling, and against the light of their fires I could make out Mavis, hopping this way and that, and gesturing to something on the ground.

'What's up?' Arkady called to Marian.

'Snake!' she called back, cheerfully.

It was only a snake-trail in the sand, but that was snake enough to put the women into hysterics.

The men, too, began to get twitchy. Led by Big Tom, they jumped to their feet. Alan re-cocked the .22. The two others armed themselves with sticks; scrutinised the sand; spoke in hoarse, emotional whispers; and waved their arms like hammy Shakespearean actors.

'Take no notice,' said Arkady. 'They're only showing off. All the same, I think I'll sleep on the roof of the Land Cruiser.'

'Chicken!' I said.

For myself, I rigged up a 'snakeproof' groundsheet to sleep on, tying each corner to a bush, so its edges were a foot from the ground. Then I began to cook supper.

The fire was far too hot for grilling steaks without charring them: I almost charred myself as well. Alan looked on with masterful indifference. None of the others gave one word of thanks for their food, but kept passing back their plates for more. Finally, when they were satisfied, they resumed their conference.

'You know who they remind me of?' I said to Arkady. 'A boardroom of bankers.'

'Which is what they are,' he said. 'They're deciding how little to give us.'

The steak was charred and tough, and after Hanlon's lunch we had very little appetite. We cleared up and went to join the old men's circle. The firelight lapped their faces. The moon came up. We could just discern the profile of the hill.

We sat in silence until Arkady, judging the moment, turned to Alan and asked quietly, in English, 'So what's the story of this place, old man?'

Alan gazed into the fire without twitching. The skin stretched taut over his cheekbones and shone. Then, almost imperceptibly, he tilted his head towards the man in blue, who got to his feet and began to mime (with words of pidgin thrown in) the travels of the Lizard Ancestor.

It was a song of how the lizard and his lovely young wife had walked from northern Australia to the Southern Sea, and of how a southerner had seduced the wife and sent him home with a substitute.

I don't know what species of lizard he was supposed to be: whether he was a 'jew-lizard' or a 'road-runner' or one of those rumpled, angry-looking lizards with ruffs around their necks. All I do know is that the man in blue made the most lifelike lizard you could ever hope to imagine.

He was male and female, seducer and seduced. He was glutton, he was cuckold, he was weary traveller. He would claw his lizard-feet sideways, then freeze and cock his head. He would lift his lower lid to cover the iris, and flick out his lizard-tongue. He puffed his neck into goitres of rage; and at last, when it was time for him to die, he writhed and wriggled, his movements growing fainter and fainter like the Dying Swan's.

Then his jaw locked, and that was the end.

The man in blue waved towards the hill and, with the triumphant cadence of someone who has told the best of all possible stories, shouted: 'That . . . that is where he is!'

The performance had lasted not more than three minutes.

The death of the lizard touched us and made us sad. But Big Tom and Timmy had been in stitches since the wife-swapping episode and went on hooting and cackling long after the man in blue sat down. Even the resigned and beautiful face of old Alan composed itself into a smile. Then one by one they yawned, and spread out their swags, and curled up and went to sleep.

'They must have liked you,' Arkady said. 'It was their way of saying thanks for the food.'

We lit a hurricane lamp and sat on a couple of camping-chairs, away from the fire. What we had witnessed, he said, was not of course the *real* Lizard song, but a 'false front', or sketch performed for strangers. The real song would have named each waterhole the Lizard Man drank from, each tree he cut a spear from, each cave he slept in, covering the whole long distance of the way.

He had understood the pidgin far better than I. This is the version I then jotted down:

The Lizard and his wife set off to walk to the Southern Sea. The wife was young and beautiful and had far lighter skin than her husband. They crossed swamps and rivers until they stopped at a hill – the hill at Middle Bore – and there they slept the night. In the morning they passed the camp of some Dingoes, where a mother was suckling a brood of pups. 'Ha!' said the Lizard. 'I'll remember those pups and eat them later.'

The couple walked on, past Oodnadatta, past Lake Eyre, and came to the sea at Port Augusta. A sharp wind was blowing off the sea, and the Lizard felt cold and began to shiver. He saw, on a headland nearby, the campfire of some Southerners and said to his wife, 'Go over to those people and borrow a firestick.'

She went. But one of the Southerners, lusting after her lighter skin, made love to her – and she agreed to stay with him. He made his own wife paler by smearing her from head to foot with yellow ochre and sent her, with the firestick, to the solitary traveller. Only when the ochre rubbed off did the Lizard realise

his loss. He stamped his feet. He puffed himself up in fury, but,
being a stranger in a distant country, he was powerless to take
revenge. Miserably, he turned for home with his uglier, substitute
wife. On the way he stopped to kill and eat the Dingo puppies but
these gave him indigestion and made him sick. On reaching the
hill at Middle Bore, he lay down and died . . .

And that, as the man in blue told us, was where he was.

Arkady and I sat mulling over this story of an antipodean
Helen. The distance from here to Port Augusta, as the crow flew,
was roughly 1,100 miles, about twice the distance – so we
calculated – from Troy to Ithaca. We tried to imagine an Odyssey
with a verse for every twist and turn of the hero's ten-year voyage.

I looked at the Milky Way and said, 'You might as well count
the stars.'

Most tribes, Arkady went on, spoke the language of their
immediate neighbour, so the difficulties of communication
across a frontier did not exist. The mystery was how a man of
Tribe A, living up one end of a Songline, could hear a few bars
sung by Tribe Q and, without knowing a word of Q's language,
would know exactly what land was being sung.

'Christ!' I said. 'Are you telling me that Old Alan here would
know the songs for a country a thousand miles away?'

'Most likely.'

'Without ever having been there?'

'Yes.'

One or two ethnomusicologists, he said, had been working on
the problem. In the meantime, the best thing was to imagine a
little experiment of our own.

Supposing we found, somewhere near Port Augusta, a song-
man who knew the Lizard song? Suppose we got him to sing his
verses into a tape-recorder and then played the tape to Alan in
Kaititj country? The chances were he'd recognise the melody at
once – just as we would the 'Moonlight' Sonata – but the meaning
of the words would escape him. All the same, he'd listen very
attentively to the melodic structure. He'd perhaps even ask us to
replay a few bars. Then, suddenly, he'd find himself in sync and be
able to sing his own words over the 'nonsense'.

'His own words for country round Port Augusta?'

'Yes,' said Arkady.

'Is that what really happens?'

'It is.'

'How the hell's it done?'

No one, he said, could be sure. There were people who argued for telepathy. Aboriginals themselves told stories of their song-men whizzing up and down the line in trance. But there was another, more astonishing possibility.

Regardless of the words, it seems the melodic contour of the song describes the nature of the land over which the song passes. So, if the Lizard Man were dragging his heels across the salt-pans of Lake Eyre, you could expect a succession of long flats, like Chopin's 'Funeral March'. If he were skipping up and down the MacDonnell escarpments, you'd have a series of arpeggios and glissandos, like Liszt's 'Hungarian Rhapsodies'.

Certain phrases, certain combinations of musical notes, are thought to describe the action of the Ancestor's *feet*. One phrase would say, 'Salt-pan'; another 'Creek-bed', 'Spinifex', 'Sand-hill', 'Mulga-scrub', 'Rock-face' and so forth. An expert song-man, by listening to their order of succession, would count how many times his hero crossed a river, or scaled a ridge – and be able to calculate where, and how far along, a Songline he was.

'He'd be able', said Arkady 'to hear a few bars and say, "This is Middle Bore" or "That is Oodnadatta" – where the Ancestor did X or Y or Z.'

'So a musical phrase', I said, 'is a map reference?'

'Music', said Arkady, 'is a memory bank for finding one's way about the world.'

'I shall need some time to digest that.'

'You've got all night,' he smiled. 'With the snakes!'

The fire was still blazing in the other camp and we heard the burble of women's laughter.

'Sleep well,' he said.

'And you.'

'I never had so much fun', he said, 'as I do with my old men.'

I tried to sleep but couldn't. The ground under my sleeping-bag was hard and lumpy. I tried counting the stars around the Southern Cross, but my thoughts kept returning to the man in blue. He reminded me of someone. I had the memory of another man miming an almost identical story, with the same kind of animal gestures. Once, in the Sahel, I had watched some dancers mime the antics of antelopes and storks. But that was not the memory I was looking for.

Then I had it.

'Lorenz!'

22

THE AFTERNOON I met Konrad Lorenz he was working in his garden at Altenberg, a small town on the Danube near Vienna. A hot east wind was blowing from the steppe. I had come to interview him for a newspaper.

The 'Father of Ethology' was a gristly silver-spade-bearded man with arctic blue eyes and a face burned pink in the sun. His book *On Aggression* had outraged liberal opinion on both sides of the Atlantic – and was a gift to the 'conservatives'. His enemies had then unearthed a half-forgotten paper, published in 1942, the year of the Final Solution, in which Lorenz had pressed his theory of instinct into the service of racial biology. In 1973 he had been awarded the Nobel Prize.

He introduced me to his wife, who set down her weeding basket and smiled, distantly, from beneath the brim of her straw hat. We made polite conversation about the difficulty of propagating violets.

'My wife and I', he said, 'have known each other since childhood. We used to play at iguanodons in the shrubbery.'

He led the way towards the house – a grandiose, neo-baroque mansion built by his father, a surgeon, in the good old days of Franz Josef. As he opened the front door, a pack of rangy, brown-coated mongrels rushed out, set their paws on my shoulder and licked my face.

'What *are* these dogs?' I asked.

'Pariah dogs!' he muttered grimly. '*Aach!* I would have killed the whole litter. You see that chow, over there? Very fine animal! Grandparent a wolf! My wife took her round all the best chow studs in Bavaria to look for a dog. She refused them all ... and then she copulated with a schnauzer!'

We sat in his study, where there was a white faience stove, a fish-tank, a toy train and a mynah bird whooping in a cage. We began with a review of his career.

At the age of six, he had read books on evolution and become a convinced Darwinian. Later, as a zoological student in Vienna, he had specialised in the comparative anatomy of ducks and geese: only to realise that they, in common with all other animals, also inherited 'blocs' or 'paradigms' of instinctive behaviour in their genes. The courtship ritual of a mallard drake was a 'set-piece'. The bird would wag its tail, shake its head, bob forward, crane its neck – performing a sequence of movements which, once triggered off, would run their predictable course and were no more separable from its nature than its webbed feet or glossy green head.

Lorenz realised, too, that these 'fixed motor patterns' had been transformed by the process of natural selection and must have played some vital role in the survival of the species. They could be measured, scientifically, as one measured anatomical changes between one species and the next.

'And that was how I discovered ethology,' he said. 'Nobody taught me. I thought it was a matter of course with all psychologists, because I was a child and full of respect for other people. I had not realised I was one of the pioneers.'

'Aggression', as Lorenz defined it, was the instinct in animals and man to seek and fight – though not necessarily to kill – a rival of their own kind. Its function was to ensure the equable distribution of a species over its habitat, and that the genes of the 'fittest' passed to the next generation. Fighting behaviour was not a reaction but a 'drive' or appetite – which, like the drives of hunger or sex, would build up and demand expression either on to the 'natural' object, or, if none were available, on to a scapegoat.

Unlike man, wild animals seldom fought to the death. Rather, they would 'ritualise' their squabbles in displays of tooth, plumage, scratch-marks or vocal calls. The intruder – providing, of course, he was the *weaker* intruder – would recognise these 'Keep Out!' signs and withdraw without a scene.

A defeated wolf, for example, had only to bare the nape of his neck and the victor *could* not press home his advantage.

Lorenz presented *On Aggression* as the findings of an experienced naturalist who knew a lot about fighting in animals and had seen a lot of fighting among men. He had served as an orderly on the Russian Front. He had spent years in a Soviet prisoner-of-war camp, and had concluded that man was a 'dangerously aggressive' species. War, as such, was the collective outpouring of his frustrated fighting 'drives': behaviour which had seen him through bad times in the primeval bush, but was lethal in an age of the H-Bomb.

Our fatal flaw, or Fall, he insisted, was to have developed 'artificial weapons' instead of natural ones. As a species, we thus lacked the instinctive inhibitions which prevented the 'professional carnivores' from murdering their fellows.

I had expected to find in Lorenz a person of old-fashioned courtesy and blinkered convictions, someone who had marvelled at the order and diversity of the animal kingdom and decided to shut out the painful, chaotic world of human contacts. I could not have been more mistaken. Here was a man as perplexed as any other, who, whatever his previous convictions, had an almost childlike compulsion to share the excitement of his discoveries, and to correct faults of fact or emphasis.

He was a perfect mimic. He could project himself beneath the skin of any bird or beast or fish. When he imitated the jackdaw at the bottom of the 'pecking order', he *became* the wretched jackdaw. He *became* the pair of greylag ganders, entwining their necks as they performed the 'triumph ceremony'. And when he demonstrated the sexual see-saw of chiclid fish in his aquarium – whereby a 'Brunhilde of a fish' refused the timid advances of her partner, yet turned into a simpering, all-too-submissive maiden the instant a real male entered the tank – Lorenz became, in turn, the 'Brunhilde', the weakling and the tyrant.

He complained of being misinterpreted by people who read into the theory of aggression an excuse for endless war. 'This', he said, 'is simply libellous. "Aggressivity" is not necessarily to do harm to your neighbour. It may just be a "pushing-away" behaviour. You can effect the same consequences simply by disliking your neighbour. You can say, "*Wauch!*" and walk away when he croaks back. That's what frogs do.'

Two singing frogs, he went on, would remove themselves as far as possible from each other, except at spawning time. The same was true of polar bears, which, fortunately for them, had a thin population.

'A polar bear', he said, 'can afford to walk away from the other chap.'

Similarly, in the Orinoco, there were Indians who would suppress tribal warfare with 'ritual' exchanges of gifts.

'But surely', I butted in, 'this "gift exchange" is not a ritual to *suppress* aggression. It *is* aggression ritualised. Violence only breaks out when the parity of these exchanges is broken.'

'Yes, yes,' he answered enthusiastically. 'Of course, of course.'

He took a pencil from his desk and waved it towards me. 'If I give you this gift,' he said, 'that means "I'm territorial here." But it also means, "I *have* a territory and I am no threat to yours." All we're doing is fixing the frontier. I say to you, "Here I put my gift. I'm not going any further." It would be an offence if I put my gift too far.

'Territory, you see,' he added, 'is not necessarily the place you feed in. It's the place in which you *stay* . . . where you know every nook and cranny . . . where you know by heart every refuge . . . where you are invincible to the pursuer. I've even measured it with sticklebacks.'

He then gave an unforgettable performance of two angry male sticklebacks. Both were unbeatable at the centre of their territory. Both became progressively more fearful and vulnerable as they strayed from it. They would skirmish to and fro until they found an equilibrium and, afterwards, kept their distance. As he told the story, Lorenz crossed his hands under his chin splaying his fingers to imitate the stickleback spines. He coloured at the gills. He paled. He inflated and deflated, lunged and fled.

It was this imitation, of the impotent, retreating stickleback, that reminded me, here at Middle Bore, of the cuckolded Lizard Man, who strayed from his own home country and lost his lovely wife to a stranger.

23

WHEN I WOKE NEXT morning I was lying in the middle of the bright blue groundsheet, and the sun was up. The old men wanted more meat for breakfast. The ice in the 'Eski' had melted in the night and the steaks were swimming in blood-coloured water. We decided to cook them before they went 'off'.

I re-lit the embers of the fire while Arkady held a conference with Alan and the man in blue. He showed them on the survey map how the railway would miss the Lizard Rock by at least two miles and got them, reluctantly, to agree to this. Next, he pointed to the twenty-five-mile stretch of country through which he intended to drive.

For most of the morning the vehicles edged slowly north-wards over broken ground. The sun was blinding and the vegetation parched and drear. To the east, the land dropped away and lifted towards a ridge of pale sandhills. The valley in between was covered with a continuous thicket of mulga trees, leafless at this season, silver-grey like a blanket of low-lying mist.

Nothing moved except the shimmering heatwaves.

We kept crossing the path of fires. In places, all that survived of the bushes were upright, fire-hardened spikes, which staked our tyres as we ran over them. We had three flats, and Marian had two in the Land-Rover. Whenever we stopped to change a wheel, dust and ash blew in our eyes. The women would jump down, delightedly, and go off to look for bush-tucker.

Mavis was in a very boisterous mood, and wanted to repay me for the thongs. She grabbed my hand and dragged me towards a limp, green bush.

'Hey! Where are you two going?' Arkady called.

'Get him some bush-bananas,' she shouted back. 'He don't

know bush-bananas.' But the bananas, when we got to them, had shrivelled up to nothing.

Another time, she and Topsy tried to run down a goanna, but the reptile was far too quick for them. At last, she found a plant of ripe solanum berries and showered them on me in handfuls. They looked and tasted like unripe cherry-tomatoes. I ate some to please her and she said, 'There you are, dearie,' and reached out her chubby hand and stroked my cheek.

When anything in the landscape even half-resembled a 'feature' Arkady would brake and ask Old Alan, 'What's that one?' or, 'Is this country clear?'

Alan glared from the window at his 'domain'.

Around noon, we came to a clump of eucalyptus: the only patch of green in sight. Nearby there was an outcrop of sandstone, about twenty feet long and scarcely visible above the surface. It had shown up on the aerial survey, and was one of three identical outcrops lying in line along the ridge.

Arkady told Alan that the engineer might want to quarry this rock for ballast. He might want to blast it with dynamite.

'How about that, old man?' he asked.

Alan said nothing.

'No story here? Or nothing?'

He said nothing.

'So the country's clear, then?'

'No,' Alan took a deep sigh. 'The Babies.'

'Whose babies?'

'Babies,' he said – and in the same weary voice, he began to tell the story of the Babies.

In the Dreamtime, the Bandicoot Man, Akuka, and his brother were hunting along this ridge. Because it was the dry season, they were terribly hungry and thirsty. Every bird and animal had fled. The trees were stripped of leaves and bushfires swept across the country.

The hunters searched everywhere for an animal to kill until, almost at his final gasp, Akuka saw a bandicoot bolting for its burrow. His brother warned him not to kill it, for to kill one's own kind was taboo. Akuka ignored the warning.

He dug the bandicoot from the burrow, speared it, skinned

and ate it, and immediately felt cramps in his stomach. His stomach swelled and swelled, and then it burst, and a throng of Babies spewed forth and started crying for water.

Dying of thirst, the Babies travelled north up to Singleton, and south back to Taylor Creek, where the dam now is. They found the soakage, but drank up all the water and returned to the three rocky outcrops. The rocks were the Babies, huddled together as they lay down to die – although, as it happened, they did not die yet.

Their uncle, Akuka's brother, heard their cries and called on his western neighbours to make rain. The rain blew in from the west (the grey expanse of mulga was the thunderstorm metamorphosed into trees). The Babies turned on their tracks and wandered south again. While crossing a creek not far from Lizard Rock, they fell into the floodwaters and 'melted'.

The name of the place where the Babies 'went back' was *Akwerkepentye*, which means 'far-travelling children'.

When Alan came to the end of the story, Arkady said softly, 'Don't worry, old man. It'll be all right. Nobody's going to touch the Babies.'

Alan shook his head despairingly.

'Are you happy then?' asked Arkady.

No. He wasn't happy. Nothing about this wicked railway was going to make him happy: but at least the Babies might be safe.

We moved ahead.

'Australia', Arkady said slowly, 'is the country of lost children.'

Another hour and we reached the northern boundary of Middle Bore Station. We now had one spare tyre for the Land Cruiser: so rather than risk returning the way we'd come, we decided to make a detour. There was an old dirt road which went east and then south and came out behind Alan's settlement. On the last lap we ran in with the railway people.

They were clearing the country along the proposed line of track. Their earth-movers had cut a sweep through the mulga, and a strip of churned-up soil about a hundred yards wide now stretched away into the distance.

The old men looked miserably at the stacks of broken trees.

We stopped to talk to a black-bearded titan. He was more than seven feet tall and might have been made of bronze. Stripped to the waist, in a straw hat and stubbies, he was driving in marker-posts with a hammer. He was off, in an hour or two, to Adelaide on leave. 'Oh boy,' he said. 'Am I ever glad to get out of here?'

The road had gone. Our vehicles crawled and slewed in the loose red dirt. Three times we had to get out and push. Arkady was whacked. I suggested we stop for a break. We turned aside into the sketchy shade of some trees. There were ant-hills every-where, splashed with bird shit. He unpacked some food and drink, and rigged up the groundsheet as an awning.

We had expected the old men, as always, to be hungry. But they all sat huddled together, moping, refusing either to eat or to talk: to judge from their expressions you would have said they were in pain.

Marian and the ladies had parked under a different tree, and they, too, were silent and gloomy.

A yellow bulldozer went by in a cloud of dust.

Arkady lay down, covered his head with a towel, and started snoring. Using my leather rucksack as a pillow, I leaned back against a tree-trunk and leafed through Ovid's *Metamorphoses*.

The story of Lykaeon's transformation into a wolf took me back to a blustery spring day in Arkadia and seeing, in the limestone cap of Mount Lykaeon itself, an image of the crouch-ing beast-king. I read of Hyacinth and Adonis; of Deucalion and the Flood; and how the 'living things' were created from the warm Nilotic ooze. And it struck me, from what I now knew of the Songlines, that the whole of Classical mythology might represent the relics of a gigantic 'song-map': that all the to-ing and fro-ing of gods and goddesses, the caves and sacred springs, the sphinxes and chimaeras, and all the men and women who became nightingales or ravens, echoes or narcissi, stones or stars – could all be interpreted in terms of totemic geography.

I must have dozed off myself, for when I woke my face was covered with flies and Arkady was calling, 'Come on. Let's go.'

We got back to Middle Bore an hour before sunset. The Land Cruiser had hardly stopped moving before Alan and the man in blue opened their doors and walked away without a nod. Big Tom mumbled something about the railway being 'bad'.

Arkady looked crushed. 'Hell!' he said. 'What's the use?'

He blamed himself for letting them see the earth-movers.

'You shouldn't,' I said.

'But I do.'

'They were bound to see it one day.'

'I'd rather not with me.'

We freshened up under a hosepipe, and I revived our hearth of the day before. Marian joined us, sitting on a sawn-off tree stump and unravelling her tangle of hair. She then compared notes with Arkady. The women had told her of a Songline called 'Two Dancing Women', but it never touched the line of the railway.

We looked up to see a procession of women and children on their way back from foraging. The babies swayed peacefully in the folds of their mothers' dresses.

'You never hear them cry,' Marian said, 'as long as the mother keeps moving.'

She had touched, unwittingly, on one of my favourite topics. 'And if babies can't bear to lie still,' I said, 'how shall we settle down later?'

She jumped to her feet. 'Which reminds me, I've got to go.'

'Now?'

'Now. I promised Gladys and Topsy they'd be home tonight.'

'Can't they stay here?' I asked. 'Couldn't we all spend the night here?'

'You can,' she said, playfully sticking out her tongue. 'I can't.'

I looked at Arkady, who shrugged, as if to say, 'When she gets an idea into her head, no power on earth's going to stop her.' Five minutes later, she had rounded up the women and, with a cheerful wave, was gone.

'That woman', I said, 'is the Pied Piper.'

'Dammit!' said Arkady.

He reminded me of our promise to look in on Frank Olson.

At the station-house, a large woman with heat-ravaged skin came shuffling to the front door, peered through the fly-screen and opened up.

'Frank's gone down to Glen Armond,' she said. 'An emergency! Jim Hanlon's taken sick!'

'When was that?' asked Arkady.

'Last night,' said the woman. 'Collapsed in the pub.'

'We should get the chaps and go,' he said.

'Yes,' I agreed. 'I think we'd better go.'

24

THE BARMAN OF THE MOTEL at Glen Armond said that Hanlon had come in around nine the night before and bragged of renting his caravan to an English 'literary gent'. On the strength of this transaction, he put back five double Scotches, fell and banged his head on the floor. Expecting him to be sober by morning, they carried him to a room out back. There, in the early hours, a truckie heard him groaning and they found him, on the floor again, clutching his abdomen, with his shirt torn to ribbons.

They called his mate, Frank Olson, who drove him down to Alice. He was on the operating table by eleven.

'Some talk of a blockage,' said the barman sententiously. 'Usually means one thing.'

There was a pay-phone on the bar. Arkady put through a call to the hospital. The nurse on duty said Hanlon was comfortable, and asleep.

'So what's the matter?' I asked.

'She wouldn't say.'

The bar itself was made up of disused wooden railway-sleepers and above it hung a notice: ALL LIQUOR MUST BE CONSUMED ON THE PREMISES.

I looked at a picture on the wall. It was an artist's impression, in watercolour, of the proposed *Glen Armond Memorial Dingo Complex*. The word 'memorial' referred to the dingo which either ate, or did not eat, the infant Azaria Chamberlain. The plans called for a fibreglass dingo about sixty feet high, with a spiral staircase up its forelegs and a dark-red restaurant inside its belly.

'Incredible,' I said.

'No,' said Arkady. 'Humorous.'

The night bus to Darwin drew up outside, and the bar filled up with passengers. There were Germans, Japanese, a pink-kneed Englishman and the usual cast of Territorians. They ate pie and ice-cream, drank, went outside to piss, and came back to drink again. The stopover lasted fifteen minutes. Then the driver called and they all trooped out, leaving the bar to its core of regulars.

At the far end of the room, a fat Lebanese was playing pool with a gaunt, fair-haired young man who had one wall-eye and was trying to explain, in a stutter, how Aboriginal kinship systems were 'so . . . so . . . co-com . . . fu . . . fuckin'-plex'. At the bar, a big man with a purple birthmark on his neck was methodically swilling Scotches through his rotted teeth, and talking to the police patrolman whom we had met the day before at Burnt Flat.

He had changed into jeans, a gold neck-chain and a clean white singlet. Out of uniform, he appeared to have shrunk. His arms were thin and white above the line of his shirt cuffs. His Alsatian lay very still, leashed to the bar-stool, eyeing some Aboriginals, its ears pricked up and tongue extended.

The policeman turned to me, 'So what'll it be?'

I hesitated.

'What are you drinking?'

'Scotch and soda,' I said. 'Thank you.'

'Ice?'

'Ice.'

'So you're a writer, eh?'

'News gets around.'

'What kind of writing?'

'Books,' I said.

'Published?'

'Yes.'

'Science fiction?'

'NO!'

'Ever write a best-seller?'

'Never.'

'I'm thinking of writing a best-seller myself.'

'Good on you.'

'You wouldn't believe some of the stories I hear.'

'I certainly would.'

'Unbelievable stories,' he said in his thin, petulant voice. 'It's all there.'

'Where?'

'In my head.'

'The great thing's to get it on to paper.'

'I got a great title.'

'Good.'

'You want me to tell you?'

'If you like.'

He dropped his jaw and gaped at me, 'You must be joking, mate. You think I'd give away my title. You might use it! That title's worth money.'

'Then you should hang on to it.'

'A title', he said, with great feeling, 'can make or break a book.'

Think of Ed McBain! *Killer's Pay-Off*! Think of *Shark City*! Or *Eden's Burning*! Think of *The Day of the Dog*! Great titles. The cash value of his title he estimated at 50,000 US dollars. With a title like that, you could make a great movie. Even without the book!

'Even without the story?' I suggested.

'Could do,' he nodded.

Titles changed hands for millions, he said, in the United States. Not that *he* was going to sell off his title to a movie company. The title and the story belonged together.

'No,' he shook his head, thoughtfully. 'I wouldn't want to part them.'

'You shouldn't.'

'Maybe we could collaborate?' he said.

He visualised an artistic and business partnership. He would provide the title and the story. I would write the book because he, as a policeman, did not have the leisure for writing.

'Writing takes time,' I agreed.

'Would you be interested?'

'No.'

He looked disappointed. He was not prepared, yet, to tell me the title, but to whet my appetite he proposed to let me in on the plot. The plot of this unbelievable story began with an Aboriginal being flattened by a road-train.

'And?'

'I better tell you,' he said.

He moistened his lips. He had come to a big decision.

'*Body Bag*,' he said.

'*Body Bag*?'

He closed his eyes and smiled.

'I never told anyone before,' he said.

'But *Body Bag*?'

'The bag you put the body in. I told you the story starts with a dead coon on the highway.'

'You did.'

'You like it?' he asked, anxiously.

'No.'

'I mean the title.'

'I know you mean the title.'

I turned to the man with the purple birthmark, who was sitting on my left. He had been stationed in England, during the war, near Leicester. He had fought in France and then married a girl from Leicester. The wife came to live in Australia, but went back with their child, to Leicester.

He had heard we were surveying sacred sites.

'Know the best thing to do with a sacred site?' he drawled.

'What?'

'Dynamite!'

He grinned and raised his glass to the Aboriginals. The birthmark oscillated as he drank.

One of the Aboriginals, a very thin hill-billy type with a frenzy of matted hair, leaned both elbows on the counter, and listened.

'Sacred sites!' the big man leered. 'If all what them says was sacred sites, there'd be three hundred bloody billion sacred sites in Australia.'

'Not far wrong, mate!' called the thin Aboriginal.

Over on my right I could hear Arkady talking to the policeman. They had both lived in Adelaide, in the suburb of St Peters. They had gone to the same school. They'd had the same maths master, but the policeman was five years older.

'It's a small world,' he said.

'It is,' said Arkady.

'So why do you bother with them?' The policeman jerked his thumb at the Aboriginals.

'Because I like them.'

'And *I* like them,' he said. 'I *like* them! I like to do what's right by them. But they're different.'

'In what way different?'

The policeman moistened his lips again, and sucked the air between his teeth.

'Made differently,' he said at last. 'They've got different urinary tracts to the white man. Different waterworks! That's why they can't hold their booze!'

'How do you know?'

'It's been proved,' said the policeman. 'Scientifically.'

'Who by?'

'I don't recall.'

The fact was, he went on, there should be two different drinking laws: one for whites and one for blacks.

'You think so?' said Arkady.

'Penalise a man for having better waterworks?' said the policeman, his voice lifting in indignation. 'It's unfair. It's unconstitutional.'

The Alsatian whined, and he patted it on the head.

From having different waterworks was an easy step to having different grey-matter. An Aboriginal brain, he said, was different to that of Caucasians. The frontal lobes were flatter.

Arkady narrowed his eyes to a pair of Tatar slits. He was now quite nettled.

'I like them,' the policeman repeated. 'I never said I didn't like them. But they're like children. They've got a childish mentality.'

'What makes you think so?'

'They're incapable of progress,' he said. 'And that's what's wrong with you Land Rights people. You're standing in the way of progress. You're helping them destroy white Australia.'

'Let me buy you a drink?' I interrupted.

'No, thanks,' the policeman snapped. His face was working wrathfully. His fingernails, I noticed, were bitten to the quick.

Arkady waited a moment or two, until he'd got control of his temper, and then began to explain, slowly and reasonably, how the surest way of judging a man's intelligence was his ability to handle words.

Many Aboriginals, he said, by our standards would rank as linguistic geniuses. The difference was one of outlook. The whites were forever changing the world to fit their doubtful vision of the future. The Aboriginals put all their mental energies into keeping the world the way it was. In what way was that inferior?

The policeman's mouth shot downwards.

'You're not Australian,' he said to Arkady.

'I bloody am Australian.'

'No, you're not. I can tell you're not Australian.'

'I was born in Australia.'

'That doesn't make you Australian,' he taunted. 'My people have lived in Australia for five generations. So where was your father born?'

Arkady paused and, with quiet dignity, answered, 'My father was born in Russia.'

'Hey!' the policeman tightened his forelip and turned to the big man. 'What did I tell you, Bert? A Pom and a Com!'

25

THE CLOUDS CAME UP in the night and the morning was overcast and muggy. We had bacon and eggs for breakfast in the bar of the motel. The owner's wife made us sandwiches for a picnic, and gave us ice for the 'Eski'. Arkady again called the hospital.

'They still won't say what's wrong,' he said as he hung up. 'I think it's bad.'

We debated whether to go back to Alice, but there was nothing we could do, so we decided to press on to Cullen. Arkady spread the map over the table. The drive, he calculated, would take two days. We'd cut across country and spend the night at Popanji, and then go on to Cullen.

The woman drinking coffee at the next banquette overheard us and asked, apologetically, if by any chance we were going past Lombardy Downs.

Arkady glanced at the map.

'It's on the way,' he said. 'Can we give you a lift?'

'Oh no!' the woman cringed. 'No. No. I don't want to go there. I wondered if you'd take something for me. A letter.'

She was an awkward, frayed young woman with lacklustre hair and unswerving amber eyes. She enunciated her syllables in a ladylike fashion, and wore a fawn-coloured dress with long sleeves.

'I've got it written,' she said. 'You wouldn't mind, would you? I'll go and fetch it if you –'

'Of course, we'll take it,' said Arkady.

She ran off and came running back, out of breath, with the letter. She pushed it away from her, vehemently, on to the table. Then she began to finger a tiny gold crucifix around her neck.

'It's for Bill Muldoon,' she said, staring dully at the name on the envelope. 'He's station-manager at Lombardy. He's my husband. Ask anyone to give it him. But if you see him . . . if he asks you if you've seen me . . . tell him I'm well.'

She looked frail and miserable and sick.

'Don't worry,' I said. 'We will.'

'Thanks,' she said in a constricted voice, and sat down to finish her coffee.

We drove for three hours across a featureless plain. Showers had fallen in the night and laid the dust on the road. We saw some emus a long way off. The wind was rising. We saw something swinging from a solitary tree. It was a huge knitted teddy bear, with royal blue trousers and a scarlet cap. Someone had slashed it at the neck, and the kapok stuffing was spilling out. On the ground, there was a cross made from twigs, rubbed with ochre and its arms lashed together with hair-string.

I picked up the cross and held it out to Arkady.

'Aboriginal business,' he said. 'I wouldn't touch that if I were you.'

I dropped it and got back into my seat. Up ahead, the sky was darkening.

'It could be', said Arkady, 'that we're in for a storm.'

We turned off at the sign marked Lombardy Downs. After a mile or so the track skirted round the end of a runway. An orange windsock blew horizontally in the whirring wind, and there was a light aircraft in the distance.

The man who owned the station owned an airline.

The homestead was a sprawling white house set back among some stunted trees, but closer to the strip there was a smaller, brick-built house alongside an open hangar. In the hangar were housed the owner's collection of vintage aeroplanes and cars. Parked beside a Tiger Moth were a Model 'T' Ford and a Rolls-Royce farm truck, its wooden sides painted brown with black trim.

I told Arkady my father's story about the Rolls-Royce and the sheep millionaire.

'Not so far-fetched after all,' I said.

A blowsy woman appeared at the door in a green-spotted housecoat. Her blonde hair was up in curlers.

'You boys looking for someone?' she called out.

'Bill Muldoon,' I called back against the wind. 'We've got a letter for him.'

'Muldoon's out,' she said. 'Come on in and I'll make you a coffee.'

We went into a messy kitchen. Arkady put the letter on the table, on the red-checked oilcloth cover, next to some women's magazines. We sat down. An oil painting of Ayer's Rock hung aslant on the wall. The woman glanced at the writing on the envelope and shrugged. She was the other woman.

While the kettle boiled, she unwrapped a half-eaten candy bar, nibbled off an inch or so, wrapped it up again, and licked the chocolate off her lips.

'God, I am bored!' she said.

The owner of the station, she told us, had flown up from Sydney for the weekend, so Muldoon was on call. She poured out our coffees and said again that she was bored.

We were on the point of leaving when Muldoon came in – an athletic, red-faced man dressed from head to foot in black: black hat, boots, jeans and a black shirt open to the navel. He imagined we had come on business and shook our hands. The instant he saw the letter, he paled and clenched his jaw.

'Get out of here,' he said.

We left.

'Unfriendly,' I said.

'The pastoral ethic,' said Arkady. 'Same the world over.'

Half an hour later we crossed a cattle-grid which marked the end of Lombardy Downs. We had narrowly missed a cloudburst and watched the chutes of rain slanting sideways towards a line of hills. We then joined the road from Alice to Popanji.

The sides of the road were littered with abandoned cars, usually upside down, in heaps of broken glass. We stopped beside a rusty blue Ford with a black woman squatting beside it. The bonnet was open and a small boy, naked, stood sentinel on the roof.

'What's up?' Arkady leaned from the window.

'Plugs,' said the woman. 'Gone to get new plugs.'

'Who has?'

'He has.'

'Where to?'

'The Alice.'

'How long's he been gone?'

'Three days.'

'You all right there?'

'Yup,' the woman sniffed.

'You got water and everything?'

'Yup.'

'You want a sandwich?'

'Yup.'

We gave the woman and boy three sandwiches. They grabbed them and ate them greedily.

'You sure you're all right, then?' Arkady persisted.

'Yup,' the woman nodded.

'We can take you back to Popanji.'

She gave a grumpy shake of the head and waved us away.

Around lunchtime we crossed a creek with river-red-gums growing in its bed. It was a good place to picnic. We picked our way over waterworn boulders, and pools of stagnant yellow water with leaves afloat on the surface. The country to the west was grey and treeless, and cloud shadows were moving across it. There were no cattle, no fences, no wind-pumps: this country was too arid for grazing. We had left behind the cow shit: there were no more flies.

As we walked up to one of the gum trees, a flock of black cockatoos flew out, squawking like rusty hinges, and settled on a dead gum up ahead. I took out my glasses and saw the flash of scarlet feathers glowing under their tails.

We spread the picnic in the shade. The sandwiches were uneatable so we chucked them to the crows. But we had biscuits and cheese, olives and a can of sardines, and five cold beers between us.

We talked politics, books and Russian books. He said how strange it was to feel oneself Russian in a country of Anglo-Saxon prejudice. Spend an evening in a roomful of Sydney 'intellectuals', and they'd all end up dissecting some obscure event within the first Penal Settlement.

He looked around at the immense sweep of country.

'Pity we didn't get here first,' he said.

'We the Russians?'

'Not only Russians,' he shook his head. 'Slavs, Hungarians, Germans even. Any people who could cope with wide horizons. Too much of this country went to islanders. They never understood it. They're afraid of space.

'We', he added, 'could have been proud of it. Loved it for what it was. I don't think we'd have sold it off so easily.'

'Yes,' I said. 'Why, in this country of untold resources, do Australians go on selling them off to foreigners?'

'They'd sell off anything,' he shrugged.

He then changed the subject and asked if ever, on my travels, I'd been with a hunting people.

'Once,' I said. 'In Mauritania.'

'Where's that?'

'The western Sahara. They weren't so much a hunting tribe as a hunting caste. They were called the Nemadi.'

'And hunted?'

'Oryx and addax antelopes,' I said. 'With dogs.'

In the city of Walata, once a capital of the Almoravid Empire and now a jumble of blood-coloured courtyards, I spent three whole days pestering the Governor to allow me to meet the Nemadi.

The Governor, a morose hypochondriac, had been longing for someone to share the memory of his student days in Paris, or to argue doctrinal points of *la pensée maotsetungienne*. His favourite words were *tactique* and *technique*, but whenever I raised the question of the Nemadi, he'd let fly a brittle laugh and murmur, 'It is forbidden.'

At mealtimes, a pink-fingered lutanist would serenade us through the couscous while the Governor reconstructed, with my prompting, a street map of the Quartier Latin. From his palace – if four mud-brick rooms were a palace – I could see a tiny white tent of the Nemadi beckoning me across the hillside.

'But why do you wish to see these people?' the Governor shouted at me. 'Walata, yes! Walata is a historical place. But this Nemadi is nothing. It is a dirty people.'

Not only were they dirty, they were a national disgrace. They were infidels, idiots, thieves, parasites, liars. They ate forbidden food.

'And their women', he added, 'are prostitutes!'

'But beautiful?' I suggested, if only to annoy him.

His hand shot out from the folds of his blue robes.

'Ha!' he wagged a finger at me. 'Now I know! Now I see it! But let me tell you, young Englishman, those women have terrible diseases. Incurable diseases!'

'That's not what I heard,' I said.

On our third evening together, having browbeaten him with the name of the Minister of the Interior, I saw signs he was beginning to relent. At lunch the day after, he said I was free to go, providing I was accompanied by a policeman, and providing I did nothing which might encourage them to hunt.

'They must *not* hunt,' he bellowed. 'Do you hear me?'

'I do hear you,' I said. 'But they *are* hunters. They were hunting before the time of the Prophet. What else can they do but hunt?'

'Hunting', he folded his fingers sententiously, 'is forbidden by the law of our Republic.'

A few weeks earlier, as I was rooting through the literature on Sahara nomads, I had come across an account of the Nemadi, based on the findings of a Swiss ethnologist, which classed them 'among the most destitute people on earth'.

They were thought to number about three hundred and they would wander, in bands of thirty or so, along the edge of El Djouf, the Saharan Empty Quarter. The report gave them fair skin and blue eyes and assigned them to the eighth and lowest grade of Moorish society, 'Outcasts of the Wilderness': lower than the Harratin, who were tied, black, agricultural slaves.

The Nemadi professed neither food taboos nor reverence for Islam. They ate locusts and wild honey, and wild boar if they got the chance. They sometimes earned a pittance from the nomads by selling *tichtar*, the dried meat of antelopes which, when crumbled, gives a gamey flavour to couscous.

The men earned a little more money carving saddle-trees and milk-bowls from acacia wood. They insisted they were the rightful owners of the land, and that the Moors had stolen it from them. Because the Moors treated them as pariahs, they were forced to camp far from the town.

As for their origins, they were possibly survivors of a Mesolithic hunting population. Almost certainly, they were the 'Messoufites', one of whom – blind in one eye, half blind in the other – guided Ib'n Battūta across the sands in 1357. 'The desert here', wrote the world traveller, 'is beautiful and brilliant, and the soul finds its ease. Antelopes abound. A herd often passes so close to our caravan that the Messoufites hunt them with arrows and with dogs.'

By the 1970s, shooting parties with Land-Rovers and long-range rifles had made sure that the oryx and addax, far from being abundant, were dying out. The government called for a general ban on hunting, in which the Nemadi were included.

Knowing themselves to be as gentle as the Moors were violent and vindictive; knowing also that it was herding which led to violence, the Nemadi wanted none of it. Their favourite songs spoke of flights into the desert where they would wait for better times.

The Governor told me how he and his colleagues had bought the Nemadi a total of a thousand goats. 'One thousand goats!' he went on shouting. 'You know what that means? *Many* goats! And what did they do with those goats? Milk them? No! Ate them! Ate the lot! *Ils sont im-bé-ciles!*'

The policeman, I'm glad to say, liked the Nemadi. He said they were *braves gens* and, surreptitiously, that the Governor was off his head.

Walking towards the white tent, we first heard the sound of laughter and then came on a party of twelve Nemadi, adults and children, resting in the shade of an acacia. They were none of them sick or dirty. Everyone was immaculate.

The headman got up to welcome us.

'Mahfould,' I said, and shook his hand.

I knew his face from the Swiss ethnographer's photos: a flat, beaming face wound about with a cornflower-blue turban. He had hardly aged in twenty years.

Among the party were several women in indigo cotton and a negro with a club foot. There was an ancient, blue-eyed cripple who manoeuvred himself on his hands. The chief hunter was a square-shouldered man whose expression spoke of rigour and reckless gaiety. He was whittling a saddle-tree from a block of wood while his favourite dog, a sleek piebald terrier not unlike a Jack Russell, nuzzled up against his knee.

Nemadi means 'master of dogs'. The dogs are said to eat even when their owners go hungry; their training would be the pride of any circus. A pack consists of five: the 'king' and four followers.

The hunter, having tracked a herd of antelopes to its grazing ground, will lie with his dogs on the downward scarp of a dune, and instruct them which animal to go for. At a signal, the 'king' then hurtles down the slope, fastens its teeth around the antelope's muzzle, and the others go for each of the legs. A single knife thrust, a rapid prayer to ask the antelope for its forgiveness – and the hunt is over.

The Nemadi despise the use of firearms as a sacrilege. And since the soul of the dead beast is thought to reside in its bones, these are reverently buried in case the dogs defile them.

'The antelopes were our friends,' said one of the women with a dazzling white smile. 'Now they have gone far away. Now we have nothing, nothing to do but laugh.'

They all roared with laughter when I asked about the Governor's goats.

'And if you will buy us a goat,' said the chief hunter, 'we will kill that also, and eat it.'

'Right,' I said to the policeman. 'Let's go and buy them a goat.'

We walked across the wadi to where a herdsman was watering his flock. I paid a little more than he asked for a yearling, and the hunter coaxed it back to the camp. A gurgle from behind a bush announced that its life had ended and there would be meat for supper.

The women laughed, beat a tam-tam on some old tin basins, and sang a soft burbling song to thank the foreigner for the gift of meat.

There is a story of a Moorish emir, who, driven to frenzy by a Nemadi woman's smile, kidnapped her, clothed her in silks and never saw her smile again until the day she spotted, through the lattice of her prison, a Nemadi man strolling through the market. To the emir's credit, he let her go.

What, I asked the women, was the secret of their famous smile?

'Meat!' they cried cheerfully, gnashing their teeth in unison. 'Meat is what gives us our beautiful smiles. We chew the meat and we cannot help smiling.'

In the little white tent, sewn from strips of Sudanese cotton, there lived an old woman with two dogs and a cat. Her name was Lemina. She was very old when the Swiss came nearly twenty years earlier. The policeman said she was more than a hundred.

Tall and unstooping, in blue, she came through the thorn trees towards the cause of the excitement.

Mahfould stood to greet her. She was deaf and dumb. They stood against the deepening sky, flicking their fingers in sign language. Her skin was white, like sheets of tissue paper. Her eyes were hooded and cloudy. Smiling, she raised her withered arms towards me and uttered a succession of warbling notes.

She held the smile a full three minutes. Then she turned on her heels, snapped a twig from an acacia, and went back to her tent.

Among these pale-skinned people, the negro was the odd man out. I asked how he had come to join the band.

'He was alone,' said Mahfould. 'So he came with us.'

I then learned, through the policeman, that it was possible for a man to join the Nemadi: a woman never. Yet, since their numbers were so low, and since no self-respecting outsider would demean himself by 'marrying down', these women always had their eyes open for 'fresh white blood'.

One of the young mothers, a grave and lovely girl with a cowl of blue cotton over her head, was suckling a baby. She was married to the hunter. You would have said she was about twenty-five: but when I mentioned the name of the Swiss ethnologist, the husband grinned and, gesturing towards his wife, said, 'We have one of his.'

He set aside his carpentry and whistled across to the second camp. A minute or two later, a lithe, bronze-skinned young man with glinting green eyes came striding through the bushes with a pair of dogs and a hunting spear. He wore a short leather breech-clout. His hair was fair-to-reddish and cut in a kind of cocks-comb. The instant he saw a European, he lowered his eyelids.

He sat down in silence between his mother and foster-father. Anyone might mistake them for the Holy Family.

When I came to the end of the story, Arkady made no comment, but stood up and said, 'We'd better get going.' We buried the debris and walked back to the car.

'You may think it sounds silly,' I said, trying to pump him for a reaction. 'But I live with that old woman's smile.'

The smile, I said, was like a message from the Golden Age. It had taught me to reject out of hand all arguments for the nastiness of human nature. The idea of returning to an 'original simplicity' was not naive or unscientific or out of touch with reality.

'Renunciation', I said, 'even at this late date, can work.'

'I'd agree with that,' said Arkady. 'The world, if it has a future, has an ascetic future.'

26

IN THE POLICE STATION at Popanji, two Aboriginal girls in dirty floral dresses were standing before the counter swearing oaths before the officer in charge. They needed his official stamp before they could sign on for welfare. They had interrupted his weight-training session.

He took the hand of the taller girl and pressed it on the Bible.

'Right,' he said. 'Now repeat what I say, after me. I, Rosie . . .'

'I, Rosie . . .'

'Swear by Almighty God . . .'

'Swear by Almighty God . . .'

'That'll do,' he said. 'Now it's your turn, Myrtle.'

The policeman reached for the other girl's hand, but she cringed and whipped it from his grasp.

'Come on, sweetheart,' he said in a wheedling voice. 'No need to act the giddy-goat.'

'Oh, come on, Myrtle,' said her sister.

But Myrtle shook her head vigorously and locked her hands behind her back. Rosie then gently uncurled her sister's forefinger and tugged it towards the binding.

'I, Myrtle . . .' said the policeman.

'I, Myrtle . . .' she repeated, as though the words were going to choke her.

'OK,' he said. 'That'll do for you.'

He stamped their application forms and scrawled a signature across each. On the wall behind, there were pictures of the Queen and Duke of Edinburgh. Myrtle sucked her thumb and stared, bug-eyed, at the Queen's diamonds.

'Now what do you want?' he asked.

'Nothing,' said Rosie for her sister.

The girls skipped away, past the flagstaff and across the rain-sodden lawn. It had been raining all day. They splashed on through puddles towards a gang of boys booting at a football.

The policeman was short, scarlet in the face, with stumpy legs and almost unbelievable muscles. He was dripping with sweat, and his carroty curls were flattened on to his forehead. He wore short, ice-blue leotards with a satiny sheen. His pectoral muscles were so heftily developed that the shoulder-straps had bunched into the cleavage, leaving his nipples bare.

'Hello there, Ark,' he said.

'Red,' said Arkady, 'I want you to meet my friend, Bruce.'

'Pleased to meet you, Bruce,' said Red.

We were standing behind the plate-glass window looking out at the blank horizon. Water lay in sheets on the ground, flooding several Aboriginal humpies to the depth of a foot or more. The owners had heaped their gear on to the roofs. The water was awash with refuse.

A short way off to the west was the old administrator's house, of two storeys, which had since been given over to the community. The roof was still on and there were floors and fireplaces. But the walls, the window sashes and the staircase had all been burnt for firewood.

We looked through this X-ray house into the yellow sunset. On both upper and lower floors sat a ring of dark figures, warming themselves over a smoky fire.

'They don't give a fuck for walls,' said Red, 'but they do like a roof for the rain.'

Arkady told him we were on our way to Cullen. 'Little dispute between Titus and the Amadeus Mob.'

'Yes,' Red nodded. 'I heard about that.'

'Who's Titus?' I asked.

'You'll see,' said Arkady. 'You'll see.'

'I'll be out that way myself next week,' Red said. 'Got to go and look for the grader.'

Clarence Japaljarrayi, the Chairman at Cullen, had borrowed the Popanji grading-machine to make a road from the settlement to a soakage.

'That was nine months ago,' Red said. 'Now the fucker says he's lost it.'

'Lost a grader?' Arkady laughed. 'For Christ's sakes, you can't lose a grader.'

'Well, if anyone's going to lose a grader,' said Red, 'it'll be Clarence.'

Arkady asked what the road was like up ahead. Red toyed with the buckle of his security belt.

'You'll be all right,' he said. 'Stumpy Jones nearly got bogged in the big storm Thursday. But Rolf and Wendy went through yesterday, and they radioed this morning they'd arrived.'

He was shifting uneasily from foot to foot. You could tell he was aching to get back to his weights.

'Just one thing,' said Arkady. 'You haven't seen old Stan Tjakamarra? I thought we'd take him along. He's on quite good terms with Titus.'

'I think Stan's gone walkabout,' Red said. 'They've been initiating all week. It's been a right mess, I can tell you. You ask Lydia.'

Lydia was one of two school-teachers stationed here. We had radioed a message for her to expect us.

'See you in a while,' Red said. 'She's cooking tonight.'

The police post at Popanji was a low concrete building divided into three equal parts: a public office, the officer's private quarters, and the room Red used for weight-training. In the yard at the back there was a gaol.

The weight-training room had a wall-to-wall window and the weights themselves were the same electric blue as Red's leotards. We watched him enter. He lay down on the bench-press and gripped the bar. A small boy whistled to his mates, who dropped their football and rushed, naked, to the window, yelling and making funny faces and pressing their noses to the glass.

'One of the sights of the Territory,' said Arkady.

'I'll say,' I said.

'Not a bad bloke, Red,' he said. 'Likes a bit of discipline. Speaks Aranda and Pintupi like a native. Bit of a nut-case, really. I'll give you one guess what his favourite book is.'

'I hate to think.'

'Guess!'

'*Pumping Iron,*' I said.

'Way off.'

'Tell me.'

'The *Ethics* of Spinoza.'

27

WE FOUND LYDIA in the schoolroom, trying to restore a semblance of order to the papers, paint pots, plastic alphabets and picture-books that lay scattered over the tables or trampled into the floor by muddy feet. She came to the doorway.

'Oh God,' she cried. 'What *am* I to do?'

She was a capable and intelligent woman in her early forties: a divorcee with two young boys. Her hair was grey and cut in a fringe above a pair of steady brown eyes. She was so capable and plainly so used to rising above every crisis that she refused to admit, to herself or others, that her nerves were frayed to breaking.

In the middle of the morning, she had gone to take a radio-call from her mother, who was sick in Melbourne. When she came back, the kids had dipped their hands into a can of green paint and slapped it round the walls.

'Well, at least they didn't shit on the desks,' she said. 'This time!'

Her boys, Nicky and David, were playing with their black friends in the schoolyard in their underpants, muddied from head to toe, and swinging like monkeys from the aerial roots of a fig tree. Nicky, frantic with excitement, shouted obscenities at his mother and stuck out his tongue.

'I'm going to *drown* you,' she shouted back.

She stretched her arms across the doorway, as though to prevent us from entering, but then said, 'Come in. Come in. I'm only being silly.'

She stood in the middle of the room, paralysed by the chaos.

'Let's have a bonfire,' she said. 'The only thing to do's to have a bonfire and burn the lot. Burn and begin again.'

Arkady comforted her in the reverberative Russian voice he usually reserved for women, to calm them. Lydia then led us towards a sheet of fibreboard, on which was pinned up the work of the art class.

'The boys paint horses and helicopters,' she said. 'But can I get them to do a house? Never! Only girls do houses . . . and flowers.'

'Interesting,' said Arkady.

'Do look at these,' she smiled. 'These are funny.'

They were a pair of crayon drawings, one of an Emu Monster with atrocious claws and beak. The other was a hairy 'Ape Man' with a jawful of fangs and flashing yellow eyes, like headlights.

'Where's Graham?' Arkady asked, suddenly.

Graham was Lydia's assistant. He was the boy I had seen in Alice as I was leaving the motel.

'Just don't *speak* to me about Graham,' she shuddered. 'I don't want to know about Graham. If anyone says the word "Graham" again I may do something violent.'

She made another half-hearted effort to clear up one of the desks, but stopped and took a deep breath.

'No,' she said. 'It's no use. I'd much rather face it in the morning.'

She locked up, called to the boys, and made them put on their Space Invader t-shirts. They were bare-foot. They trailed us reluctantly across the compound, but since there were so many thorns and bits of broken glass we decided to carry them piggyback.

We passed the Lutheran chapel, boarded up now for three years. We then passed the Community Centre: a blue-metal hangar on which there was painted a cartoon procession of honey-ants. From inside came the sound of country and western music. An evangelical meeting was in progress. I put David down and poked my head around the door.

Onstage stood a pale Aboriginal half-caste in tight, white bell-bottom pants and a shiny scarlet shirt. His hairy chest was festooned with gold chains. His pot-belly seemed to have been added as an afterthought, and he was swivelling on his high heels doing his best to rouse a rather grumpy congregation.

'OK,' he crooned. 'Come on now! Give it voice! Give voice to Je-e-e-sus!'

(138)

The verses, projected on slides, came up one by one on to a screen:

> Jesus is the sweetest name I know
> And he's the same as his name
> And that's why I love him so . . .

'Now you see', said Arkady, 'what some of us have to contend with.'

'Bathos,' I said.

Lydia and the boys lived in a shabby, prefabricated house of three rooms, which had been set down in the shade of an ironwood. She threw her briefcase on to an armchair.

'And now', she said, 'I've got to face the kitchen sink.'

'We've got to face it,' said Arkady. '*You*'ve got to put your feet up.'

He took some toys off the daybed and guided her feet firmly on to it. There were three days' dirty dishes in the kitchen and the ants were everywhere. We scoured the grease from aluminium saucepans, and boiled a kettle. I cut up some steak and onions for a stew. Over a second pot of tea, Lydia began to unwind and to talk, quite rationally, about Graham.

Graham had come straight to Popanji from a teacher-training college in Canberra. He was twenty-two. He was innocent, intolerant, and had a smile of irresistible charm. He could turn quite nasty if anyone called him 'angelic'.

He lived for music – and Pintupi boys were born musicians. One of his first acts, on arrival, was to start the Popanji Band. He scrounged the sound equipment from a moribund radio-station in Alice. They practised in the disused doctor's surgery, which still had its electric wiring intact.

Graham took the drums for himself. There were two guitarists, sons of Albert Tjakamarra. The keyboard player was a fat boy who styled himself 'Danny Roo'. The singer, and star, was a whiplike sixteen-year-old, 'Long-fingers' Mick.

Mick had his hair in rasta plaits and was a mesmerising mimic. After five minutes of watching a video, he could 'do' Bob Marley, or Hendrix or Zappa. But his best performance was to

roll his syrupy eyes and spread his huge, pouty mouth into a grin
– and 'become' his namesake, Jagger himself.

Travelling and sleeping in Graham's old Volkswagen van, the
Band toured the settlements from Yuendumu to Ernabella and
even as far afield as Balgo.

They sang a dirge about police killings called 'The Ballad of
Barrow Creek'. They had an upbeat number called 'Abo Rasta':
another, more morally uplifting, against petrol-sniffing. They
made a tape, and then a seven-inch disc, and then they had a hit
on their hands.

'Grandfather's Country' became the song of the Out-Station
Movement. Its theme was eternal, 'Go west, young man! Go
west!' Away from cities and government camps. Away from
drink, glue, hash, smack, gaol. Out! Back to the desert from
which grandfather was hounded. The refrain, 'Mobs of
people . . . Mobs of People . . .', had a slightly liturgical tone,
like 'Bread of Heaven . . . Bread of Heaven . . .' – and drove the
audiences wild. At the Alice Rock Festival, where they played it,
ancient Aboriginal greybeards were seen skittering and bopping
with the kids.

A promoter from Sydney took Graham aside, and seduced
him with the blather of show business.

Graham went back to his job at Popanji, but was hardly there
in spirit. He had visions of his music sweeping Australia and the
rest of the world. He pictured himself starring in a 'road movie'.
He was soon lecturing Lydia about agents, agents' fees,
recording rights and movie rights. She heard him out in silence,
with misgivings.

She was – she was too honest not to admit it – jealous. She
had mothered Graham, fed him, sewn the patches on his jeans,
tidied his house and listened to his idealistic hot talk.

What she loved most in him was his seriousness. He was a
do-er: the opposite of her ex-husband, whose idea it had been to
'work for Aboriginals' and who'd then nipped off to Bondai.
What she dreaded, above all, was the thought that Graham
might leave.

To be alone, without home or money, with two boys to bring
up, nagged with worry that the government might cut back
funds and she be made redundant: none of that mattered as long
as Graham was around.

She was afraid, too, for Graham himself. He and his black friends would 'go bush' for days on end. She never pressed him for details, yet she suspected, just as she'd suspected her husband of heroin, that Graham was mixed up in Aboriginal 'business'.

Eventually, he couldn't resist telling her. He described the dancing and singing, the blood-letting and sacred diagrams; and told her how he'd been painted all over, in bands of white and ochre.

She warned him that Aboriginals' friendship was never 'pure'. They would always look on whites as a 'resource'. Once he was 'one of them' he'd have to share everything.

'They'll have the Volkswagen off you,' she said.

He turned on her with a smile of amused contempt and said, 'Do you think I'd care?'

Her second set of fears she kept to herself. She was afraid that, once you joined, you joined: whether it was a secret society or a spy-ring, your life from then on was marked. At her previous post in Groote Eylandt, a young anthropologist had been given ritual secrets, but when he published them in his thesis, he suffered from headaches and depressions – and could now live only outside Australia.

Lydia willed herself not to believe the stories of 'bone-pointing' and of sorcerers who could 'sing' men to their doom. All the same, she had an idea that the Aboriginals, with their terrifying immobility, had somehow got Australia by the throat. There was an awesome power in these apparently passive people who would sit, watch, wait and manipulate the white man's guilt.

One day, after Graham had gone missing for a week, she asked him, straight, 'Do you, or don't you, want to teach?'

He folded his arms. 'I want to. Yes,' he replied with inconceivable insolence. 'But not in a school run by racists.'

She gasped, wanted to block her ears, but he went on, mercilessly. The education programme, he said, was systematically trying to destroy Aboriginal culture and to rope them into the market system. What Aboriginals needed was land, land and more land – where no unauthorised European would ever set foot.

He ranted on. She felt her answer rising in her throat. She knew she shouldn't say the words, but the words came bursting out, 'In South Africa they've a name for that! Apartheid!'

Graham walked from the house. The break, from then on, was total. In the evenings the bam-bam-bam of the Band struck her as something evil and menacing.

She could have reported him to the education authority. She could have had him fired. Instead, she shouldered all his work and taught both classes herself. Sometimes she came into the schoolroom and found 'Lydia loves Graham' scrawled up on the blackboard.

Early one morning, as she watched the sunlight spread over the bedsheets, she heard Graham's voice in the front room. He was laughing with Nicky and David. She closed her eyes, smiled and dozed off again.

Later, she heard him tinkering in the kitchen. He came in with a cup of tea, sat on the end of her bed, and gave her the news.

'We've made it,' he said.

'Grandfather's Country' was number 3 in the National Hit Parade. The Band was to be given star billing in Sydney, at The Place, all air fares and hotels paid.

'Oh!' she said, and let her head fall back on the pillow. 'I'm glad. You deserve it. You do, you know. Every bit of it.'

Graham had accepted to play the first concert in Sydney on February 15th – and in his haste to sign the contract had put all other considerations aside.

He forgot – or pretended to forget – that the rains came in February, and that February was the month for initiations. He forgot his friend Mick was due to be initiated into the Bandicoot Clan. And he put out of his mind the fact that he, Graham, in a moment of bravura, had agreed to be initiated with him.

Initiation ceremonies the world over are staged as a symbolic battle in which the young man – to prove his virility and 'fitness' for marriage – must bare his sexual organs to the jaws of a bloodthirsty ogre. The knife of the circumciser is a substitute for the carnivore's fang. In Aboriginal Australia, the puberty rites will also include 'head-biting' – at which the Elders gnaw at the boys' skulls or jab at them with sharpened points. Sometimes, the boys pull out their own fingernails and stick them back on with their blood.

The ceremony takes place in secret, at a Dreaming site far from the eyes of strangers. Afterwards, at a seminar made unforgettable by pain, the sacred couplets are dinned into the heads of the initiates – who, meanwhile, are made to crouch over fires of smouldering sandalwood. The smoke is said to have anaesthetic properties which assist the wounds to heal.

For a boy to delay his initiation is to risk being stranded in a lifeless, asexual limbo: to evade it altogether was, until recently, unheard of. The performance can drag on for weeks, if not months.

Lydia was a little vague as to what happened. Graham, it seems, was frantic with worry they would miss the first concert: Mick made a terrible scene, and accused Graham of abandoning him.

Eventually, everyone arrived at a compromise: whereby Graham would only suffer token 'cuts' and Mick would be allowed to shorten his period of isolation. He would return to Popanji in order to practise with the Band, but would have to spend several hours each day in session with the Elders. He also promised not to leave until two days before the concert.

At first, everything went without a hitch and, on February 7th, as soon as Mick was fit to walk, he and Graham returned to the settlement. The weather was damp and sultry, and Mick insisted on rehearsing in a pair of skin-tight blue jeans. On the night of February 9th, he woke from a nightmare to find the wound had gone horribly septic.

Graham then panicked. He bundled all the sound equipment and the players into the Volkswagen and, before dawn, drove off to Alice.

Lydia got up that morning to find the house surrounded by a furious mob, some waving spears, accusing her of hiding the fugitives or helping them escape. Two carloads of men gave chase – in order to fetch Mick back.

I told Lydia I'd seen Graham, looking more or less demented, outside the motel.

'What can one do,' she said, 'except see the funny side of it?'

28

WE WERE ON THE ROAD by eight, under a blanket of low-hanging cloud. The road streaked ahead in two parallel ruts of reddish water. In places we had to cross a floodpan with low bushes breaking the surface. A cormorant flew up ahead of us, thrashing the water with its wings. We passed through a stand of desert oaks, which are a species of casuarina and look less like an oak than a cactus. They, too, were standing in water. Arkady said it was madness to go on, but we went on. The muddy water splashed up inside the cab. I gritted my teeth whenever the wheels began to spin, but then we would again lurch forward.

'The nearest I came to drowning', I said, 'was in a flashflood in the Sahara.'

Around noon we sighted Stumpy Jones's truck. He was coming back from Cullen, from delivering the weekly supplies.

He braked and leaned out of the cab.

'Hi, Ark,' he called. 'Want a shot of Scotch?'

'Wouldn't say no.'

He handed down the bottle. We each took a couple of swigs and handed it back.

'Hear you got a date with Titus?' said Stumpy.

'Yes.'

'Best of luck.'

'He *is* there, I hope?'

'Oh, he'll be there all right.'

Stumpy Jones was a grizzled, green-eyed man with enormous biceps and a 'bit of the black in him'. He was wearing a red plaid shirt. The left half of his face was yellowish scar tissue. On the trailer he was carrying a caravan which was being sent for modernisation in Alice. He got out to check his lashings. His legs were so extraordinarily short that he swung himself from the door-frame on one hand, and lowered himself gently to the ground.

'Happy landings,' he waved to us. 'You're over the worst.'

We moved ahead, through what seemed to be an endless lake.

'What happened to his face?' I asked.

'Bitten by a king-brown,' said Arkady. 'About four years back. He got down to change a wheel and the bugger'd wrapped itself around the axle. He got over that one and the thing went cancerous.'

'Christ!' I said.

'Stumpy's indestructible.'

A couple of hours later, we saw a herd of camels, soaked in the downpour, and then through the mist we began to see the rounded hump of Mount Cullen, rearing up above the level of the plain. As we came up closer, the colour of the mountain turned from grey to purple: the colour of sodden red sandstone. A mile or two beyond, there was an escarpment of sheer, faceted cliffs, upraised into a peak at one end, and then tapering away towards the north.

This, said Arkady, was Mount Liebler.

On a saddle between these two mountains lay the settlement of Cullen.

We drove along the airstrip, past the caravans of the white advisers, towards a building of galvanised sheet. There was a petrol pump outside it. The sun had come out and it was hot and sticky. Packs of dogs were squabbling over a few scraps of offal. There was no one about.

Dispersed among the bushes were a number of humpies, but most of the Pintupi preferred to live in windbreaks of thorn. A few bits of washing were hanging out to dry.

'Who would guess', said Arkady, 'that this is a flourishing community of four hundred souls?'

'Not me,' I said.

The store was locked.

'We'd better go and rout out Rolf.'

'Who is this Rolf?'

'Rolf Niehart,' he said. 'You'll see.'

He pointed the Land Cruiser towards a caravan set in some trees. There was a generator purring in a shed alongside. Arkady sidestepped the puddles and rapped on the door.

(145)

'Rolf?' he called.

'Who's that?' someone answered in a sleepy voice.

'Ark!'

'Ha! The Great Do-Gooder himself!'

'That'll do.'

'Your humble servant.'

'Open up.'

'Clothed or unclothed?'

'Clothed, you little monster!'

After a few moments of rummaging about, Rolf appeared at the caravan door, scrubbed and immaculate, like someone off the beach in St Tropez, in cut-off jeans and a striped French sailor's shirt. He was built on a minuscule scale, and can't have been more than four foot ten. He had a prominent bridge to his nose, but what was so arresting was the colour scheme: uniform amber – golden, sandy amber – the eyes steady and mocking; the hair *en brosse*, very French; the skin tanned, oiled, unlined, without a pimple or blemish anywhere. And when he opened his mouth, he displayed a set of glittering triangular teeth, like a baby shark's.

He was the store manager.

'Enter,' he said, ceremoniously.

Inside the caravan, you could hardly move for books: novels mostly, in shelves and in stacks; hardback and paperback; English and American novels; novels in French and German; from the Czech, the Spanish, the Russian; unopened packages from the Gotham Book Mart; heaps of the *Nouvelle Revue Française* and the *New York Review*; literary journals; journals of literature in translation, dossiers, files, card indexes . . .

'Sit!' he said, as if there was anywhere to sit until we'd cleared a space.

By the time we had done so, Rolf had poured three cups of coffee from the espresso machine, lit himself a Gauloise, and was holding forth, in a staccato rat-tat-tat, against the whole of contemporary fiction. One after the other, the big names were set up on the block of this literary executioner, played with, and put down with a single syllable, 'Shit!'

The Americans were 'bores'. The Australians were 'infantile'. The South Americans were 'over'. London was a 'cesspit', Paris not much better. The only half-decent work was being done in Eastern Europe.

'Providing', he snapped, 'they stay there!'

He next turned his venom on to publishers and agents until Arkady could take it no longer.

'Look, little monster. We *are* tired.'

'You look tired,' he said. 'You also look filthy.'

'Where are we going to sleep?'

'In a lovely, air-conditioned caravan.'

'Whose caravan?'

'Put specially at your disposal by the Cullen Community. With clean sheets on the beds, cool drinks in the fridge . . .'

'I said whose caravan?'

'Glen's,' he said. 'He hasn't moved into it yet.'

Glen was a community adviser.

'So where's Glen?'

'In Canberra,' said Rolf. 'For a conference. Silly ponce!'

He nipped outside, jumped into the Land Cruiser and headed us towards a brand-new, smartly painted caravan a few hundred yards away. Hanging from the branch of a ghost-gum, there was a canvas bucket-shower, with two water containers under it.

Rolf lifted the lid of one and dipped his finger in.

'Still warm,' he said. 'We were expecting you earlier.'

He handed Arkady the key. Inside the caravan there was soap, there were towels, there were sheets.

'I'll leave you to it,' he said. 'Look over at the store a bit later. We close at five.'

'How's Wendy?' Arkady asked.

'In love with me,' Rolf grinned.

'Monkey!'

Arkady raised his fist as if to cuff him, but Rolf jumped down the steps and strolled off, inconsequentially, through the bushes.

'That one needs some explaining,' I said.

'It's what I always tell people,' said Arkady. 'Australia is a land of wonders.'

'For a start,' I said, 'how old is he?'

'Anything from nine to ninety.'

We showered, changed, put our feet up and then Arkady outlined what he knew of Rolf's background.

He belonged, on his father's side, to a lineage of Barossa Valley Germans – eight generations of Prussians, solid Lutheran with solid money, the most rooted community in Australia. The mother was a Frenchwoman who had landed up in Adelaide during the war. Rolf was trilingual, in English, German and French. He got a grant to go to the Sorbonne. He wrote a thesis on 'structural linguistics' and later had a job as 'cultural correspondent' for a Sydney newspaper.

This experience gave him so rabid a hatred for the press, press-lords and the media in general that, when his girlfriend Wendy suggested they maroon themselves at Cullen, he agreed on one condition: he'd have as much time as he liked to read.

'And Wendy?' I asked.

'Oh, she's a serious linguist. She's collecting material for the Pintupi dictionary.'

By the end of the first year, he went on, Rolf had read himself to a standstill when the job of storekeeper came up.

The previous storekeeper, another lunatic called Bruce, believing himself more Aboriginal than the Aboriginals, made the mistake of picking a quarrel with an unhinged old man called Wally Tjangapati, and had his skull split open by Wally's boomerang.

Unfortunately, a splinter of mulga wood, needle-thin or thinner, escaped the eyes of the X-ray operator in Alice Springs, and made a traverse through Bruce's brain.

'Affecting', said Arkady, 'not only his speech but his lower bodily functions.'

'Why did Rolf take it on?'

'Perversity,' he said.

'What does he do with himself?' I asked. 'Does he write?'

Arkady frowned.

'I wouldn't mention that,' he said. 'I think it's a sore subject. I think he had his novel turned down.'

We had an hour's siesta and then walked over to the dispensary, where the radio-telephone was. Estrella, the Spanish nursing sister, was bandaging a woman whose leg had been bitten by a dog. On the roof of the dispensary, several galvanised sheets had worked loose and were clattering up and down in the wind.

Arkady asked if there'd been any messages.

'No,' Estrella yelled above the din. 'I don't hear nothing.'

'Any messages?' Arkady bellowed, pointing at the radio.

'No. No. No messages!'

'The first thing I'm going to do tomorrow', I said as we walked away, 'is to fix that roof.'

We walked towards the store.

Because Stumpy Jones had brought a consignment of melons – rock-melons and water-melons – about fifty people were squatting or sitting around the petrol-pump, eating melon.

The dogs were disgusted by melon rind.

We went inside.

The lights of the store had fused and the shoppers were groping about in semi-darkness. Some were ferreting in the deep-freeze. Someone had spilt a bag of flour. A child was howling for a lost lolly, and a young mother, her baby cinched inside her scarlet jumper, was taking swigs from a tomato-sauce bottle.

The 'mad boomeranger', a gaunt, hairless man with rings of fat around his neck, stood in front of the till, angrily demanding cash for his welfare cheque.

There were two cash registers. One was manually operated; the other was electric and therefore out of order. Behind the first one, an Aboriginal girl sat totting up the bills with deft-fingered competence. Behind the second, head down, oblivious to the noise and the stink, was Rolf.

He was reading.

He looked up and said, 'Oh, there you are!' He was reading Proust.

'I'm about to shut,' he said. 'Need anything? We got a great line in coconut shampoo.'

'No,' I said.

He was, to be precise, nearing the end of the Duchesse de Guermantes's interminable dinner party. His head swayed from side to side as his eyes ran across the page. Then, with the satisfaction of concluding a Proustian paragraph, he let out an involuntary 'Ah!', inserted the bookmark and slapped the Pléiade shut.

He jumped to his feet.

'Out!' he barked at the shoppers. 'Out! Out! Scram!'

He allowed the women already standing in line to complete their purchases. All other customers, even the 'boomeranger', he sent packing for the door. With a moan of anguish, the young mother shielded her basket from him. He was unrepentant.

(149)

'Out!' he repeated. 'You've had all day. Come back at nine tomorrow.'

He grabbed the basket and returned her tins of ham and pineapple to the shelves. Finally, when he had shoved the last customer through the door, he pointed to an 'Eski' hidden behind his cash till.

'Hardship rations,' he said. 'Courtesy of Stumpy Jones. Come on, you two big thugs. Give us a hand.'

He allowed Arkady and me to carry the container to his caravan. Wendy had not yet come back.

'See you later,' he nodded. 'Eight sharp.'

We read for a couple of hours, and at eight sharp walked across to find Rolf and Wendy grilling chicken over a charcoal fire. There were sweet-potatoes baking in silver-foil. There were greens and salad. And in defiance of the regulations, there were four bottles of ice-cold Barossa Valley 'Chablis'.

The moment I set eyes on Wendy I could hear myself saying, 'Not another one!' Not another of these astonishing women! She was tall, calm, serious yet amused, with golden hair done up in braids. She seemed less demonstrative than Marian, but less highly strung, happier in her work, less 'lost'.

'I'm glad you've come,' she said. 'Rolf badly needs someone to talk to.'

29

TITUS TJILKAMATA, the man Arkady had come to see, lived about twenty-five miles south-west of Cullen settlement, in a shanty beside a soakage.

Apparently he was in such a foul mood that Arkady, who had been bracing himself for the ordeal, suggested I stay behind until he'd 'taken the temperature'. He enlisted the support of Titus's 'manager', a soft-spoken man with a limp and the nickname 'Limpy'. The two of them set off in the Land Cruiser at nine.

The day was very hot and windy and there were scribbles of cirrus blowing across the sky. I walked over to the dispensary. The noise from the roof was deafening.

'They fix-ed it once,' Estrella yelled. 'Costed two thousand dollars! Imagine!' She was a tiny young woman with a very humorous face.

I climbed up to inspect the damage. The job had been hopelessly botched. All the roof timbers were askew: in the not unforeseeable future, the building was going to collapse.

Estrella sent me over to Don, the works manager, to ask him for a hammer and roofing nails. 'None of your business,' he said. 'Or mine.'

The work had been done by some 'shit-artist' from Alice.

'That doesn't lessen the risk', I said, facetiously, 'of one suicidal Spanish nun. Or a child cut in two when a sheet blows off.'

Don relented with bad grace and gave me all the nails he had. I spent a couple of hours hammering down the sheets and, when the job was done, Estrella smiled, with approval.

'At leasted I can hear myself think now,' she said.

On my way back from returning the hammer, I looked in on Rolf at the store.

Nearby, sheltering from the wind behind a ring of empty drums, a party of men and women were playing poker for very high stakes. A man had lost 1,400 dollars and was resigned to losing more. The winner, a giantess in a yellow jumper, was slapping her cards on to the groundsheets with the droop-mouthed, hungry expression of ladies at a casino.

Rolf was still reading Proust. He had left the Duchesse de Guermantes's dinner party and was following the Baron de Charlus through the streets to his apartment. He had a Thermos of black coffee, which he shared with me.

'I've got someone here you should meet,' he said.

He handed a toffee to a small boy and told him to run and fetch Joshua. About ten minutes later, a middle-aged man appeared in the doorway, all leg and less body, very dark-skinned in a black cowboy hat.

'Ha!' said Rolf. 'Mr Wayne himself.'

'Boss!' said the Aboriginal, in a gravelly American accent.

'Listen, you old scrounger. This is a friend of mine from England. I want you to tell him about the Dreamings.'

'Boss!' he repeated.

Joshua was a famous Pintupi 'performer', who could always be counted on to give a good show. He had performed in Europe and the United States. On flying into Sydney for the first time, he mistook the ground lights for stars – and asked why the plane was flying upside down.

I followed him home along a winding path through the spinifex. He had no hips to speak of, and his pants kept falling down to reveal a pair of neat, calloused buttocks.

'Home' lay on the highest point of the saddle between Mount Cullen and Mount Liebler. It consisted of a gutted station-wagon which Joshua had rolled on to its roof so he could lie under the bonnet, in the shade. The cab was wrapped in black plastic sheet. A bundle of hunting spears poked out from one window.

We sat down cross-legged in the sand. I asked him if he'd mind pointing out some local Dreamings.

'Ho! Ho!' he broke into a wheezy cackle. 'Many Dreamings! *Many!*'

'Well, who –', I asked, waving towards Mount Liebler, 'who is that?'

'Ho! Ho!' he said. 'That one a Big One. A Walk One. A Perenty One.'

The perenty, or lace-monitor, is the largest lizard in Australia. It can reach a length of eight feet or more, and has a burst of speed to run down a horse.

Joshua stuck his tongue in and out like a lizard's and, twisting his fingers into claws, dug them crabwise into the sand to imitate the perenty's walk.

I looked up again at the cliffline of Mount Liebler and found I could 'read' into the rock the lizard's flat, triangular head, his shoulder, his foreleg and hindleg, and the tail tapering away towards the north.

'Yes,' I said. 'I see him. So where was this Perenty Man coming from?'

'Come long way,' said Joshua. 'Come long, long way. Some way up Kimberley.'

'And where's he going on to?'

He raised his hand towards the south, 'Out that country people.'

Having established that the Perenty Songline followed a north–south axis, I then swivelled round and pointed to Mount Cullen.

'OK,' I said. 'Who's this one?'

'Women,' Joshua whispered. 'Two women.'

He told the story of how the Two Women had chased Perenty up and down the country until, at last, they cornered him here and attacked his head with digging-sticks. Perenty, however, had dug himself into the earth, and escaped. A hole on the summit of Mount Liebler, like a meteorite crater, was all that remained of the head wound.

South of Cullen the country was green after the storms. There were isolated rocks jutting out of the plain like islands.

'Tell me, Joshua,' I asked, 'who are those rocks over there?'

Joshua listed Fire, Spider, Wind, Grass, Porcupine, Snake, Old Man, Two Men and an unidentifiable animal 'like a dog but a white one'. His own Dreaming, the Porcupine (or echidna), came down from the direction of Arnhem Land, through Cullen itself and on towards Kalgoorlie.

I looked back again towards the settlement, at the metal roofs and the spinning sails of the wind-pump.

'So Porcupine's coming up this way?' I said.

'Same one, Boss,' Joshua smiled. 'You seeing him good.'

He traced the line of the Porcupine track across the airstrip, past the school and the pump, then on along the foot of the Perenty cliff before it swooped down on to the plain.

'Can you sing him for me?' I asked. 'Can you sing him coming up this way?'

He glanced round to make sure no one was in earshot and then, in his chesty voice, sang a number of Porcupine couplets, keeping time by flicking his fingernail against a piece of cardboard sheet.

'Thank you,' I said.

'Boss.'

'Tell me another story,' I said.

'You like them stories?'

'I like them.'

'OK, Boss!' he tilted his head from side to side. 'Story 'bout the Big Fly One.'

'Dragonfly?' I asked.

'Bigger one.'

'Bird?'

'Bigger.'

Aboriginals, when tracing a Songline in the sand, will draw a series of lines with circles in between. The line represents a stage in the Ancestor's journey (usually a day's march). Each circle is a 'stop', 'waterhole', or one of the Ancestor's campsites. But the story of the Big Fly One was beyond me.

It began with a few straight sweeps; then it wound into a rectangular maze, and finally ended in a series of wiggles. As he traced each section, Joshua kept calling a refrain, in English, 'Ho! Ho! They got the money over there.'

I must have been very dim-witted that morning: it took me ages to realise that this was a Qantas Dreaming. Joshua had once flown into London. The 'maze' was London Airport: the Arrival gate, Health, Immigration, Customs, and then the ride into the city on the Underground. The 'wiggles' were the twists and turns of the taxi, from the tube station to the hotel.

In London, Joshua had seen all the usual sights – the Tower of London, Changing of the Guard and so on – but his real destination had been Amsterdam.

The ideogram for Amsterdam was even more perplexing. There was a circle. There were four smaller circles around it: and there were wires from each of these circles which led to a rectangular box.

Eventually, it dawned on me that this was some kind of round-table conference at which he, Joshua, had been one of four participants. The others, in a clockwise direction, had been 'a white one, a Father one', 'a thin one, a red one', 'a black one, a fat one'.

I asked if the 'wires' were microphone cables; Joshua shook his head vigorously. He knew all about microphones. They *had* microphones, on the table.

'No! No!' he shouted, pointing his fingers at his temples.

'Were they electrodes or something?'

'Hey!' he cackled. 'You got him.'

The picture I pieced together — true or false I can't begin to say — was of a 'scientific' experiment at which an Aboriginal had sung his Dreaming, a Catholic monk had sung the Gregorian Chant, a Tibetan lama had sung his mantras, and an African had sung whatever: all four of them singing their heads off, to test the effect of different song styles on the rhythmic structure of the brain.

The episode struck Joshua, in retrospect, as so unbelievably funny that he had to hold his stomach for laughing.

So did I.

We laughed ourselves into hysterics and lay gasping for breath on the sand.

Weak from laughter, I got to my feet. I thanked him, and said goodbye.

He grinned.

'Couldn't you buy a man a drink?' he growled in his John Wayne accent.

'Not at Cullen,' I said.

30

ARKADY CAME BACK in the late afternoon, tired and worried. He showered, wrote up some notes and lay on his bunk. The visit to Titus had not gone well. No, that is not true. He and Titus had got on very well, but what Titus had to tell him was a depressing story.

Titus's father was Pintupi, his mother was Loritja, and he was forty-seven or forty-eight years old. He had been born not far from his shanty, but around 1942 — attracted by the white man's jam, tea and flour — his parents had migrated out of the desert and taken refuge at the Lutheran Mission on Horn River. The pastors recognised in Titus a child of outstanding intelligence, and took him for education.

Even as late as the 1950s, the Lutherans ran their schools on the lines of a Prussian academy — and Titus was a model pupil. There are pictures of him at his desk, his hair neatly parted, in grey flannel shorts and spit-and-polished shoes. He learned to speak fluent English and German. He learned calculus. He mastered all kinds of mechanical skills. As a young lay preacher, he once astonished his teachers by delivering a sermon, in German, on the theological consequences of the Edict of Worms.

Twice a year, in June and again in November, he would get out his double-breasted suit, board the train for Adelaide, and spend a few weeks catching up with modern life. In the Public Library he would read back-numbers of *Scientific American*. One year, he took a course in petrochemical technology.

The 'other' Titus was the ultra-conservative song-man who lived, half-naked, with his dependants and his dogs; who hunted with a spear and never a rifle; who spoke six or seven Aboriginal languages and was famous, up and down the Western Desert, for his judgments on tribal law.

To have the stamina to keep both systems going was proof – if proof were lacking – of an incredible vitality.

Titus had welcomed the Land Rights Act as a chance for his people to go back to their country – and their only hope of getting rid of alcoholism. He detested the activities of the mining companies.

Under the Act, the government reserved the right to all minerals under the ground and to grant licences for prospecting. Yet the companies, if they wished to make soundings in Aboriginal country, were at least obliged to consult the 'traditional owners' and, if mining operations started, to pay them a royalty.

Titus, after weighing the pros and cons, took the line that money from minerals was bad money – bad for whites and bad for blacks. It had corrupted Australia and given it false values and false standards of living. When a company got permission to put seismic lines through his country, he gave them the scorn of his passive non-co-operation.

This attitude was not calculated to win him friends, either among white businessmen or ambitious blacks in Alice. It was also the reason for the present dispute.

Around 1910 Titus's grandfather, in dealings with a Loritja clan who, now living on the Amadeus Mission, call themselves the Amadeus Mob, had exchanged two sets of unmarked tjuringas. The exchange gave each the right of access to the other's hunting ground. Since the tjuringas had never been returned, the agreement was still in force.

One day, at a time when the mining company despaired of dealing with Titus, a deputation from Amadeus turned up in Alice to say that they, not he, were the 'owners' of the country and its songs – and were therefore entitled to mining royalties. What they had done was to tamper with the tjuringas; engraving them with their own totemic designs. They had, in other words, forged the title deeds to Titus's birthright.

Titus, who knew of Arkady by reputation only, had sent a message for help.

Arkady, at his briefing in Alice, had been assured that this was simply a squabble about money. But Titus, it turned out, didn't give a hoot for money. The crisis was much more dangerous since, by altering the tjuringas, the Amadeus Mob had attempted to re-write the Creation.

Titus told Arkady how, at nights, he heard his Ancestors howling for vengeance – and how he felt forced to obey them.

Arkady, for his part, realised the urgency of getting the offenders to 'withdraw' their sacrilege, but could only think of playing for time. He suggested Titus take a holiday in Alice. 'No,' said Titus, grimly, 'I'll stay.'

'Then promise me one thing,' Arkady said. 'Do nothing until I get back to you.'

'I promise.'

Arkady was sure he meant to keep the promise; but what he found so shocking was the idea that, from now on, Aboriginals themselves were going to twist their own law in order to line their pockets.

'And if that's going to be the future,' he said, 'I might as well give up.'

That evening Estrella insisted on cooking an '*estofado* for the roofing man', and while we were waiting in her caravan we heard a few pecks of rain on the roof. I looked out to see, hanging over Mount Liebler, a solid barrage of cloud with bolts of lightning fizzling at the edges.

A few minutes later, the storm broke in sheets of water.

'Christ,' said Arkady, 'we'll be bogged in here for weeks.'

'I'd like that,' I said.

'Would you?' he snapped. 'I wouldn't.'

First, there was the Titus business to attend to. Then there was Hanlon. Then Arkady was due in Darwin in four days' time for a meeting with the railway engineer.

'You never told me,' I said.

'You never asked.'

The trip-switch of the generator then failed, and we were left in semi-darkness. The rain slammed down for half an hour or so, and stopped as abruptly as it started.

I went outside. 'Ark,' I called, 'you must come out.'

A pair of rainbows hung across the valley between the two mountains. The cliffs of the escarpment, which had been a dry red, were now purplish-black and striped, like a zebra, with vertical chutes of white water. The cloud seemed even denser than the earth, and, beneath its lower rim, the last of the sun broke through, flooding the spinifex with shafts of pale green light.

'I know,' said Arkady. 'Like nowhere else in the world.'

It poured again in the night. Next morning, before light, he shook me awake.

'We've got to get going,' he said. 'Quick.'

He had listened to the weather forecast. There was worse weather on the way.

'Must we?' I said, sleepily.

'I must,' he said. 'You stay, if you want.'

'No,' I said. 'I'll come.'

We had tea and tidied the caravan. We wiped the mud stains from the floor and scribbled a note for Wendy and Rolf.

We drove off through the puddles along the airstrip and joined the road that comes from Lake Mackay. The dawn was murky and sunless. We came off a ridge of higher ground . . . and the road disappeared into a lake.

'Well, that', said Arkady, 'is that.'

It was pouring by the time we got back to Cullen. Rolf was standing outside the store, in a rainproof poncho.

'Ha!' he leered at me. 'Thought you could sneak off without saying goodbye? I haven't done with you. Yet!'

Arkady spent the rest of the morning on the radio. The reception was terrible. All the roads to Alice were closed and would be for at least ten days. There were two seats on the mail plane – if the pilot would only make a detour.

Around noon there was a message that the plane would try to land.

'You coming?' said Arkady.

'No,' I said. 'I'll stay.'

'Good for you,' he said. 'Make sure the kids don't monkey around with the Land Cruiser.' He parked the vehicle under the trees, by our caravan, and handed me the key.

At the dispensary, Estrella had a woman in agony with an abscess. She would have to go to hospital in Alice, and would have to have my seat on the plane.

Another storm seemed to be brewing behind Mount Liebler when the crowd began waving at a black speck coming from the

(159)

south. The Cessna splashed down on to the runway, spattering the fuselage with mud, and taxied towards the store.

'Get a fuckin' move on,' the pilot bawled from the cockpit.

Arkady gripped my hand. 'See you, mate,' he said. 'About ten days, if all goes well.'

'See you,' I said.

'Bye 'bye, Little Monster,' he said to Rolf, and escorted the moaning woman to the plane.

They took off, easing out of the valley just ahead of the incoming storm.

'How does it feel', Rolf asked, 'to be stuck here with me?'

'I'll survive.'

For lunch we had beer and a salami sandwich. The beer made me sleepy, so I slept until four. When I woke, I started rearranging the caravan as a place to work in.

There was a plyboard top which pulled out over the second bunk to make a desk. There was even a swivelling office chair. I put my pencils in a tumbler and my Swiss Army knife beside them. I unpacked some exercise pads and, with the obsessive neatness that goes with the beginning of a project, I made three neat stacks of my 'Paris' notebooks.

In France, these notebooks are known as *carnets moleskines*: 'moleskine', in this case, being its black oilcloth binding. Each time I went to Paris, I would buy a fresh supply from a *papeterie* in the Rue de l'Ancienne Comédie. The pages were squared and the end-papers held in place with an elastic band. I had numbered them in series. I wrote my name and address on the front page, offering a reward to the finder. To lose a passport was the least of one's worries: to lose a notebook was a catastrophe.

In twenty odd years of travel, I lost only two. One vanished on an Afghan bus. The other was filched by the Brazilian secret police, who, with a certain clairvoyance, imagined that some lines I had written – about the wounds of a Baroque Christ – were a description, in code, of their own work on political prisoners.

Some months before I left for Australia, the owner of the *papeterie* said that the *vrai moleskine* was getting harder and harder to get. There was one supplier: a small family business in Tours. They were very slow in answering letters.

'I'd like to order a hundred,' I said to Madame. 'A hundred will last me a lifetime.'

She promised to telephone Tours at once, that afternoon.

At lunchtime, I had a sobering experience. The headwaiter of Brasserie Lipp no longer recognised me, 'Non, Monsieur, il n'y a pas de place.' At five, I kept my appointment with Madame. The manufacturer had died. His heirs had sold the business. She removed her spectacles and, almost with an air of mourning, said, 'Le vrai moleskine n'est plus.'

I had a presentiment that the 'travelling' phase of my life might be passing. I felt, before the malaise of settlement crept over me, that I should reopen those notebooks. I should set down on paper a résumé of the ideas, quotations and encounters which had amused and obsessed me; and which I hoped would shed light on what is, for me, the question of questions: the nature of human restlessness.

Pascal, in one of his gloomier *pensées*, gave it as his opinion that all our miseries stemmed from a single cause: our inability to remain quietly in a room.

Why, he asked, must a man with sufficient to live on feel drawn to divert himself on long sea voyages? To dwell in another town? To go off in search of a peppercorn? Or go off to war and break skulls?

Later, on further reflection, having discovered the cause of our misfortunes, he wished to understand the reason for them, he found one very good reason: namely, the natural unhappiness of our weak mortal condition; so unhappy that when we gave to it all our attention, nothing could console us.

One thing alone could alleviate our despair, and that was 'distraction' (*divertissement*): yet this was the worst of our misfortunes, for in distraction we were prevented from thinking about ourselves and were gradually brought to ruin.

Could it be, I wondered, that our need for distraction, our mania for the new, was, in essence, an instinctive migratory urge akin to that of birds in autumn?

All the Great Teachers have preached that Man, originally, was a 'wanderer in the scorching and barren wilderness of this world' – the words are those of Dostoevsky's Grand Inquisitor

– and that to rediscover his humanity, he must slough off attachments and take to the road.

My two most recent notebooks were crammed with jottings taken in South Africa, where I had examined, at first hand, certain evidence on the origin of our species. What I learned there – together with what I now knew about the Songlines – seemed to confirm the conjecture I had toyed with for so long: that Natural Selection has designed us – from the structure of our brain-cells to the structure of our big toe – for a career of seasonal journeys *on foot* through a blistering land of thorn-scrub or desert.

If this were so; if the desert were 'home'; if our instincts were forged in the desert; to survive the rigours of the desert – then it is easier to understand why greener pastures pall on us; why possessions exhaust us, and why Pascal's imaginary man found his comfortable lodgings a prison.

FROM THE NOTEBOOKS

OUR NATURE LIES *in movement; complete calm is death.*
Pascal, Pensées

◆

A study of the Great Malady; horror of home.
Baudelaire, Journaux Intimes

◆

The most convincing analysts of restlessness were often men who, for one reason or another, were immobilised: Pascal by stomach ailments and migraines, Baudelaire by drugs, St John of the Cross by the bars of his cell. There are French critics who would claim that Proust, the hermit of the cork-lined room, was the greatest of literary voyagers.

◆

The founders of monastic rule were forever devising techniques for quelling wanderlust in their novices. 'A monk out of his cell', said St Anthony, 'is like a fish out of water.' Yet Christ and the Apostles walked *their journeys through the hills of Palestine.*

◆

What is this strange madness, Petrarch asked of his young secretary, this mania for sleeping each night in a different bed?

◆

What am I doing here?
Rimbaud writing home from Ethiopia

◆

Sleepless night in the Charm Hotel. The sleeping-sickness bug is endemic to this region, which has one of the highest infant-mortality rates in the world. At breakfast-time, the proprietor, instead of serving my eggs, thwacked his fly-swat on to my plate and removed a mottled brown insect by the leg.

'Mata gente,' he said gloomily. 'It kills people.'

The stucco façade is painted a pale mint green with the words CHARM HOTEL *in bold black letters. A leaking gutter pipe has washed away the letter C, so that it now reads . . .*

◆

Djang, Cameroon

There are two hotels in Djang: the Hotel Windsor and, across the street, the Hotel Anti-Windsor.

◆

British Embassy, Kabul, Afghanistan

The Third Secretary is also Cultural Attaché. His office is stacked with copies of Orwell's Animal Farm: *the British government's contribution to the teaching of English in Afghan schools and an elementary lesson on the evils of Marxism, as voiced through the mouth of a pig.*

'But pigs?' I said. 'In an Islamic country? Don't you think that kind of propaganda might backfire?'

The Cultural Attaché shrugged. The Ambassador thought it was a good idea. There was nothing he could do.

◆

He who does not travel does not know the value of men.
                                                    Moorish proverb

◆

Miami, Florida

On the bus from Downtown to the Beach there was a lady in pink. She must have been eighty, at least. She had bright pink hair with pink flowers in it, a matching pink dress, pink lips, pink nails, pink handbag, pink earrings, and, in her shopping-basket, there were boxes of pink Kleenex.

In the wedges of her clear plastic heels a pair of goldfish were lazily floating in formaldehyde.

I was too intent on the goldfish to notice the midget in horn-rimmed glasses who was standing on the seat beside me.

'Permit me to ask you, sir,' he asked in a squeaky voice, 'which of the human qualities do you value the most?'

'I haven't thought,' I said.

'I used to believe in empathy,' he said, 'but I have recently moved over to compassion.'

'I'm glad to hear it.'

'Permit me to ask you, sir? At which of the professions are you presently engaged?'

'I'm studying to be an archaeologist.'

'You amaze me, sir. I'm in that line of country myself.'

He was a sewer-rat. His friends would lower him, with a metal-detector, into the main sewer beneath the hotels of Miami Beach. There, he would prospect for jewellery flushed, accidentally, down the toilets.

'It is not, I can assure you, sir,' he said, 'an unrewarding occupation.'

◆

On the night express from Moscow to Kiev, reading Donne's third 'Elegie':

> To live in one land, is captivitie,
> To runne all countries, a wild roguery

◆

This life is a hospital in which each sick man is possessed by a desire to change beds. One would prefer to suffer by the stove. Another believes he would recover if he sat by the window.

I think I would be happy in that place I happen not to be, and this question of moving house is the subject of a perpetual dialogue I have with my soul.

Baudelaire, 'Any Where Out of this World!'

◆

Bekom, Cameroon

The names of taxis: The Confidence Car. Baby Confidence. The Return of the Gentleman Chauffeur. Le Chauffeur Kamikaze.

◆

In the air, Paris–Dakar

Dinner last night at the Rue l'Abée de l'Epée. Malraux was there. A ventriloquist! He gave a faultless imitation of the door to Stalin's office as it slammed on Gide's face. He and Gide had gone to complain about the treatment of homosexuals in Russia, and Stalin had got wind of their intention.

◆

Dakar

The Hotel Coq Hardi is also a brothel. Its owner, Madame Martine, owns a fishing-boat, and so we have langouste for dinner. Of the two resident whores, my friend Mamzelle Yo- Yo wears a mountainous puce pink turban and has piston rods for legs. The other, Madame Jacqueline, has two regular clients: Herr Kisch, a hydrologist, and the Ambassador of Mali.

Yesterday was Kisch night. She appeared on her balcony, bangled and gleaming, the Mother-of-all-Africa in flowing robes of indigo. She blew him a kiss, tossed down a sprig of bougainvillaea, and cooed, 'Herr Kisch, I come.'

Tonight, when the Ambassador's Mercedes pulled up outside, she flew out in a curvaceous, café-au-lait suit, a peroxide wig and white high-heeled shoes, shouting stridently, 'Monsieur l'Ambassadeur, je viens!'

◆

Gorée, Senegal

On the terrace of the restaurant a fat French couple have been stuffing themselves with fruits de mer. *Their dachshund, leashed to the woman's chair leg, keeps jumping up in the hope of being fed.*

Woman to dachshund, 'Taisez-vous, Roméo! C'est l'entracte.'

(166)

Internal burning . . . wandering fever . . .

Kalevala

In The Descent of Man *Darwin notes that in certain birds the migratory impulse is stronger than the maternal. A mother will abandon her fledglings in the nest rather than miss her appointment for the long journey south.*

◆

Sydney Harbour

On the ferry back from Manly a little old lady heard me talking.

'You're English, aren't you?' she said, in an English North Country accent. 'I can tell you're English.'

'I am.'

'So am I!'

She was wearing thick, steel-framed spectacles and a nice felt hat with a wisp of blue net above the brim.

'Are you visiting Sydney?' I asked her.

'Lord, love, no!' she said, 'I've lived here since 1946. I came out to live with my son, but a very strange thing happened. By the time the ship got here, he'd died. Imagine! I'd given up my home in Doncaster, so I thought I might as well stay! *So I asked my second son to come out and live with me. So he came out . . . emigrated . . . and do you know what?'*

'No.'

'He died. He had a heart attack, and died.'

'That's terrible,' I said.

'I had a third son,' she went on. 'He was my favourite, but he died in the war. Dunkirk, you know! He was very brave. I had a letter from his officer. Very brave, he was! He was on the deck . . . covered in blazing oil . . . and he threw himself into the sea. Oooh! He was a sheet of living flame!'

'But that is terrible!'

'But it's a lovely day,' she smiled. 'Isn't it a lovely day?'

(167)

*It was a bright sunny day with high white clouds and a breeze
coming in off the ocean. Some yachts were beating out towards
The Heads, and other yachts were running under spinnaker.
The old ferry ran before the whitecaps, towards the Opera
House and the Bridge.*

'*And it's so lovely out at Manly!*' *she said.* '*I loved to go out
to Manly with my son . . . before he* died! *But I haven't been
for twenty years!*'

'*But it's so near,*' *I said.*

'*But I haven't been out of the house for sixteen. I was* blind,
*love! My eyes was covered with cataracts, and I couldn't see a
thing. The eye surgeon said it was hopeless, so I sat there. Think
of it! Sixteen years in the dark! Then along comes this nice social
worker the other week and says, "We'd better get those
cataracts looked at." And look at me now!*'

*I looked through the spectacles at a pair of twinkling — that is
the word for them — twinkling blue eyes.*

'*They took me to hospital,*' *she said.* '*And they cut out the
cataracts! And isn't it lovely? I can see!*'

'*Yes,*' *I said.* '*It's wonderful!*'

'*It's my first time out alone,*' *she confided.* '*I didn't tell a soul.
I said to myself at breakfast, "It's a* lovely *day. I'll take the bus
to Circular Quay, and go over on the ferry to Manly . . . just
like we did in the old days." I had a fish lunch. Oh, it was
lovely!*'

She hunched her shoulders mischievously, and giggled.

'*How* old *would you say I was?*' *she asked.*

'*I don't know,*' *I said.* '*Let me look at you. I'd say you were
eighty.*'

'*No. No. No,*' *she laughed.* '*I'm ninety-three . . . and I can
see!*'

◆

*Darwin quotes the example of Audubon's goose, which,
deprived of its pinion feathers, started out to walk the journey
on foot. He then goes on to describe the sufferings of a bird,
penned up at the season of its migration, which would flail its
wings and bloody its breast against the bars of its cage.*

◆

Robert Burton – sedentary and bookish Oxford don – devoted an immense amount of time and scholarship to showing that travel was not a curse, but a cure for melancholy: that is, for the depressions brought on by settlement:

The heavens themselves run continually round, the sun riseth and sets, the moon increaseth, stars and planets keep their constant motions, the air is still tossed by the winds, the waters ebb and flow, to their conservation no doubt, to teach us that we should ever be in motion.

Or:

There is nothing better than a change of air in this malady [melancholia], than to wander up and down, as those Tartari Zalmohenses that live in hordes, and take the opportunity of times, places, seasons.

The Anatomy of Melancholy

◆

My health was menaced. Terror came. For days on end I fell asleep and, when I woke, the dark dreams continued. I was ripe for death. My debility led me along a route of dangers, to the world's edge, to Cimmeria, the country of black fog and whirlwinds.

I was forced to travel, to ward off the apparitions assembled in my brain.

Rimbaud, Une Saison en enfer

He was a great walker. Oh! An astonishing walker, his coat open, a little fez on his head in spite of the sun.

Righas, on Rimbaud in Ethiopia

. . . along horrible tracks like those presumed to exist on the moon.

Rimbaud, writing home

'L'Homme aux semelles de vent.' 'The man with footsoles of wind.'

Verlaine on Rimbaud

(169)

Sheikh S lives in a small house overlooking the tomb of his grandfather, the Mahdi. On sheets of paper joined with Scotch tape to make a scroll, he has written a poem of five hundred stanzas, in the style and metre of Grey's Elegy, *entitled 'Lament for the Destruction of the Sudanese Republic'. He has been giving me lessons in Arabic. He says I have the 'light of faith' on my forehead, and hopes to convert me to Islam.*

I say I will convert to Islam if only he will conjure up a djinn.

'Djinns', he says, 'are difficult. But we can try.'

After an afternoon of combing the Omdurman souk for the right kinds of myrrh, frankincense and perfume, we are now all prepared for the djinn. The Faithful have prayed. The sun has gone down, and we are sitting in the garden, under a papaya, in a mood of reverent expectation, in front of a charcoal brazier.

The sheikh first tries a little myrrh. A wisp of smoke curls upward.

No djinn.

He tries the frankincense.

No djinn.

He tries everything we have bought, in turn.

Still no djinn!

He then says, 'Let's try the Elizabeth Arden.'

—

An ex-Légionnaire, a veteran of Dien Bien Phu with grey hair en brosse *and a toothy grin, is outraged at the US government for avoiding the blame for the My Lai massacre.*

'There is no such thing as a war crime,' he said. 'War is the crime.'

He is even more outraged by the court sentence that condemned Lieutenant Calley for the murder of 'human Orientals' – as if 'Oriental' needed 'human' to qualify it.

His definition of a soldier is as follows, 'A professional man, who, for thirty years, is employed to kill other men. After that, he prunes his roses.'

◆

Above all, do not lose your desire to walk: every day I walk myself into a state of well-being and walk away from every illness; I have walked myself into my best thoughts, and I know of no thought so burdensome that one cannot walk away from it . . . but by sitting still, and the more one sits still, the closer one comes to feeling ill . . . Thus if one just keeps on walking, everything will be all right.
    Søren Kierkegaard, letter to Jette (1847)

◆

Solvitur ambulando. *'It is solved by walking.'*

◆

Atar, Mauritania

'Have you seen the Indians?' asked the son of the Emir of Adrar.
'I have.'
'Is it a village, or what?'
'No,' I said. 'It's one of the greatest countries in the world.'
'Tiens! I always thought it was a village.'

◆

Nouakchott, Mauritania

A scatter of concrete buildings dumped down in the sand and now surrounded by a bidonville *of nomads, who, like Jacob and his sons, have been forced into settlement 'when the famine was sore in the land'.*
    Until last year's drought, about 80 per cent of the people in this country lived in the tents.

The Moors have a passion for the colour blue. Their robes are blue. Their turbans are blue. The tents of the bidonville *are patched with blue cotton; and the shanties, cobbled together from packing cases, are bound to have some blue paint somewhere.*
    This afternoon I followed a wizened old crone who was picking over the garbage dump in search of blue rag. She picked

(171)

up one piece. She picked up another. She compared them. She chucked the first piece away. At last she found a scrap which was exactly the shade she was looking for – and she went away singing.

On the edge of town three tiny boys stopped booting their football and ran up to me. But instead of asking for money or my address, the tiniest began a very grave conversation. What was my opinion of the war in Biafra? What were the causes of the Arab-Israeli conflict? What did I think of the persecution of the Jews by Hitler? The Pharaonic monuments of Egypt? The Ancient Empire of the Almoravids?

    'But who*', I asked, 'are you?'*

    He saluted stiffly.

    'Sall' 'Zakaria sall Muhammad,' he trilled in a high-pitched treble. 'Son of the Minister of the Interior!'

    'And how old are you?'

    'Eight.'

    Next morning a jeep arrived to take me to the Minister.

    'I believe, cher Monsieur,' he said, 'that you have met my son. A most interesting conversation, he tells me. I, for my part, would like you to dine with us, and to know if I can assist you in any way.'

◆

For a long time I prided myself I would possess every possible country.

                       Rimbaud, Une Saison en enfer

◆

Mauritania, on the road to Atar

There were about fifty people on top of the truck, huddled against sacks of grain. We were half-way to Atar when a sandstorm hit. Next to me was a strong-smelling Senegalese. He said he was twenty-five. He was stocky and over-muscled, and his teeth were orange from chewing cola nuts.

    'You are going to Atar?' he asked.

    'You too?'

    'No. I am going to France.'

    'What for?'

'To continue my profession.'
'What is your profession?'
'Installation sanitaire.'
'You have a passport?'
'No,' he grinned. 'I have a paper.'
He unfolded a soggy scrap of paper on which I read that Don
Hernando So-and-so, master of the trawler such-and-such, had
employed Amadou . . . surname blank . . . etc. etc.
'I will go to Villa Cisneros,' he said. 'I will take a ship to
Tenerife or Las Palmas in the Gran Canaria. There I will
continue my profession.'
'As a sailor?'
'No, Monsieur. As an adventurer. I wish to see all the peoples
and all the countries of the world.'

On the road back from Atar

There were fifteen passengers crammed into the back of a
canvas-hooded pick-up. All of them were Moors except for
myself and a person covered in a sack. The sack moved, and the
drawn and beautiful head of a young Wolof peered out. His skin
and hair were coated with white dust, like the bloom on purple
grapes. He was frightened and very upset.
'What's the matter?' I asked.
'It is finished. I was turned back at the frontier.'
'Where were you going?'
'To France.'
'What for?'
'To continue my profession.'
'What is your profession?'
'You would not understand.'
'I would,' I said. 'I know most of the métiers in France.'
'No,' he shook his head. 'This is not a profession that you
would understand.'
'Tell me.'
Finally, with a sigh that was also a groan, he said, 'I am an
ébéniste. I make bureaux-plats Louis Quinze and Louis Seize.'
This he did. In Abidjan he had learned to inlay veneer at a
furniture factory that catered to the taste of the new, black,
francophile bourgeoisie.

(173)

Although he had no passport, he had in his bag a book on French eighteenth-century furniture. His heroes were Cressent and Reisener. He had hoped to visit the Louvre, Versailles and the Musée des Arts Décoratifs. He had hoped, if possible, to apprentice himself to a Parisian 'master', assuming that such a person existed.

◆

London

With Bertie to a dealer in French furniture. The dealer had offered a Reisener commode to Paul Getty, who had called on Bertie for his expertise.

The commode had been over-restored to its original condition.

Bertie looked at it and said, 'Oh!'

'Well?' asked the dealer, after a long pause.

'Well, I wouldn't put it in the maid's bedroom. *But it'll do for* him.'

◆

It is good to collect things, but it is better to go on walks.
                                                    Anatole France

◆

My possessions fly away from me. Like locusts they are on the wing, flying . . .
                        A lament on the destruction of Ur

◆

Timbuktu

The waiter brought me the menu:

> Capitaine bamakoise *(fried catfish)*
> Pintade grillée
> Dessert

'Good,' I said. 'What time can I eat?'
'We eat at eight,' he said.
'All right, then. Eight.'

(174)

'No, Monsieur. We *eat at eight*. You *must eat before* seven . . . or after ten.'
'Who's we?'
'We,' he said. 'The staff.'
He lowered his voice and whispered:
'I counsel you to eat at seven, Monsieur. We *eat up all the* food.'

Christianity was planted here about a century ago, not person-ally, by Cardinal de la Vigerie, Archbishop of Carthage and Primate of All Africa. He was a connoisseur of burgundy and had his habits made at Worth.

Among his agents in Africa were three white Fathers — Paulmier, Boerlin and Minoret — who, shortly after saying Mass in the forbidden city, had their heads struck off by the Tuareg.

The Cardinal received the news in his landau on the sea-front at Biarritz.

'Te Deum Laudamus!' he cried. 'But I don't believe it.'
'No,' said his informant. 'It's true.'
'They are really dead?'
'They are.'
'What joy for us! And for them!'

The Cardinal interrupted his morning drive to write three identical letters of condolence to the mothers, 'God used you to give them birth, and God used me to send them as martyrs to Heaven. You have that happy certainty.'

◆

In a paperback copy of Tristram Shandy *bought in the second-hand bookstore in Alice, this was scribbled in the fly-leaf,* 'One of the few moments of happiness a man knows in Australia is that moment of meeting the eyes of another man over the tops of two beer glasses.'

◆

Yunnan, China

The village schoolmaster was a chivalrous and energetic man with a shock of glinting blue-black hair, who lived with his childlike wife in a wooden house beside the Jade Stream.

A musicologist by training, he had climbed to distant

mountain villages to record the folksongs of the Na-Khi tribe. He believed, like Vico, that the world's first languages were in song. Early man, he said, had learnt to speak by imitating the calls of animals and birds, and had lived in musical harmony with the rest of Creation.

His room was crammed with bric-à-brac salvaged, heaven knows how, from the catastrophes of the Cultural Revolution. Perched on chairs of red lacquer, we nibbled melon seeds while he poured into thimbles of white porcelain a mountain tea known as 'Handful of Snow'.

He played us a tape of a Na-Khi chant, sung antiphonally by men and women around the bier of a corpse: Wooo . . . Zeee! Wooo . . . Zeee! The purpose of the song was to drive away the Eater of the Dead, a fanged and malicious demon thought to feast upon the soul.

He surprised us by his ability to hum his way through the mazurkas of Chopin and an apparently endless repertoire of Beethoven. His father, a merchant in the Lhasa caravan trade, had sent him in the 1940s to study Western music at the Kunming Academy.

On the back wall, above a reproduction of Claude Lorrain's L'Embarquement pour Cythère, there were two framed photos of himself: one in white tie and tails behind a concert grand; the other, conducting an orchestra in a street of flag-waving crowds – a dashing and energetic figure, on tiptoe, his arms extended upwards and his baton down.

'1949,' he said. 'To welcome the Red Army into Kunming.'

'What were you playing?'

'Schubert's "Marche militaire".'

For this – or rather, for his devotion to 'Western culture' – he got twenty-one years in jail.

He held up his hands, gazing at them sadly as though they were long-lost orphans. His fingers were crooked and his wrists were scarred: a reminder of the day when the Guards strung him up to the roof-beams – in the attitude of Christ on the Cross . . . or a man conducting an orchestra.

◆

One commonly held delusion is that men are the wanderers and women the guardians of hearth and home. This can, of course, *be so. But women, above all, are the guardians of continuity: if the hearth moves, they move with it.*

It is the gipsy women who keep their men on the road. Similarly, in the gale-lashed waters of the Cape Horn archipelago, it was the women of the Yaghan Indians who kept their embers alight in the bottom of their bark canoes. The missionary Father Martin Gusinde compared them to the 'Ancient Vestals' or to 'fidgety birds of passage who were happy and inwardly calm only when they were on the move'.

◆

In Central Australia, women are the driving force behind the return to the old ways of life. As one woman said to a friend of mine, 'Women are ones for country.'

◆

Mauritania

Two days out from Chinguetti we had to cross a gloomy grey canyon with not a green thing in sight. On the valley floor there were several dead camels, their desiccated hides flapping rat . . . tat . . . tat . . . against the ribcages.

It was almost dark by the time we'd climbed the opposite cliff. A sandstorm was brewing. The camels were restless. One of the guides then pointed to some tents: three of goat-hair and one of white cotton, about half a mile away among the dunes.

We approached slowly. The guides screwed up their faces, trying to decide if the tents were of a friendly tribe. Then one of them smiled, said 'Lalakhlal!' and put his camels into a trot.

A tall young man drew back the tent-flap and beckoned us forward. We dismounted. His robes were blue and he was wearing yellow slippers.

An old woman brought us dates and goats' milk, and the sheikh gave orders for a kid to be killed.

'Nothing has changed', I said to myself, 'since the days of Abraham and Sarah.'

The sheikh, Sidi Ahmed el Beshir Hammadi, spoke perfect French. After supper, as he poured the mint tea, I asked him, naively, why life in the tents, for all its hardship, was irresistible.

'Bah!' he shrugged. 'I'd like nothing better than to live in a house in town. Here in the desert you can't keep clean. You can't take a shower! It's the women who make us live in the desert. They say the desert brings health and happiness, to them and to the children.'

◆

Timbuktu

The houses are built of grey mud. Many of the walls are covered with graffiti, written in chalk in the neatest of copybook hands:

Les noms de ceux qui voyagent dans la nuit sont Sidi et Yéyé.
Hélas! Les Anges de l'Enfer.
Beauté . . . Beau . . .
La poussière en Décembre . . .

◆

Useless to ask a wandering man
Advice on the construction of a house.
The work will never come to completion.

After reading this text, from the Chinese Book of Odes, I realised the absurdity of trying to write a book on Nomads.

◆

Psychiatrists, politicians, tyrants are forever assuring us that the wandering life is an aberrant form of behaviour; a neurosis; a form of unfulfilled sexual longing; a sickness which, in the interests of civilisation, must be suppressed.

Nazi propagandists claimed that gipsies and Jews – peoples with wandering in their genes – could find no place in a stable Reich.

Yet, in the East, they still preserve the once universal concept: that wandering re-establishes the original harmony which once existed between man and the universe.

◆

(178)

There is no happiness for the man who does not travel. Living in the society of men, the best man becomes a sinner. For Indra is the friend of the traveller. Therefore wander!
                                        Aitareya Brāhmana

You cannot travel on the path before you have become the Path itself.
                                        Gautama Buddha

Walk on!
                                His last word to his disciples

In Islam, and especially among the Sufi Orders, siyaḥat *or 'errance' – the action or rhythm of walking – was used as a technique for dissolving the attachments of the world and allowing men to lose themselves in God.*

The aim of a dervish was to become a 'dead man walking': one whose body stays alive on the earth yet whose soul is already in Heaven. A Sufi manual, the Kashf-al-Mahjub, *says that, towards the end of his journey, the dervish becomes the Way not the wayfarer, i.e. a place over which something is passing, not a traveller following his own free will.*

Arkady, to whom I mentioned this, said it was quite similar to an Aboriginal concept, 'Many men afterwards become country, in that place, Ancestors.'

By spending his whole life walking and singing his Ancestor's Songline, a man eventually became the track, the Ancestor and the song.

The Wayless Way, where the Sons of God lose themselves and, at the same time, find themselves.
                                        Meister Eckhart

(179)

He is by nature led
To peace so perfect that the young behold
With envy, what the old man hardly feels.
                    Wordsworth, 'Old Man Travelling'

◆

A very brief life of Diogenes:
   He lived in a tub. He ate raw octopus and lupins. He said,
'Kosmopolites eimi'. 'I am a citizen of the world.' He compared
his wanderings through Greece to the migration of storks:
north in summer, south to avoid the winter cold.'

◆

We Lapps have the same nature as the reindeer: in the
springtime we long for the mountains; in winter we are
drawn to the woods.

Turi's Book of Lappland

◆

In ancient India the monsoon made travel impossible. And since
the Buddha did not want his followers to wade up to their necks
in floodwater, He allowed them a 'rain retreat', the Vassa.
During this time, the homeless pilgrims were to congregate on
higher ground and live in huts of wattle and daub.
   It was from these sites that the great Buddhist monasteries
arose.

◆

In the early Christian Church there were two kinds of pilgrim-
age: 'to wander for God' (ambulare pro Deo) *in imitation of*
Christ or of Father Abraham who quit the city of Ur and went to
live in a tent. The second was the 'penitential pilgrimage': in
which criminals guilty of 'enormous crimes' (peccata enormia)
were required, in accordance with a fixed set of tariffs, to
assume the role of travelling beggar – with hat, purse, baton and
badge – and work out their salvation on the road.
   The idea that walking dissolved crimes of violence goes back
to the wanderings forced on Cain to atone for the murder of his
brother.

(180)

The camel-men wore flaying knives instead of rosaries around their necks, and had served as auxiliaries with the Legion. At sunset, they took me to a house on the edge of town in order to hear the bhagi.

The bhagi *was a holy wanderer who would walk from oasis to oasis in the company of his toothless old father. His eyes were clouded blue almonds. He had been blind from birth and the father had to lead him everywhere.*

He knew the whole of the Koran by heart and, when we found him, he was crouched against the mud-brick wall, chanting the suras *with an uplifted smile while the father turned the pages of the Book. The words came faster and faster until they tailed off into a continuous hammering rhythm, like a drum solo. The father flipped over the pages, and the people in the crowd began to sway with a 'lost' look, as though they were on the verge of trance.*

Suddenly, the bhagi *stopped. There was a moment of absolute silence. The next verse he began to enunciate very, very slowly, twisting his tongue around the gutturals, flinging the words, one by one, at the audience, who caught them as messages from 'out there'.*

The father rested his head against his son's shoulder, and let out a deep sigh.

◆

Life is a bridge. Cross over it, but build no house on it.
                                                        Indian proverb

◆

On the spring migration, province of Fars

Between Firuzabad and Shiraz, the Quashgai migration is in full swing: mile on mile of sheep and goats, like ant-trails if you watch them from the hillsides. Hardly a blade of grass: a dusting of green on the mountains but along the route only a white broom in flower, and a grey-leaved artemisia. The animals thin and weak, skin-covered bone but little more. Now and then one falls out of line, like a soldier fainting on parade, totters and falls, and then it's a race between the vultures and the dogs.

Slavering mastiffs! Red-headed vultures! But are their heads really red or red with blood? Both! They are both red and blooded. And when you look along the way we've come, there are spirals of vultures, wheeling.

The Quashgai men were lean, hard-mouthed, weatherbeaten and wore cylindrical caps of white felt. The women were in all their finery: bright calico dresses bought especially for the springtime journey. Some rode horses and donkeys; some were on camels, along with the tents and tent poles. Their bodies ebbed and flowed to the pitching saddles. Their eyes were blinkered to the road ahead.

A woman in saffron and green rode by on a black horse. Behind her, bundled up together on the saddle, a child was playing with a motherless lamb; copper pots were clanking, and there was a rooster tied on with a string.

She was also suckling a baby. Her breasts were festooned with necklaces, of gold coins and amulets. Like most nomad women, she wore her wealth.

What, then, are a nomad baby's first impressions of this world? A swaying nipple and a shower of gold.

◆

The Huns burn with an insatiable lust for gold.
                                    Ammianus Marcellinus

◆

For they had golden earrings, because they were Ishmaelites.
                                    Judges 8:24

◆

A good horse is a member of the family.
                                    Quashgai saying

◆

The old man crouched beside his dying chestnut mare: on migration, the horses are the first to drop. He had found a patch of fresh grass. He had coaxed the mare on to it and was trying to ram a handful between her teeth. It was too late. She lay on her side, tongue out, with the glazed eyes of approaching death.

The old man bit his lip and cried, sparingly, a drop or two down either cheek. Then he shouldered the saddle without a backward glance, and together we walked to the road.

Along the road we were picked up by one of the khans in his Land-Rover.

He was a straight-backed old gentleman, with a monocle and some knowledge of Europe. He owned a house and orchards in Shiraz: but every spring, he put himself on call to help his kin.

He took me to a tent where his fellow khans were meeting to discuss their strategy. One was a very chic type in a padded yellow ski jacket. He had what I took to be a skier's tan. I suspected him of coming straight from St Moritz, and he mistrusted me on sight.

The khan they all deferred to was a wiry, hook-nosed man with a growth of grey stubble on his chin, who sat on a kelim, listening to the others' arguments without moving a muscle. Then he reached for a scrap of paper and, on it, drew some wiggly lines in ball-point.

This was the order of precedence in which the different clans were to move through the next stretch of country.

—

The same scene is described in Genesis 13:9 when Abraham the bedouin sheikh becomes worried that his cowboys will start fighting with the cowboys of Lot, 'Is not the whole land before thee? Separate thyself, I pray thee, from me: If thou wilt take the left hand, then I will go to the right; or if thou depart to the right hand, then I will go to the left.'

—

Any nomad migration must be organised with the precision and flexibility of a military campaign. Behind, the grass is shrivelling. Ahead, the passes may be blocked with snow.

(183)

Most nomads claim to 'own' their migration path (in Arabic Il-Rāh, 'The Way'), but in practice they only lay claim to seasonal grazing rights. Time and space are thus dissolved around each other: a month and a stretch of road are synonymous.

But a nomad's migration – unlike that of a hunter – is not his own. It is, rather, a guided tour of animals whose instinctive sense of direction has been blunted by domestication. It calls for skill and risk-taking. A man, like Job, can be ruined in a single season: as were the nomads of the Sahel, or the Wyoming cattle companies in the Great White Winter of 1886–7.

In a bad season, a nomad's temptation to stray from his path is irresistible; but the army is waiting for him with sub-machine guns.
    'The Army', said my friend, the old khan, 'has now replaced the lion and the wolf.'

Nomos *is Greek for 'pasture', and 'the Nomad' is a chief or clan elder who presides over the allocation of pastures.* Nomos *thus came to mean 'law', 'fair distribution', 'that which is allotted by custom' – and so the basis of all Western law.*
    The verb nemein *– to 'graze', 'to pasture', 'to range' or 'to spread' – has a second sense as early as Homer: 'to deal', 'to apportion' or 'to dispense' – especially of land, honour, meat or drink.* Nemesis *is the 'distribution of justice' and so of 'divine justice'.* Nomisma *means 'current coin': hence 'numismatics'.*

The nomads known to Homer were the 'mare-milking' Scythians who roamed with their wagons across the south Russian steppe. They were a people who buried their chiefs under grave mounds, with horses and treasures of gold.
    But the origins of nomadism are very hard to assess.

◆

Bandiagara, Mali

Madame Dieterlen, an old Africa hand, gave me coffee in her caravan on the edge of the Dogon cliff. I asked her what traces

(184)

the Bororo Peul – cattle herders of the Sahel – would leave for an archaeologist once they had moved off a campsite.

She thought for a moment, and answered, 'They scatter the ashes of their fires. No. Your archaeologist would not find those. But the women do weave little chaplets from grass stems, and hang them from the branch of their shade tree.'

―

Max Weber traces the origins of modern capitalism to certain Calvinists who, disregarding the parable of the camel and the eye of the needle, preached the doctrine of the just rewards of work. Yet the concept of shifting and increasing one's 'wealth on the hoof' has a history as old as herding itself. Domesticated animals are 'currency', 'things that run', from the French courir. In fact, almost all our monetary expressions – capital, stock, pecuniary, chattel, sterling – perhaps even the idea of 'growth' itself – have their origins in the pastoral world.

―

> Is it not passing brave to be a King,
> And ride in triumph through Persepolis?
> Marlowe, Tamburlaine the Great, *Part I, 1,758*

―

Persepolis, Fars

We were walking to Persepolis in the rain. The Quashgais were soaked and happy, and the animals were soaked; and when the rain let up, they shook the water from their coats and moved on, as though they were dancing. We passed an orchard with a mud wall around it. There was a smell of orange blossom, after rain.

A boy was walking beside me. He and a girl exchanged a flashing glance. She was riding behind her mother on a camel, but the camel was moving faster.

About three miles short of Persepolis we came to some huge domed tents under construction, to which the Shah-i-Shah had invited a riff-raff of royalty for his coronation in June. The tents were designed by the Paris firm of decorators, Jansen.

Someone was yelling, in French.

I tried to get the Quashgai boy to comment, or even to look at the tents. But he shrugged and looked the other way – and so we went on to Persepolis.

Passing Persepolis I looked at the fluted columns, the porticoes, lions, bulls, griffins; the sleek metallic finish of the stone, and the line on line of megalomaniac inscription: 'I . . . I . . . I . . . The King . . . The King . . . burned . . . slew . . . settled . . .'

My sympathies were with Alexander for burning it.

Again I tried to get the Quashgai boy to look. Again he shrugged. Persepolis might have been made of matchsticks for all he knew or cared – and so we went up to the mountains.

◆

Pyramids, arches, obelisks, were but the irregularities of vain-glory, and wild enormities of ancient magnanimity.
Sir *Thomas Browne,* Urne Buriall

◆

London

Franco S., returning from Iran for the first time since the fall of the Shah, says that, among the side effects of the Khomeini Revolution, the Quashgai have recovered their strength and their mobility.

◆

The tradition of the camp-fire faces that of the pyramid.
Martin Buber, Moses

◆

Before addressing the crowds at the Nuremberg Rallies, the Führer would commune with himself in a subterranean chamber modelled on the tomb in the Great Pyramid.

◆

'Look! I've drawn a skull on the top of the Pyramid.'
'Why did you do that, Sedig?'
'I like drawing scary things.'
'What's the skull doing on the Pyramid?'

'Because a giant's buried in there, and his skull's popping out.'
'What do you think of that giant?'
'Bad.'
'Why?'
'Because he eats people up.'
        Conversation with Sedig el Fadil el Mahdi, aged six

◆

Jahweh's horror of hewn masonry, 'And if thou wilt make me an altar of stone, thou shalt not build it of hewn stone: for if thou lift up thy tool upon it, thou hast polluted it.'
                                    Exodus 20:25

◆

. . . but no man knoweth of his sepulchre unto this day.
                                    Deuteronomy 34:6

In the last of the moonlight a dog howls and falls silent. The firelight flutters and the watchman yawns. A very old man walks silently past the tents, feeling his way with a stick to make sure he doesn't trip on the tent ropes. He walks on. His people are moving to a greener country. Moses has an appointment with the jackals and vultures.

◆

Pompey in Jerusalem, after barging his way into the Temple, demanded to be shown the Holy of Holies, and was surprised to find himself in an empty room.

◆

Herodotus records the visit of some Greeks to Egypt, who, on seeing the man-made mountains of limestone, called them pyramides *because their shape reminded them of little wheaten cakes that were sold on street stalls. He adds that the local inhabitants preserved a memory of their construction as a time of horror and were unable to pronounce the names of the builders, Cheops and Chephren, preferring to call them*

(187)

'Philitis', after the name of a shepherd who had once pastured his flock in their shadow.

◆

Masonry, and is it man's? . . . I shudder at the thought of the ancient Egyptians.

Herman Melville, Journey up the Straits

◆

Djinguereber Mosque, Timbuktu

Row on row of gloomy mudbrick arches. Bat guano. Wasps' nests in the rafters. Shafts of sunlight falling on reed mats like the beams of a burning glass.

The marabout interrupted his prayers to ask me a few questions.

'There is a people call the Mericans?' he asked.

'There is.'

'They say they have visited the Moon.'

'They have.'

'They are blasphemers.'

◆

A very short History of the Skyscraper:

Everyone knows that the Tower of Babel was conceived as an attack on Heaven. The officials in charge of the construction were few. The work-force was innumerable: and in order that commands might not be misconstrued, every worker was required to speak the same language.

Little by little, as the courses of masonry succeeded one another, the Highest Authority became anxious that the concept of a war against Heaven might be meaningless: worse, that God in His Heaven might not exist. At an emergency session of the Central Committee, it was decided to launch a probe into the sky. Salvoes of missiles were fired off, vertically; and when these returned to Earth, bloodstained, here was proof that God, after all, was mortal; and that work on the Tower should proceed.

(188)

He, for His Part, resented being pricked in the backside. One morning, with a disdainful puff, He unsteadied the arm of a mason on one of the uppermost terraces, causing him to drop a brick on to the head of a fellow mason below. It was an accident. Everyone knew it was an accident, but the mason below began shouting threats and insults. His comrades tried to calm him, in vain. Everyone took sides in the quarrel without knowing what the quarrel was about. Everyone, in his righteous anger, refused to listen to what his neighbour was saying, and used language intended to confuse. The Central Committee was helpless: and the work gangs, each of whom now spoke a different language, took refuge from each other in remotest regions of the Earth.

After Josephus, Jewish Antiquities, *i, iv*

◆

Without Compulsion no settlement could be founded. The workers would have no supervisor. The rivers would not bring the overflow.

Sumerian text

◆

To the Babylonian 'bab-il' meant 'Gate of God'. To the Hebrews the same word meant 'confusion', perhaps 'cacophonous confusion'. The ziggurats of Mesopotamia were 'Gates of God', painted the seven colours of the rainbow and dedicated to Anu and Enlil, divinities representing Order and Compulsion.

It was surely a marvellous intuition on the part of the ancient Jews – sandwiched as they were between bullying empires – to have conceived the State as Behemoth or Leviathan, as a monster which threatened human life. They were, perhaps, the first people to understand that the Tower was chaos, that order was chaos, and that language – the gift of tongues which Jahweh breathed into the mouth of Adam – has a rebellious and wayward vitality compared to which the foundations of the Pyramid are as dust.

◆

He was on his way to see his old father, who was a rabbi in Vienna. He was short and fat. He had pallid white skin and ginger ringlets, and wore a long serge greatcoat and beaver hat. He was very shy. He was so shy he found it impossible to undress with anyone else in the compartment. The sleeping-car attendant had assured him he would be alone.

I offered to go into the corridor. The train was passing through a forest. I opened the window and breathed in the smell of pines. When I came back, ten minutes later, he was lying on the upper bunk, relaxed and eager to talk.

For sixteen years he had been studying at a Talmudic Academy in Brooklyn: he had not seen his father since. The morning would reunite them.

Before the war his family had lived at Sibiu in Romania and, when the war came, they hoped they were safe. Then, in 1942, Nazis painted a star on their house.

The rabbi shaved his beard and cut his ringlets. His Gentile servant fetched him a peasant costume: a felt hat, a belted tunic, a sheepskin jacket and boots. He embraced his wife, his two daughters and the baby boy: all four of them would die in Birkenau. He took his first-born son in his arms, and dashed for the woods.

The rabbi walked through the Carpathian beech forests with his son. Shepherds sheltered them and gave them meat: the way the shepherds slaughtered sheep did not offend his principles. Eventually, they crossed the Turkish frontier and made their way to America.

The rabbi never felt at ease in America. He could sympathise with Zionism, but never bring himself to join. Israel was an idea, not a country. Wherever was the Torah, there was the Kingdom also. He had left, in despair, for Europe.

Now father and son were returning to Romania, since, only a few weeks earlier, the rabbi had received a sign. Late one night, in his apartment in Vienna, he reluctantly answered the doorbell. On the landing stood an old woman with a shopping basket. She had bluish lips and wispy white hair. Dimly, he recognised his Gentile servant.

'I have found you,' she said. 'Your house is safe. Your books

are safe, your clothes even. For years I pretended it was now a
Gentile house. I am dying. Here is the key.'

◆

Shahrak, Afghanistan

The Tajiks say they are the oldest people in the land. They plant
wheat, flax and melons. They have long, resigned faces, and
exhaust themselves in tending irrigation ditches. They keep
fighting partridges, and do not know how to look after horses.
    In the valley above the Tajik village, we came to a camp of
Firuzkuhi Aimaqs. Their yurts had domed white roofs, and the
sides were painted with lozenges, scrolls and chequers in every
conceivable colour, like a field of chivalry. Horses were grazing
in a meadow of cornflowers, and there were white-leaved
willows along the stream. We saw a fat-tailed sheep with a tail
so big it had to be strapped to a cart. Outside the yurts, some
women in purple were carding wool.
    This is the time of year when the farmers and nomads, after a
season of acrimony, are suddenly the best of friends. The
harvest is in. The nomads buy grain for the winter. The villagers
buy cheese and hides and meat. They welcome the sheep on to
their fields: to break up the stubble and manure it for autumn
planting.

◆

Nomad and planter are the twin arms of the so-called 'Neolithic
Revolution,' which, in its classic form, took place around 8,500
BC *on the slopes of the Fertile Crescent, the well-watered 'land*
of hills and valleys' that stretches in an arc from Palestine to
south-western Iran. Here, at altitudes of 3,000 feet or so, the
wild ancestors of our sheep and goats would browse over stands
of wild wheat and barley.
    Gradually, as each of these four species was domesticated,
the farmers spread downhill on to the alluvial floodplains, from
which the first cities would arise. The herdsmen, for their part,
took to the summer uplands and founded a rival order of their
own.

◆

The Amorite who knows not grain . . . A people whose onslaught is like a hurricane . . . A people who have never known a city . . .

Sumerian text

◆

Ouissa, Mountains of Air, Niger

The garden was circular. Its soil was black. Around the perimeter ran a palisade of thorn bush, to keep away the camels and goats. At the centre stood two ancient date palms, flanking the well-shaft and a tank.

Four irrigation ditches divided the garden into quarters. The quarters were further divided into a maze of vegetable beds and planted with peas, beans, onions, carrots, greens, squashes and tomatoes.

The gardener was a negro slave, naked but for a breechclout. He was lost in concentration on his work. He would heave the leather bucket up the shaft and watch the water threading round the labyrinth. When one crop had had its fill, he would dam up the channel with his hoe, and divert the current on to the next patch.

A short way up the valley, there were other circular palisades of thorn, into which the Tuareg drove their goats at night.

The Negro in command of his seedlings shares a common destiny with the first dictators. Sumerian and Egyptian archives tell us that the earliest rulers of civilisation saw themselves as 'Lords of the Fertilising Waters' – who would either bring life to their wilting subjects or turn the taps off.

◆

Abel, in whose death the Church Fathers saw the martyrdom of Christ prefigured, was a keeper of sheep. Cain was a settled farmer. Abel was the favourite of God, because Jahweh himself was a 'God of the Way' whose restlessness precluded other gods. Yet Cain, who would build the first city, was promised dominion over him.

A verse of the Midrash, *commenting on the quarrel, says that the sons of Adam inherited an equal division of the world: Cain the ownership of all land, Abel of all living creatures – whereupon Cain accused Abel of trespass.*

The names of the brothers are a matched pair of opposites. Abel comes from the Hebrew 'hebel', meaning 'breath' or 'vapour': anything that lives and moves and is transient, including his own life. The root of 'Cain' appears to be the verb 'kanah': to 'acquire', 'get', 'own property', and so 'rule' or 'subjugate'.

'Cain' also means 'metal-smith'. And since, in several languages – even Chinese – the words for 'violence' and 'subjugation' are linked to the discovery of metal, it is perhaps the destiny of Cain and his descendants to practise the black arts of technology.

A possible synopsis for the Murder:
Cain is a painstaking fellow, bent double from constant digging. The day is hot and cloudless. Eagles are floating high above in the blue. The last of the snowmelt still cascades down the valley, but the hillsides are already brown and parched. Flies cluster at the corners of his eyes. He wipes the sweat from his forehead, and resumes his work. His hoe has a wooden handle, with a stone blade hafted on to it.

Somewhere, higher up the slope, Abel is resting in the cool of a rock. He trills at his flute: again and again, the same insistent trills. Cain pauses to listen. Stiffly, he straightens his back. Then, raising his hand against the glare, he peers at his fields along the stream. The sheep have trampled his morning's work. Without having time to think, he breaks into a run . . .

A less excusable version of the story says that Cain lay in ambush for Abel and heaved a rock on to his head – in which case the killing was the fruit of brewed-up bitterness and envy: the envy of the prisoner for the freedom of open spaces.

Jahweh allows Cain to make atonement, only if he pays the price. He denies him the 'fruits of the earth' and forces him to wander 'a fugitive and a vagabond' in the Land of Nod: 'Nod' meaning 'wilderness' or 'desert', where Abel once wandered before him.

'Travel': same word as 'travail' – 'bodily or mental labour', 'toil, especially of a painful or oppressive nature', 'exertion', 'hardship', 'suffering'. A 'journey'.

Cain's City built with Human Blood, not Blood of Bulls and Goats.

> *William Blake, 'The Ghost of Abel'*

'Alone and amid the nations', masters of the raid, avid for increase yet disgusted by possessions, driven by the fantasy of all travellers to pine for a stable home – no people but the Jews have ever felt more keenly the moral ambiguities of settlement. Their God is a projection of their perplexity. Their Book – the Old Testament and the New – may be read, on one level at least, as a monumental dialogue between Him and His People in the rights and wrongs of living in the Land.

Was it to be a land for fields and houses? A land of corn and wine? Of cities which they had not built and vineyards which they did not plant? Or was it to be a country of black tent and goat path? A nomad's country of milk and wild honey? A Kingdom where the people 'may dwell in a place of their own, and move no more?' (II Samuel 7:10) Or was it, as Heine surmised, 'a portable kingdom' which could only exist in men's hearts?

Jahweh, in origin, is a God of the Way. His sanctuary is the Mobile Ark, His House a tent, His Altar a cairn of rough stones. And though He may promise His Children a well-watered land – as blue and green are a bedouin's favourite colours – He secretly desires for them the Desert.

He leads them out of Egypt, away from the fleshpots and the overseer's lash, a journey of three days into the harsh clean air of Sinai. There He gives them their Solemn Feast, the Passover: a feast of roasted lamb and bitter herbs, of bread baked not in an oven but on a hot stone. And He commands them to eat it 'in

(194)

haste', with shodden feet and sticks in hand, to remind them, for ever, that their vitality lies in movement.

He gives them their 'ring dance', the hag: *a dance that mimes the antics of goats on their spring migration 'as when one goeth with a pipe into the mountains of the Lord'. He appears in the Burning Bush and in the Pillar of Fire. He is everything that Egypt is not. Yet He will allow himself the doubtful honour of a Temple – and regret it: 'They have set their abominations in the house which is called by my name, to pollute it.' (Jeremiah 7:30)*

The ghettos of Eastern Europe were each a little patch of desert 'where no green thing would grow'. Jews were forbidden by their Christian masters to own land or houses; to grow their own vegetables, or practise any trade but usury. And though they were allowed to gather sticks for firewood, they might not saw a plank, in case this led to building.

The Gentiles, who imposed these restrictions, believed they were punishing the Jews for the crime of killing Christ – as Jahweh had punished Cain. Orthodox Jews believed that, by accepting them, they were re-living the journey through Sinai, when the People had found favour with their Lord.

The prophets Isaiah, Jeremiah, Amos and Hosea were nomadic revivalists who howled abuse at the decadence of civilisation. By sinking roots in the land, by 'laying house to house and field to field', by turning the Temple into a sculpture gallery, the people had turned from their God.

How long, O Lord, how long? . . . 'Until the cities be wasted . . .' The prophets looked to a Day of Restoration when the Jews would return to the frugal asceticism of nomadic life. In the Vision of Isaiah they are promised a Saviour, whose name would be Emmanuel, and who would be a herdsman.

When Nebuchadnezzar, King of Babylon, had the Jews penned up behind the walls of Jerusalem, Jeremiah reminded them of the Rechabites, the only tribe to have resisted the blandishments of settled life:

> *We will drink no wine: for Jonadab the son of Rechab our father commanded us, saying, Ye shall drink no wine, neither*

*ye nor your sons for ever: Neither shall ye build house, nor
sow seed, nor plant vineyard, nor have any: but all your days
ye shall dwell in tents; that ye may live many days in the land
where ye be strangers.*

Jeremiah 35:6–7

*The Rechabites alone, by preserving tactical mobility, would
escape the horrors of siege warfare.*

—

In the Muqaddimah *or 'Universal History', of Ib'n Khaldūn, a
philosopher who surveyed the human condition from a
nomadic viewpoint, we read:*

The Desert People are closer to being good than settled
peoples because they are closer to the First State and are more
removed from all the evil habits that have infected the hearts
of settlers.

*By 'desert people', Ib'n Khaldūn means the bedouin such as
those he once recruited, as mercenaries from the heart of the
Sahara, in the days of his warlike youth.*

*Years later, when he had gazed into the slanting eyes of
Tamerlane and witnessed the piles of skulls and smouldering
cities, he, too, like the Old Testament prophets, felt the fearful
anxiety of civilisation, and looked back with longing to life in
the tents.*

*Ib'n Khaldūn based his system on the intuition that men decline,
morally and physically, as they drift towards cities.*

*The rigours of the desert, he suggested, had preceded the
softness of cities. The desert was thus a reservoir of civilisation,
and desert peoples had the advantage over settlers because they
were more abstemious, freer, braver, healthier, less bloated, less
craven, less liable to submit to rotten laws, and altogether easier
to cure.*

—

Monastery of Simonaspetras, Mount Athos

A young Hungarian, exhausted after climbing the Holy Mountain, came and sat on the balcony and stared at the stormy sea below. He had trained as an epidemiologist but had given up this work in order to climb the sacred mountains of the world. He hoped to climb Mount Ararat and to circumambulate Mount Kailash in Tibet.

'Man', he said suddenly, without warning, 'was not meant to settle down.'

This was something he had learnt from his study of epidemics. The story of infectious disease was a story of men brewing in their own filth. He also made the observation that Pandora's Box of Ills had been a Neolithic pottery urn.

'Make no mistake,' he said. 'Epidemics are going to make nuclear weapons seem like useless toys.'

◆

Hong Kong

Paddy Booz tells of meeting a Taoist Grand Master on the streets of a provincial Chinese city. The man was wearing his Grand Master's blue robes and high hat. He and his young disciple had walked the length and breadth of China.

'But what', Paddy asked him, 'did you do during the Cultural Revolution?'

'I went for a walk in the Kun L'ung Mountains.'

◆

Driving with Arkady I remembered a passage in Vernadsky's Early Russia, *which describes how Slav peasants would submerge themselves in a marsh, breathing through hollow reeds until the sound of the horsemen died away.*

'Come home and meet my Dad,' he said. 'He and his mates did that when the Panzers came through the village.'

◆

Quadrupedante putrem sonitu quatit ungula campum. *Virgil's exemplary hexameter, to describe the thud of horse hooves over a plain, has its Persian equivalent in the utterance of a survivor from the Mongol sack of Bokhara,*

Amdand u khandand u sokhtand u kushtand u burdand u raftand. *'They came and they sapped and they burned and they slew and they trussed up their loot and were gone.'*

In his History of the World Conqueror *Juvaini says that all his writing, and all the horror of those times, is contained in this one line.*

From Henry Yule's Marco Polo *1, 233*

◆

On the cruelty of Nomads:

> *I do not have a mill with willow trees*
> *I have a horse and a whip*
> *I will kill you and go.*

Yomut Turkoman

◆

In 1223 the Novgorod Chronicle recorded the arrival from Tartary of a sorceress and two men with her, who demanded one-tenth of everything: 'of men, princes, horses, treasure, of everything one-tenth'.

The Russian princes said no. The Mongol invasion was on.

◆

Leningrad

A picnic in the office of a Professor of Archaeology: caviar, black bread, slabs of smoked sturgeon, onions, radishes and a bottle of Stolichnaya – for two.

For most of the morning, I had been canvassing his views on the mechanics of nomad invasions. Toynbee held to the theory that a phase of drought, somewhere on the Central Asian steppe, would dislodge a tribe from its grazing grounds and cause a 'house of cards' effect, with ripples from Europe to China.

It had struck me, however, that nomads were at their most invasive, not in times of want but abundance; *in times of maximum growth, when the grass was greenest and the herdsmen allowed their stock to increase beyond the point of stability.*

As for the Professor, his nomads seemed to have moved in nice, tight, obedient circles, without troubling their neighbours or trespassing on what are now the boundaries of the Socialist Republics.

Later, after a few more shots of vodka, he enfolded me in a fraternal, pan-European embrace, and, pushing the corners of his eyes into a pair of slits, said, 'What we hate is this, isn't it?'

'Not me,' I said.

◆

Le Désert est monothéiste. Renan's aphorism implies that blank horizons and a dazzling sky will clear the mind of its distractions and allow it to concentrate on the Godhead. But life in the desert is not like that!

To survive at all, the desert dweller — Tuareg or Aboriginal — must develop a prodigious sense of orientation. He must forever be naming, sifting, comparing a thousand different 'signs' — the tracks of a dung beetle or the ripple of a dune — to tell him where he is; where the others are; where rain has fallen; where the next meal is coming from; whether if plant X is in flower, plant Y will be in berry, and so forth.

It is a paradox of the monotheistic faiths that, although they arose within the ambit of the desert, the desert people themselves show an indifference towards the Almighty that is decidedly cavalier. 'We will go up to God and salute him,' said a bedu to Palgrave in the 1860s, 'and if he proves hospitable, we will stay with him: if otherwise, we will mount our horses and ride off.'

Muhammad said, 'No man becomes a prophet who was not first a shepherd.' But, as he had to confess, the Arabs of the desert were 'the most hardened in infidelity and hypocrisy'.

Until recently, a bedouin who migrated within sight of Mecca would not think it worthwhile, even once in a lifetime, to circumambulate the shrines. Yet the Hadj, or 'Sacred Journey', was itself a 'ritual' migration: to detach men from their sinful homes and reinstate, if temporarily, the equality of all men before God.

A pilgrim on the Hadj has resumed Man's first condition: if he dies on the Hadj he goes straight, as a martyr, to Heaven. Similarly, Il-Rāh 'The Way' was first used as a technical term for 'road' or 'migration path' – before being adopted by the mystics to denote 'the Way to God.'

The concept has its equivalent in the Central Australian languages where tjurna djugurba *means 'the footprints of the Ancestor' and 'the Way of the Law'.*

It would seem there exists, at some deep level of the human psyche, a connection between 'path-finding' and 'law'.

—

To the Arabian bedouin, Hell is a sunlit sky and the sun a strong, bony female – mean, old and jealous of life – who shrivels the pastures and the skin of humans.

The moon, by contrast, is a lithe and energetic young man, who guards the nomad while he sleeps, guides him on night journeys, brings rain and distils the dew on plants. He has the misfortune to be married to the sun. He grows thin and wasted after a single night with her. It takes him a month to recover.

—

The Norwegian anthropologist, Frederick Barth, writes of how the Basseri, another tribe of Iranian nomads, were, in the 1930s, forbidden by Reza Shah to move from their winter grazing ground.

In 1941, the Shah was deposed, and they were free once again to make the 300-mile journey to the Zagros. Free they were, but they had no animals. Their fine-fleeced sheep had suffocated on the southern plains: yet they set off all the same.

They became nomads again, which is to say, they became human again. 'The supreme value to them', wrote Barth, 'lay in the freedom to migrate, not in the circumstances that make it economically viable.'

When Barth came to account for the dearth of ritual among the Basseri – or of any rooted belief – he concluded that the Journey itself was the ritual, that the road to summer uplands was the

Way, and that the pitching and dismantling of tents were prayers more meaningful than any in the mosque.

◆

Raids are our agriculture.

Bedouin proverb

◆

I against my brother
I and my brother against our cousin
I, my brother and our cousin against the neighbours
All of us against the foreigner

Bedouin proverb

◆

Alois Musil, the Arabist cousin of Robert, calculated in 1928 that, among the Rwala bedouin, four-fifths of the men fell in war or vendettas or died from wounds received.

Hunters, on the other hand, who practise an art of the minimum, deliberately limit their numbers and enjoy far greater security of life and land. Of the Central Australian native, Spencer and Gillen wrote that, though he might occasionally quarrel or fight, the idea of annexing fresh territory would never enter his head: an attitude to be explained 'by the belief that his Alcheringa (Dreamtime) ancestors occupied precisely the same country as he does now'.

◆

The pastoral ethic in Australia:

Someone in the Department of Aboriginal Affairs – I think it was the Minister himself – has said that, in the Northern Territory, 'foreign-owned cattle' have more rights than Australian citizens.

The pastoral ethic in Ancient Ireland:

Since I took my spear in my hand, I have not been without killing a Connaught man every single day.

Conall Cernach, an Ulster cattle-man

(201)

Any nomad tribe is a military machine in embryo whose impulse, if it is not fighting other nomads, is to raid or threaten the city.

Settlers, therefore, since the beginning of history, have recruited nomads as mercenaries: either to stave off a nomad threat, as the Cossacks fought the Tatars for the Tsars; or, if there were no nomads, to fight other States.

◆

In Ancient Mesopotamia, these 'mercenaries' first transformed themselves into a caste of military aristocrats, then into directors of the State. It can be argued that the State, as such, resulted from a kind of 'chemical' fusion between herdsman and planter, once it was realised that the techniques of animal coercion could be applied to an inert peasant mass.

Apart from their role as 'Lords of the Fertilising Waters', the first Dictators called themselves 'Shepherds of the People'. Indeed, all over the world, the words for 'slave' and 'domesticated animal' are the same. The masses are to be corralled, milked, penned in (to save them from the human 'wolves' outside), and, if need be, lined up for slaughter.

The City is thus a sheepfold superimposed over a Garden.

A further possibility – not without application to the games theory of warfare – is that the army, any professional army or war department, is, without knowing it, a tribe of surrogate nomads, which has grown up inside the State; which preys off the State; without whom the State would crumble; yet whose restlessness is, finally, destructive of the State in that, like gadflies, they are forever trying to goad it into action.

◆

Hesiod's Works and Days *provides a metaphorical model for the decline of man in relation to technological progress. His stages of human culture pass from the Ages of Gold to those of Silver, Bronze and Iron. The Bronze and Iron Ages were an archaeological reality, which Hesiod knew from experience and which had culminated in a crescendo of violence and strife.*

*Obviously, he was unaware of 'Palaeolithic' and 'Neolithic',
so the Gold and Silver Ages were conceived symbolically.
Arranged in the reverse order of metallic perfection, they
represent a degeneration from the incorruptible to the
tarnished, the corroded and the rusty.*

*The Men of the Golden Race, Hesiod says, lived in an age
when Cronos, or 'Natural Time', ruled in Heaven. The earth
provided them with abundance. They lived happy, carefree
lives, wandering freely over their lands, without possessions,
houses or war. They ate their meals in common, with one
another and the immortal gods. They died with hands and feet
unfailing as if sleep had come upon them.*

*In the Christian era, Origen (Contra Celsum, IV, 79) would
use Hesiod's text to argue that, at the beginning of human
history, men were under supernatural protection, so there was
no division between their divine and human natures: or, to
rephrase the passage, there was no contradiction between a
man's instinctual life and his reason.*

◆

*In the part of Libya where the wild beasts are found live the
Garamantes, who avoid all intercourse with men, possess no
weapons of war, and do not know how to defend themselves.*
Herodotus, IV, 194

◆

*Early Christians believed that, by returning to the desert, they
could assume Our Lord's agony in the Wilderness.*

*They wander in the deserts as if they were wild animals
themselves. Like birds they fly about the hills. They forage
like beasts. Their daily round is inflexible, always predictable, for they feed on roots, the natural product of the Earth.*
From the Spiritual Meadow *of St John Moscus,
a description of hermits known as 'the Browsers'*

◆

*Every mythology remembers the innocence of the first state:
Adam in the Garden, the peaceful Hyperboreans, the Uttar-
akurus or 'the Men of Perfect Virtue' of the Taoists. Pessimists*

often interpret the story of the Golden Age as a tendency to turn our backs on the ills of the present, and sigh for the happiness of youth. But nothing in Hesiod's text exceeds the bounds of probability.

The real or half-real tribes which hover on the fringe of ancient geographies – Atavantes, Fenni, Parrossits or the dancing Spermatophagi – have their modern equivalents in the Bushman, the Shoshonean, the Eskimo and the Aboriginal.

One characteristic of the Men of the Golden Age: they are always remembered as migratory.

On the coast of Mauritania, not far from where the Méduse *(of Géricault's* Radeau de la Méduse*) was wrecked, I saw the flimsy shelters of the Imraguen: a caste of fishermen who catch mullet in seine nets and enjoy, with cheerfulness and grace, the same pariah status as the Nemadi.*

Similar fishermen's huts will have stood on the shore of Lake Galilee: 'Come with me and I will make you fishers of men.'

An alternative to the vision of the Golden Age is that of the 'anti-primitivists': who believe that man, in becoming a hunter, became the hunter and killer of his kind.

This is a very convenient doctrine if: a) you wish to murder others; b) you wish to take 'draconian' measures to prevent their murderous impulses from getting out of hand.

Whichever way, the Savage must be seen as vile.

In his Meditations on Hunting *Ortega y Gasset makes the point that hunting (unlike violence) is never reciprocal: the hunter hunts and the hunted tries to escape. A leopard at the kill is no more violent or angry than an antelope is angry with the grass it eats. Most accounts of the hunters emphasise that the act of killing is a moment of compassion and reverence: of gratitude to the animal that consents to die.*

A 'bushie' in the pub at Glen Armond turned to me and said: 'Want to know how the Blackfellows hunt?'

'Tell me.'

'Instinct.'

3 1

In one of my earlier notebooks I made painstaking copies from Sir George Grey's *Journal*, written in the 1830s. Grey was perhaps the first white explorer to understand that, despite occasional discomforts, the Aboriginals 'lived well'.

The best passage in the *Journal* is a description of a Blackfellow straining all his physical and mental faculties to stalk and spear a kangaroo.

The last paragraph winds into a coda:

> . . . his graceful movements, cautious advance, the air of quietude and repose which pervade his frame when his prey is alarmed, all involuntarily call forth your imagination and compel you to murmur to yourself, 'How beautiful! How very beautiful!'

I fooled myself into believing that some of this 'beauty' must survive, even today. I asked Rolf to find a man to take me hunting.

I had been sitting on my arse for a couple of weeks, and was beginning to feel the disgust for words that comes from taking no exercise.

'The best man to go with', said Rolf, 'would be old Alex Tjangapati. He speaks some English.'

Alex was an elderly man who wore his hair up in ochre-string and a lady's plum velvet overcoat with padded shoulders. I don't think he had anything on underneath. He went bush-walking every day, and, in the evenings, he'd hang about the store with his hunting spears, staring at the rest of the Cullen Mob as though they were the real *canaille*.

When Rolf asked him to take me, Alex pulled a long, regretful face, and walked away.

'Well, that', I said, 'is that.'

'Never mind,' he said. 'We'll find someone else.'

Around noon next day, Stumpy Jones drove the truck into Cullen. He was the first to make it through the flood. Even so, he'd got bogged for a day and a night this side of Popanji, and the Magellan Mining boys had to haul him out.

There was a girl with him. She was the girlfriend of Don, the works manager. 'And she's a good girl,' said Stumpy, winking.

She had cropped hair and a dirty white dress. Don seemed very pleased to see her, but she gave him a cool, appraising glance and continued to smile at Stumpy.

'Right,' she said. 'I don't whinge about being bogged.'

Don and I helped unload the crates off the truck. We had almost finished when Rolf came out.

'You want to go hunting?' he called.

'Yes,' I said.

'You want to pay for a full tank of petrol?'

'If that's what they want.'

'I've fixed it.'

'Who with?'

'Donkey-donk,' he said. 'Good bloke!'

'When?'

'Now,' he said. 'You'd better go and get your boots on. And a hat!'

I was walking across to the caravan when a rattletrap Ford Sedan came creaking and groaning up behind. At the wheel was a bearded Aboriginal with a big belly.

'You going a-hunting?' he grinned.

'With you?'

'Man!' said Donkey-donk.

We drove back to get the petrol but, the moment the tank was paid for, I realised my role in this expedition was not that of 'client' but 'slave'.

Donkey-donk made me buy extra oil, bullets, candy bars, cigarettes. He wanted me to buy him a new tyre. He made me hold his cigarette while he tinkered with the engine.

We were all set to go when a young man called Walker strolled up. Walker was a great traveller. He'd travelled up and down Australia on a most fastidious search for a wife. He had also spent time in the Amsterdam YMCA. He was very beautiful. He had a godlike profile and very dark skin. His hair and beard were the colour of spun gold.

'You want to come hunting?' Donkey-donk called to him.

'Sure,' said Walker, and sat down in the back seat.

We drove off to find the man who had the gun. He was another incredibly graceful young man, with a feckless smile and hair down to his shoulders. He was sitting outside a brushwood shelter. He had scrawled his name, 'Nero', in red ball-point all over his jeans.

Nero's wife, it turned out, was the giantess I had watched playing poker. She was a good head taller than he, and about four times as wide. She was sitting behind her shelter, by the campfire, gnawing at a charred kangaroo ham. When Nero got into the car, their small son rushed after him, and did a high dive through the open window. The mother followed, waving her kangaroo-bone bludgeon. She dragged the boy out by the hair and spat in his face.

We had been going a couple of minutes when Nero turned to the others.

'Got the matches?' he asked.

Donkey-donk and Walker shook their heads. We turned round to fetch some matches.

'Smokes,' Nero grinned. 'Case we get bogged.'

We headed south between Mounts Cullen and Liebler and dropped down towards the Gun Barrel Highway. After the rain, the scrub was breaking into yellow flowers. The track began and ended in a mirage, and the chain of rocky hills appeared to float above the plain.

I pointed to a reddish outcrop on the left.

'So what's that one?' I asked.

'Old Man,' Walker volunteered brightly.

'So where's this Old Man coming from?'

'Come long way. Aranda Mob, maybe. Maybe Sydney.'

'And where's he going to?'

'Port Hedland,' he said, decisively.

Port Hedland is an iron-ore port on the coast of western Australia about 800 miles west of Cullen, beyond the Gibson Desert.

'And what happens to that Old Man', I asked, 'when he gets to the sea?'

'End of him,' said Walker. 'Finish.'

I next pointed to a low, flat-topped hill which, Rolf had assured me, was a lump of shit the Perenty Man had shat in the Dreamtime.

'And what about that one there?'

Walker fumbled nervously with his beard.

'I'm too young,' he said bashfully – by which he meant he had *not* been initiated into that particular song.

'Ask Nero,' he went on. 'He knows it.'

Nero sniggered and tilted his head from side to side.

'Toilet Dreaming,' he said. 'Shit Dreaming.'

Donkey-donk was splitting his sides with laughter and swerving all over the track.

I turned to face the two on the back seat.

'Perenty shit?' I asked.

'No, no,' Nero giggled foolishly. 'Two Men.'

'And where do those Two Men come from?'

'Coming from nowhere,' he flapped his hands. 'Doing it there!'

Nero made a sign with his thumb and forefinger making it all too plain what the Two Men were up to.

'Brothers-in-law,' he said.

Walker frowned, pursed his lips and pressed his knees tight together.

'I don't believe you,' I said to Nero. 'You're having me on.'

'He! He!' he laughed, and let fly another helpless peal of giggles.

He and Donkey-donk were still snorting with laughter when, a mile or so farther on, we stopped by some low-lying rocks. All three jumped out of the car.

'Come on,' Nero called to me. 'Water.'

There were pools of stagnant water among the rocks and mosquito larvae wriggling about in them.

'Tapeworms,' said Nero.

'Not tapeworms,' I said. 'Mosquito larvae.'

'Dingo,' said Donkey-donk.

He gestured towards the largest rock, which really did look like a dog lying down. The smaller rocks, he said, were puppies.

They splashed around in the water for several minutes. We then quit the track and headed west across country.

Donkey-donk, I have to say, was an astounding driver. He put the car into a kind of dance through the spinifex. He knew exactly whether to swerve round a bush or flatten it. The seed-heads showered on to the windscreen.

Nero kept the barrel of his .22 sticking out of the window.

'Turkey-track,' he whispered.

Donkey-donk braked and a bush turkey – which is a kind of bustard – craned its mottled brown head above the grass stems and made off at a trot. Nero fired, once, and the bird collapsed in a whirl of flying feathers.

'Good shot!' I said.

'Another one!' shouted Walker, and a second turkey ran on ahead into a thicket. Nero fired again, and missed. By the time we got back to the first turkey, it too had vanished.

'Fuckin' turkey,' said Nero.

We held our course to the west and, before long, a kangaroo and young leaped up in front of us. Donkey-donk put his foot on the accelerator and the car thumped and bounced over the tussocks with the kangaroos bounding on ahead, gaining. Then we were out of the spinifex into burnt and open country, and *we* were gaining, and we caught up and hit the mother in the haunches – the young one had veered off sideways – and she flew, in a backward somersault, over the roof of the car and landed – dead, I prayed! – in a cloud of dust and ash.

We jumped out. Nero fired into the cloud, but the kangaroo was up and off, shaky, limping yet with a fair burst of speed and Donkey-donk, alone at the wheel now, at her tail.

We watched the car slam into the kangaroo a second time, but she landed on the bonnet, jumped clear, and came bounding in our direction. Nero took a couple of swinging shots but missed – they zinged into the bush beside me – and the kangaroo zigzagged back the way she'd come. Donkey-donk then headed off and hit her a third time, with an awful thud, and this time she didn't budge.

He opened the car door and clouted the base of her skull with a spanner – at which she reared up again on her haunches and he had to grab her by the tail. By the time we three ran up, the kangaroo was hopping forward and Donkey-donk was hanging on like a man in a tug-of-war, and then Nero put a shot through her head, and that was that.

Walker looked disgusted and miserable.

'I don't like it,' he said.

'Nor do I,' I agreed.

Nero contemplated the dead kangaroo. A stream of blood trickled from her nostrils on to the red earth.

'Old one,' he shrugged. 'Not good for eat.'

'What are you going to do with her?'

'Leave,' he said. 'Cut off tail, maybe. You got a knife?'

'No,' I said.

Nero rummaged in the car and found the lid of an old tin can. Using it as a blade, he tried to cut off the tail but couldn't saw through the vertebrae.

The back left tyre had a flat. Donkey-donk commanded me to get out the jack and change the wheel. The jack was badly bent and, when I applied a few strokes of pressure, it snapped and the axle hit the dirt.

'Now you done it,' he leered.

'What do we do?' I asked.

'Walk,' said Nero, with a titter.

'How far?'

'Two days, maybe.'

'What about the smoke?' I suggested.

'Nah!' growled Donkey-donk. 'Lift him! Lift him up, man!'

Walker and I gripped the bumper, braced our backs, and tried to lift while Donkey-donk got ready with a log to shove under the differential.

It was no use.

'Come on,' I shouted at Nero. 'Give us a hand!'

He cupped his fingers and ran them up and down one of his slender biceps, batting his eyelids and giggling.

'No force!' he said, breathlessly.

Donkey-donk handed me a digging-stick and ordered me to scoop out a hole beneath the wheel. Half an hour later, the hole was big enough to change the wheel. All three looked on as I worked. I was done in and drenched with sweat. We then rocked the car back and forth, and finally pushed it clear.

We left the kangaroo to the crows and drove back to Cullen.

'You want to come hunting tomorrow?' asked Donkey-donk.

'No,' I said.

London, 1970

AT A PUBLIC LECTURE *I listened to Arthur Koestler airing his opinion that the human species was mad. He claimed that, as a result of an inadequate co-ordination between two areas of the brain – the 'rational' neocortex and the 'instinctual' hypothalamus – Man had somehow acquired the 'unique, murderous, delusional streak' that propelled him, inevitably, to murder, to torture and to war.*

Our prehistoric ancestors, he said, did not suffer from the effects of overcrowding. They were not short of territory. They did not live in cities . . . yet they butchered one another just the same.

He went on to say that, since Hiroshima, there had been a total transformation of the 'structure of human consciousness': in that, for the first time in his history, Man had to contemplate the idea of his destruction as a species.

This millenarian claptrap made me quite angry. At question time I stuck up my hand.

Around the year 1000, I said, people all over Europe believed that a violent end of the world was imminent. How was the 'structure of their consciousness' any different from our own?

Koestler fixed me with a contemptuous stare and, to the approval of the audience, snapped:

'Because one was a fantasy and the H-Bomb is real.'

◆

Salutary reading for the end of the Second Millennium: Henri Focillon's L'An mil.

In his chapter 'The Problem of the Terrors', Focillon shows how, exactly one thousand years ago, Western man was paralysed by the same set of fears being put about today by the bigots who pass for statesmen. The phrase 'Mundus senescit' 'The world grows old,' reflected a mood of dire intellectual pessimism, as well as a 'religious' conviction that the world was a living body which, having passed the peak of its maturity, was doomed, suddenly, to die.

The sources of the Terror were threefold.

1 *That God would destroy his creation in clouds of fire and brimstone.*

2   *That the legions of the Devil would erupt out of the East.*
3   *That epidemics would wipe out the human race.*

And yet the Terror passed. The year 1000 came and went, and the new 'open' society of the Middle Ages took root. As Bishop Glaber wrote, in the loveliest of lines, 'Three years after the year 1000, the Earth was covered with a white robe of churches.'

◆

Dinner party, London, 1971

A very tall American came to dinner. He was on his way to Washington from a fact-finding mission in Vietnam. Over the past week he had flown to Hawaii, to Guam, to Tokyo and Saigon. He had overflown Hanoi on a bombing raid. He had conferred with NATO chiefs-of-staff – and this was his one night off.

He was an innocent man. Over salad he spoke of defoliants. I shall not forget the sight of raspberries passing between his lips, nor the thud of stressed syllables coming out of them: 'The Nórth Viétnamése have lóst betwéen a hálf and a thírd of a generátion of their yóung fíghting mén. This is a lóss nó nátion can afford to sustáin indéfinitely: which is whý we antícipate a mílitary víctory, in Víetnám, in the coúrse of 1972 . . .'

◆

From Sun Tzu's The Art of War.

Do not press an enemy at bay.
    Prince Fu Ch'ai said, 'Wild beasts, when at bay, fight desperately. How much more is this true of men! If they know there is no alternative, they will fight to the death.

◆

Steiermark, Austria, 1974

Hiking in the Rottenmanner Tauern before my interview with Lorenz, my rucksack weighted with his books. The days were cloudless. I spent each night in a different Alpine hut, and had sausages and beer for supper. The mountainsides were in flower: gentians and edelweiss, columbines and the turk's cap lily. The pinewoods were blue-green in the sunlight, and streaks of snow still lingered on the screes. On every meadow there were mild brown cows, the cowbells clanking and echoing across the valleys, or the chime of a church bell far below . . .

Hölderlin's line, 'In lovely blueness blooms the steeple with its metal roof . . .'

The hikers: men and women in red-and-white shirts and lederhosen and everyone calling 'Grüss Gott!' *as they passed.* One knotty little man mistook me for a German and, with the leer of a pornography salesman, reversed his jacket collar to show me his swastikas.

◆

Re-reading Lorenz made me realise why sensible people tended to throw up their hands in horror: to deny there was such a thing as human nature, and to insist that everything must be learnt.

'Genetic determinism', they felt, threatened every liberal, human and democratic impulse to which the West still clung. They recognised, too, that you couldn't pick and choose with instincts: you had to take the lot. You couldn't allow Venus into the Pantheon and bolt the door on Mars. And once you took on 'fighting', 'territorial behaviour' and 'rank order', you were back in the soup of nineteenth-century reaction.

What, in On Aggression, *caught the fancy of the Cold War warriors was Lorenz's concept of 'ritual' combat.*

The Superpowers, by implication, must *fight because it is in their nature to fight: yet could perhaps contain their squabbles in some poor, small, preferably defenceless country – just as two bucks will choose a patch of no-man's land to spar on.*

The US Secretary of Defence, I was told, kept an annotated copy by his bedside.

Men are products of their situation, and learning conditions everything they will ever say or think or do. Children are traumatised by events in their childhood; nations by crises in their history. But could this 'conditioning' mean there are no absolute *standards which transcend historical memories? No 'rights' or 'wrongs' regardless of race or creed?*

Has the 'gift of tongues' somehow done away with instinct? Is Man, in short, the proverbial 'blank slate' of the behaviourists – infinitely malleable and adaptive?

If so, then all the Great Teachers have been spouting hot air.

The most 'objectionable' passage in On Aggression *– or the one that led to catcalls of 'Nazi!' – is one in which Lorenz describes the instinctive 'fixed motor pattern' observable in young soldiers roused to battle fury: the head held high . . . chin stuck out . . . the arms rotated inwards . . . the shiver down the now non-existent hair along the spine . . . : 'One soars elated above the cares of everyday life . . . Men enjoy the feeling of absolute righteousness even when they commit atrocities . . .*

And yet . . . the mother who fights in fury to defend her child is – one would hope! – obeying the call of instinct, not the advice of some maternal guidance leaflet. And if you allow the existence of fighting behaviour in young women, why not also in young men?

Instincts are Pascal's 'reasons of the heart of which the reason knows nothing'. And to believe in the 'reasons of the heart' holds no comfort whatsoever for the reactionary – very much the reverse!

Without religion, in Dostoevsky's famous formulation, everything is permissible. Without instinct, everything would be equally permissible.

A world shorn of instinct would be a far more deadly and dangerous place than anything the 'aggression-mongers' could come up with, for here would be Limbo-land where everything could be capped by something else: good could be bad; sense, nonsense; truth, lies; knitting no more moral than child murder; and where a man might be brainwashed into thinking or saying or doing whatever might be pleasing to the powers-that-be.

A torturer can cut off a man's nose; but if the man gets a chance to breed, his child will be born with a nose. So with instinct! A core of unmodifiable instinct in man means that the brain-washers must begin their work of distortion over and over again, with each individual and each generation – and this, in the end, is a very wearisome business.

The Greeks believed there were limits to the range of human behaviour: not, as Camus pointed out, that these limits would never be surpassed, simply that they existed, arbitrarily; and that whoever had the hubris to exceed them would be struck down by Fate!

◆

Lorenz maintains there are certain crises – or instinctual rubicons – in the life of any animal when it receives a call to behave in a certain way. The call is not necessarily taken up; for if the 'natural' target of its behaviour is missing, the animal will redirect it on to a substitute – and grow up warped.

◆

Every mythology has its version of the 'Hero and his Road of Trials', in which a young man, too, receives a 'call'. He travels to a distant country where some giant or monster threatens to destroy the population. In a superhuman battle, he overcomes the Power of Darkness, proves his manhood, and receives his reward: a wife, treasure, land, fame.
 These he enjoys into late middle age when, once again, the clouds darken. Again, restlessness stirs him. Again he leaves: either like Beowulf to die in combat or, as the blind Tiresias prophesies for Odysseus, to set off for some mysterious destination, and vanish.

◆

'Catharsis': Greek for 'purging' or 'cleansing'. One controversial etymology derives it from the Greek katheiro 'to rid the land of monsters'.

◆

Myth proposes, action disposes. The Hero Cycle represents an unchangeable paradigm of 'ideal' behaviour for the human male. (One could, of course, work one out for the Heroine.)

Each section of the myth – like a link in a behavioural chain – will correspond to one of the classic Ages of Man. Each Age opens with some fresh barrier to be scaled or ordeal to be endured. The status of the Hero will rise in proportion as to how much of this assault course he completes – or is seen to complete.

Most of us, not being heroes, dawdle through life, mis-time our cues, and end up in our various emotional messes. The Hero does not. The Hero – and this is why we hail him as a hero – takes each ordeal as it comes, and chalks up point after point.

I once made the experiment of slotting the career of a modern hero, Che Guevara, on to the structure of the Beowulf epic. The result was, with a bit of tinkering here and there, that both heroes are seen to perform the same set of exploits in the same sequence: the leavetaking; the voyage across the sea; the defeat of the Monster (Grendel–Batista); the defeat of the Monster's mother ('The water-hag' – the Bay of Pigs). Both heroes receive their reward: a wife, fame, treasure (in Guevara's case a Cuban wife and the Directorship of the National Bank of Cuba), and so forth. Both end up dying in a distant country: Beowulf killed by the Scaly Worm, Guevara by the Dictator of Bolivia.

As a man, Guevara, for all his charm, strikes one as a ruthless and unpleasant personality. As a Hero, he never put a foot wrong – and the world chose to see him as a Hero.

Heroes in moments of crisis are said to hear 'angel voices' telling them what to do next. The whole of the Odyssey *is a marvellous tug of war between Athene whispering in Odysseus's ear, 'Yes, you'll make it,' and Poseidon roaring, 'No, you won't!' And if you swap the word 'instinct' for 'angel-voice', you come close to the more psychologically-minded mythographers: that myths are fragments of the soul-life of Early Man.*

The Hero Cycle, wherever found, is a story of 'fitness' in the Darwinian sense: a blueprint for genetic 'success'. Beowulf leaves . . . Ivan leaves . . . Jack leaves . . . the young Aboriginal on Walkabout leaves . . . even the antique Don Quixote leaves. And these Wanderjahre, *and combats with the Beast, are the* story-teller's version of the incest taboo; whereby a man must first prove 'fitness' and then must 'marry far'.

In practice, it scarcely matters whether myths are the coded messages of instinct, whose structures will reside in the central nervous system, or tales of instruction handed down from the Year Dot. One point cannot be emphasised too strongly. Seldom, if ever, in myth, is it desirable, morally, for a man to kill a man in cold blood.

◆

Among the military fraternities of Ancient Germany a young man, as part of his training to stifle inhibitions against killing, was required to strip naked; to dress himself in the hot, freshly flayed skin of a bear; to work himself into a 'bestial' rage: in other words, to go, quite literally, berserk.

'Bearskin' and 'berserk' are the same word. The helmets of the Royal Guards, on duty outside Buckingham Palace, are the descendants of this primitive battle costume.

◆

Homer distinguishes two kinds of 'fighting behaviour'. One is menos, the cold-blooded stand of Odysseus as he shoots the suitors. The other is lyssa, or 'wolfish rage', such as possesses Hector on the battlefield (Iliad IX, 237–9). A man in the thrall of lyssa is thought to be no longer 'human', or subject to the laws of earth and Heaven.

Lorenz's 'militant fighting enthusiasm' is a description of lyssa.

◆

The Sioux Indians are a set of miserable dirty lousy blanketed thieving lying sneaking murdering graceless faceless gut-eating SKUNKS as the Lord ever permitted to infect the earth, and whose immediate and final extermination all MEN, excepting Indian agents and traders, should pray for.

From the Topeka Weekly Daily, 1869

◆

(217)

The stranger, if he be not a trader, is an enemy.

Old English

◆

The Middle Latin wargus — *i.e. 'expulsus' or 'stranger', is also the same as the wolf; and thus the two conceptions — that of the wild beast to be hunted down, and that of the man to be treated as a wild beast — are intimately associated.*

P. J. Hamilton Grierson, The Silent Trade

◆

Nuristan, Afghanistan, 1970

The villages of Nuristan are set at so vertiginous an angle to the mountainsides that ladders of deodar wood must serve the function of streets. The people have fair hair and blue eyes, and carry battle-axes made of brass. They wear pancake hats, cross-gartering on their legs, and a dollop of kohl on each eyelid. Alexander mistook them for a tribe of long-lost Greeks, the Germans for a tribe of Aryans.

Our porters were a cringing lot, forever complaining that their poor feet could carry them no farther and casting envious eyes on our boots.

At four o'clock they wanted us to camp beside some sunless and broken houses, but we insisted on moving up the valley. An hour later, we came to a village surrounded by walnut trees. The roof-tops were orange, from apricots drying in the sun, and girls in rose-madder dresses were playing in a field of flowers.

The village headman welcomed us with a frank and open smile. We were then joined by a bearded young satyr, his hair wreathed in vine leaves and meadow-sweet, who offered us from his leather flask a thread of sharp white wine.

'Here,' I said to the leading porter, 'we will stop.'

'We will not stop,' he said.

He had learnt his English in the Peshawar bazaar.

'We will stop,' I said.

'These people are wolves,' he said.

'Wolves?'

'They are wolves.'

(218)

'And the people of that village?' I asked, pointing to a second, dejected-looking village about a mile upstream.

'They are people,' he said.

'And the village beyond that? Wolves, I suppose?'

'Wolves,' he nodded.

'What nonsense you do talk!'

'Not nonsense, sahib,' he said. 'Some people are people and some other people are wolves.'

◆

It does not take too much imagination to suppose that man, as a species, has suffered some tremendous ordeal in his evolutionary past: the fact that he scraped through so brilliantly is a measure of the magnitude of the threat.

To prove this is another matter. Yet, already twenty years ago, I felt that far too much attention was being paid to our supposedly 'fratricidal' tendencies and too little to the role of the Carnivore in shaping our character and destiny.

◆

If one had to give a general answer to the question, 'What do carnivores eat?' it would be a very simple one, 'What they can get.'

Griff Ewer, The Carnivores

◆

It has been said of the Kadars, a hunting tribe of southern India, that they were strangers to violence or displays of virility because they channelled all their antipathies outwards *on to the tiger.*

◆

Suppose, for the sake of argument, you cut all the loose talk of 'aggression' and focused on the problem of 'defence'. What if the Adversary, on the plains of Africa, had not been the other man? Not the men of the other tribe? What if the adrenal discharges that precipitate 'fighting fury' had evolved to protect us from the big cats? What if our weapons were not, primarily, for hunting game, but for saving our skins? What if we were not so much a predatory species as a species in search of a predator?

Or if, at some critical watershed, the Beast had been about to win?

◆

Here — let there be no mistake — lies the great divide.

If the first men had been brutish, murderous, cannibalistic, if their rapacity had driven them to acts of extermination and conquest, then any State, by providing an umbrella of force, will have saved men from themselves and must, inevitably, be considered beneficial. Such a State must, however frightful for the individual, be counted a blessing. And any action by individuals to disrupt, weaken or threaten the State will be a step in the direction of primaeval chaos.

If, on the other hand, the first men themselves were humbled, harried, besieged, their communities few and fragmented, forever gazing at the horizon whence help might come, clinging to life and one another through the horrors of the night — might not all the specific attributes we call 'human' — language, song-making, food-sharing, gift-giving, intermarriage — this is to say, all the voluntary graces which bring equipoise to society, which suppress the use of force among its members; and which can only function smoothly if equivalence is the rule — might not all these have evolved as stratagems for survival, hammered out against tremendous odds, to avert the threat of extinction? Would they, therefore, be any less instinctual or directionless? Would not a general theory of defence explain more readily why offensive wars are, in the long run, unfightable? Why the bullies never win?

◆

Altenberg, Austria, 1974

It was too hot in Lorenz's study and we moved into a summer-house in the garden. Above the town towered the mediaeval castle of Greiffenstein: a bastion of Christian Europe against the shifting world of Asiatic horsemen. Seeing him on his own ground made me realise that his views on fighting must, in some way, be coloured by having been brought up at the centre of a tremendous geopolitical drama.

(220)

Why was it, I asked him, that so many people still found the theory of instinct, as applied to man, unstomachable?

'There are certain things', he said, 'with which one simply cannot cope, and one of them is plain stupidity.'

'Please stop me if I'm wrong,' I said, 'but when, in any animal, you isolate a "bloc" of behaviour, the first question to ask is "What for?" How would this or that have helped to preserve the species in its original habitat?'

'True,' he nodded.

'A robin', I said, alluding to one of his experiments, 'on seeing another robin, or even a piece of red fluff, will move into the attack, because red says "territorial rival".'

'He will.'

'So the trigger which releases fighting in a robin is the sight of its own kind?'

'Of course.'

'Well, why, when it comes to fighting among men, must one or other of the fighters be not quite human? Don't you think that "militant enthusiasm", as you describe it, might have evolved as a defensive reaction against the wild beasts?'

'It could be,' he answered thoughtfully. 'It could very well be. Before hunting a lion, the Masai in Kenya drum up fighting enthusiasm quite artificially, like a Nazi music march . . . Yes. Fighting may have developed primarily against the wild beasts. Chimps, at the sight of a leopard, do the whole collective aggression stunt beautifully.'

'But surely,' I persisted, 'haven't we got the concepts of "aggression" and "defence" mixed up? Aren't we dealing with two entirely separate mechanisms? On the one hand you have the "aggressive" rituals which, in the case of human beings, are gift-giving, treaty-making and kinship arrangements. Then you have "defence", surely against the Beast?'

All war propaganda, I went on, proceeded on the assumption that you must degrade the enemy into something bestial, infidel, cancerous, and so on. Or, alternatively, your fighters must transform themselves into surrogate beasts – in which case men became their legitimate prey.

Lorenz tugged at his beard, gave me a searching look and said, ironically or not I'll never know:

'What you have just said is totally new.'

(221)

32

ONE MORNING, AS I was having breakfast with Rolf and Wendy, a tall shirtless figure came ambling towards us.

'We're honoured,' Rolf said. 'Big Foot Clarence. Chairman of the Cullen Council.'

The man was dark-skinned and rather pear-shaped, and his feet were enormous. I gave him my chair. He sat down, scowling.

'So how's you?' Rolf asked.

'Right,' said Clarence.

'Good.'

'They passed the budget in Canberra,' Clarence said, in a flat disinterested voice.

'Oh, yes.'

'Yep,' he said. 'We've got the plane.'

For over two years now, the Cullen Council had been angling for a plane.

'Yep,' Clarence repeated. 'We've got the plane now. Thought I'd tell you.'

'Thanks, Clarence.'

'Thought I'd go to Canberra Thursday,' he said. 'Thought I'd come back in the plane.'

'You do that,' said Rolf.

Clarence got to his feet and was walking away when Rolf called him back.

'Clarence,' he said.

'Yep.'

'Clarence, what have you done with the grader?'

'What grader?'

'The Popanji grader.'

'Don't know no Popanji grader.'

'Yes, you do,' Rolf said. 'The grader Red Lawson lent you.'

'When?'

'Last year,' he said. 'You and your mates went hunting on that grader. Remember?'

'No.'

'Well, Red's coming over to fetch the grader. I suggest you find it, Clarence. Or they might deduct the cost from the plane.'

'Dunno nothing about a grader,' Clarence sneered, angrily, and stamped off.

I caught Wendy's eye. She was trying not to giggle.

'That plane', Rolf turned to me, 'is going to be trouble.'

It was all very well to give them a plane, another thing to pay for its upkeep. None of the Cullen Mob saw the least point in having a plane unless they had the plane *right there*. That meant paying a pilot to live at Cullen. It also meant a child-proof hangar.

At the Amadeus Settlement, Rolf continued, the pilot had been a nice guy who liked to take the kids for a spin. Kids of eight and ten, and they soon got wise to the plane's control systems. They watched where he kept his keys, in a locked drawer in his caravan, and managed to nick them while he was taking a nap.

'He woke', Rolf said, 'to watch the aircraft moving down the runway.'

'They took off?'

'Not quite,' he said. 'Overshot the strip and landed in some bushes. The plane was a near wreck.'

It was still cool and bright in the early morning.

'I thought I'd go for a walk today,' I said.

We were expecting Arkady any day and, each morning, at work in the caravan, I promised myself a walk up Mount Liebler.

'Take water,' said Rolf. 'Take three times the water you think you need.'

I pointed out the way I planned to climb.

'Don't worry,' he said. 'We've got trackers who'd find you in a couple of hours. But you *must* take the water.'

I filled my water flask, put two extra bottles in my rucksack, and set out. On the edge of the settlement, I passed a lady's handbag hanging from a tree.

I walked over a plateau of sandhills and crumbly red rock, broken by gulches which were difficult to cross. The bushes had been burnt for game-drives, and bright green shoots were sprouting from the stumps.

I was climbing steadily, and, looking down at the plain, I understood why Aboriginals choose to paint their land in 'pointillist' dots. The land *was* dotted. The white dots were spinifex; the blueish dots were eucalyptus, and the lemon-green dots were some other kind of tufty grass. I understood, too, better than ever, what Lawrence meant by the 'peculiar, lost weary aloofness of Australia'.

A wallaby got up and went bounding downhill. I then saw, on the far side of the chasm, something big in the shade of a tree. At first I thought it might be a Giant Red, until I realised it was a man.

I shinned up the far side to find Old Alex, naked, his spears along the ground and his velvet coat wrapped in a bundle. I nodded and he nodded.

'Hello,' I said. 'What brings you here?'

He smiled, bashful at his nakedness, and barely opening his lips, said: 'Footwalking all the time all over the world.'

I left him to his reverie and walked on. The spinifex was thicker than ever. At times I despaired of finding a way through, but always, like Ariadne's thread, there *was* a way through.

I next fell for the temptation – the temptation of touching a hedgehog – to put my hand on a clump: only to find my palm was stuck with spines an inch or so before I'd expected. As I picked them out, I remembered something Arkady had said, 'Everything's spiny in Australia. Even a goanna's got a mouthful of spines.'

I clambered up the screes of the escarpment and came out on a knife edge of rock. It really did look like the perenty lizard's tail. Beyond, there was a tableland with some trees along a dried-up watercourse. The trees were leafless. They had rumpled grey bark and tiny scarlet flowers that fell to the ground like drops of blood.

I sat, exhausted, in the half-shade of one of these trees. It was infernally hot.

A short way off, two male butcher birds, black and white like magpies, were calling antiphonally across a ravine. One bird would lift his beak vertically and let out three long whooping notes, followed by three ascending shorts. The rival would then pick up the refrain, and repeat it.

'Simple as that,' I said to myself. 'Exchanging notes across a frontier.'

I was lying spreadeagled against the tree-trunk with one leg dangling over the bank, swigging greedily from the water flask. I now knew what Rolf meant by dehydration. It was madness to go on up the mountain. I would have to go back the way I'd come.

The butcher birds were silent. Sweat poured over my eyelids so that everything seemed blurred and out of scale. I heard the clatter of loose stones along the bank, and looked up to see a monster approaching.

It was a giant lace-monitor, the lord of the mountain, Perenty himself. He must have been seven feet long. His skin was pale ochre, with darker brown markings. He licked the air with his lilac tongue. I froze. He clawed his way forward: there was no way of telling if he'd seen me. The claws passed within two inches of my boot. Then he turned full-circle and, with a sudden burst of speed, shot off the way he'd come.

The perenty has a nasty set of teeth, but is harmless to man unless cornered: in fact, apart from scorpions, snakes and spiders, Australia is exceptionally benign.

All the same the Aboriginals have inherited a bestiary of monsters and bugaboos: with which to menace their children, or torment young men at initiation time. I remembered Sir George Grey's description of the Boly-yas: a flap-eared apparition, more stealthily vengeful than any other creature, which would consume the flesh, but leave the bones. I remembered the Rainbow Snake. And I remembered Arkady talking about the *Manu-manu*: a fanged, yeti-like creature which moved underground, prowled the camps at night, and made off with unwary strangers.

The first Australians, I reflected, will have known real monsters such as the *Thylacaleo*, or 'marsupial lion'. There was also a perenty lizard thirty feet long. Yet there was nothing in the Australian megafauna to contend with the horrors of the African bush.

I fell to wondering whether the violent edge of Aboriginal life – the blood-vengeance and bloody initiations – might stem from the fact of their having no proper beasts to contend with.

I dragged myself to my feet, climbed across the ridge, and looked down over Cullen settlement.

I thought I could see an easier way down, which would avoid

having to cross the gulches. This 'easy way' turned out to be a rock-slide, but I arrived at the bottom in one piece and walked home along a streambed.

There was a trickle of water in the stream, and bushes grew along it. I splashed some water over my face, and walked on. I had raised my right leg to take a step forward and heard myself saying, 'I am about to tread on something that looks like a green pine-cone.' What I had not yet seen was the head of the king-brown, about to strike, rearing up behind a bush. I put my legs into reverse and drew back, very slowly . . . one . . . two . . . one . . . two. The snake also withdrew, and slithered off into a hole. I said to myself, 'You're being very calm' – until I felt the waves of nausea.

I got back to Cullen at half past one.

Rolf looked me up and down and said, 'You look quite shattered, mate.'

ROCK-A-BYE, *baby, on the tree top,*
When the wind blows, the cradle will rock.
When the bough breaks, the cradle will fall,
And down will come baby, cradle and all.

◆

That man is a migratory species is, in my opinion, born out by
an experiment made at the Tavistock Clinic in London and
described by Dr John Bowlby in his Attachment and Loss.

Every normal baby will scream if left alone; and the best way
of silencing these screams is for the mother to take it in her arms
and rock or 'walk' it back to contentment. Bowlby rigged up a
machine which imitated, exactly, the pace and action of a
mother's walk; and found that, providing the baby was healthy,
warm and well-fed, it stopped crying at once. 'The ideal
movement', he wrote, 'is a vertical one with a traverse of three
inches.' Rocking at slow speeds, such as thirty cycles a minute,
had no effect: but once you raised the pace to fifty and above,
every baby ceased to cry and almost always stayed quiet.

◆

Day in, day out, a baby cannot have enough walking. And if
babies instinctively demand to be walked, the mother, on the
African savannah, must have been walking too: from camp to
camp on her daily foraging round, to the waterhole and on visits
to the neighbours.

◆

Apes have flat feet, we have sprung arches. According to
Professor Napier, the human gait is a long, lilting stride – 1 . . .
2, . . . 1 . . . 2 – with a fourfold rhythm built into the action of
the feet as they come into contact with the ground – 1, 2, 3,
4 . . . 1, 2, 3, 4 . . . : heel strike; weight along the outside of
the foot; weight transferred to the ball of the foot; push-off with
big toe.

◆

The question occurs to me – and quite seriously – how many
shoe soles, how many ox-hide soles, how many sandals
Alighieri wore out in the course of his poetic work, wander-
ing about on the goat paths of Italy.

The Inferno *and especially the* Purgatorio *glorify the human gait, the measure and rhythm of walking, the foot and its shape. The step, linked to the breathing and saturated with thought: this Dante understands as the beginning of prosody.*
Osip Mandelstam, Conversations about Dante,
trans. Clarence Brown

◆

Melos: *Greek for 'limb', hence 'melody.'*

◆

And think this slow-pac'd soule . . .
John Donne, 'The Second Anniversarie'

A white explorer in Africa, anxious to press ahead with his journey, paid his porters for a series of forced marches. But they, almost within reach of their destination, set down their bundles and refused to budge. No amount of extra payment would convince them otherwise. They said they had to wait for their souls to catch up.

The Bushmen, who walk distances across the Kalahari, have no idea of the soul's survival in another world. 'When we die, we die,' they say. 'The wind blows away our foot prints, and that is the end of us.'

Sluggish and sedentary peoples, such as the Ancient Egyptians – with their concept of an afterlife journey through the Field of Reeds – project on to the next world the journeys they failed to make in this one.

◆

London, 1965

The man who came to supper with Mr Rasikh was a scrubbed and balding Englishman, pink as a healthy baby and in his middle sixties. He had sandy-to-greying sideburns and clear blue eyes. His name was Alan Brady. You could tell at a glance he was a very happy man.

(228)

Mr Rasikh was the official buyer in London for the Sudanese government. He lived in a flat on top of a tower block in Victoria. He had a hennaed beard, and wore white jalabiyas and a floppy white turban. He was never off the phone collecting punters' tips for horses, and apparently never went out. Occasionally, you heard the sound of his women in another room.

His friend Brady was a travelling salesman for a firm that made typewriters and office equipment. He had customers in about thirty African countries and, every four months, would visit each in turn.

He said he preferred the company of Africans to white men. It was a pleasure to do business with them. People said Africans were impossible to deal with, always wanting something for nothing.

'But, let me tell you,' Brady said to me, 'they're a whole lot easier than my colleagues in the office.'

In twenty years of trading, he had had two bad debts. He never took a holiday. He was unafraid of revolutions, or African airlines.

He came to London three times a year, never for more than a week, and would stay in the bunk-room the company set aside for its travellers. Because he had no winter clothes, he tried to time these visits to avoid the worst of the weather: in November, in March and again in July.

Apart from the clothes he stood up in, he owned no possessions other than a spare tropical suit, a spare tie, a pullover, three shirts, underwear, socks, slippers, an umbrella and a sponge-bag. Everything fitted into a suitcase he could carry as hand-baggage.

'I don't believe in wasting time at airports,' he said.

Every time he returned to London, he went to a tropical outfitter's off Piccadilly and completely re-equipped himself: suitcase, umbrella, clothes and all. He gave the rejects to the office porter, who made a few pounds on them.

'Nothing', he said proudly, 'wears out on Alan Brady.'

He had neither English friends, nor family. Mr Rasikh's flat was the one place in London where he felt at ease.

His father had been gassed on the Somme, his mother had died during the week of Dunkirk. Sometimes, in the summers, he used to visit her grave, in a village churchyard near Nottingham. He had once had an aunt in Wigan, but now she too had died.

He was past retiring age. There were murmurings among the office staff that it was time for him to go: but his order book was always full, and the management kept him on.

'Don't you have a base?' I asked him. 'Don't you have anywhere you could call "home"?'

He blushed with embarrassment. 'I do,' he faltered. 'It is rather private.'

'I'm sorry,' I said. 'Forget it.'

'Not that I'm ashamed of it,' he went on. 'Only some people might think it silly.'

'Not me,' I said.

He said that, in the office safe, he kept an old solicitor's black tin deed box, the kind with 'The Estate of Sir Somebody So-and-So' in white lettering.

Whenever he came to London, he would lock himself in the bunk-room and spread the contents over the mattress.

In the bottom of the box he kept the bric-à-brac salvaged from an earlier existence: his parents' wedding photo; his father's medals; the letter from the King; a teddy bear; a Dresden kingfisher that had been his mother's favourite; her garnet brooch; his swimming trophy (by 1928, he no longer had attacks of bronchial asthma); his silver ashtray 'for twenty-five years' loyal service' to the firm.

In the top half of the box, separated by a layer of tissue paper, he kept his 'African' things – worthless things, each the record of a memorable encounter: a Zulu carving bought off a sad old man in the Drakensbergs; an iron snake from Dahomey; a print of the Prophet's Horse, or a letter from a boy in Burundi thanking him for the present of a football. Each time he brought back one new thing, and chucked out one old thing that had lost its significance.

Alan Brady had only one fear: that soon they would make him retire.

◆

If every newborn baby has an appetite for forward *motion, the next step is to find out why it hates lying still.*

Penetrating further into the causes of anxiety and anger in the very young, Dr Bowlby concluded that the complex instinctual bond between a mother and her child – the child's screams of alarm (quite different to the whimperings of cold or hunger or sickness); the mother's 'uncanny' ability to hear those screams; the child's fear of the dark, and of strangers; its terror of rapidly approaching objects; its invention of nightmarish monsters where none exist; in short, all those 'puzzling phobias' which Freud sought to explain but failed, could, in fact, be explained by the constant presence of predators in the primaeval home of man.

Bowlby quotes from William James's Principles of Psychology, 'The greatest source of terror in childhood is solitude.' A solitary child, kicking and yelling in its cot, is not, therefore, necessarily showing the first signs of the Death Wish, or of the Will to Power, or of an 'aggressive drive' to bash its brother's teeth in. These may or may not develop later. No. The child is yelling – if you transpose the cot on to the African thornscrub – because, unless the mother comes back in a couple of minutes, a hyena will have got it.

Every child appears to have an innate mental picture of the 'thing' that might attack: so much so that any threatening 'thing', even if it is not the real 'thing', will trigger off a predictable sequence of defensive behaviour. The screams and kicks are the first line of defence. The mother must then be prepared to fight for the child; and the father to fight for them both. The danger doubles at night, because man has no night vision and the big cats hunt at night. And surely this most Manichaean drama – of light, darkness and the Beast – lies at the heart of the human predicament.

Visitors to a baby ward in hospital are often surprised by the silence. Yet if the mother really has abandoned her child, its only chance of survival is to shut its mouth.

33

As promised, Red Lawson drove into Cullen to look for the missing grader. He came in the police vehicle; and to impress on the Cullen Mob the seriousness of his intentions, he was fully togged up, in khaki, with all the insignia of his rank and a hat strapped purposefully under his chin. His socks were stretched to bursting over his calves.

In the afternoon he made a round of the humpies, but drew a blank. No one had heard of the grader. No one knew what a grader was: except for Clarence the Chairman, who flew into a rage and said he'd confused Cullen with some place else. Even Joshua acted dumb.

'Now what?' Red asked Rolf.

He was sitting on a packing-case inside the store, mopping the sweat from his forehead.

'Let's wait for old Alex,' said Rolf. 'He'll know. And from what I know of him, he'll hate the grader and want it out.'

Alex, as usual, was bushwalking but was bound to be back at sunset – and he was.

'Leave this one to me,' said Rolf, who went over to talk to him.

Alex listened. Then, with the faintest grin, he pointed a bony finger towards the north-east.

Red's passion for Spinoza began to make better sense at supper when he told us that his mother was an Amsterdam Jewess. She, alone of her family, had survived the Nazi occupation, cooped in the attic of some Gentile neighbours. When the brutes had gone and she was free to walk the streets, she had the sensation she must either die – or go far away. She met an Australian soldier, who was kind to her and asked her to be his wife.

Red was aching to talk about Spinoza, but to my shame, I'd

only dipped into *The Ethics* and our conversation was a series of halting *non sequiturs*. My performance, plainly, was not a patch on Arkady's.

Next morning Red and I, and a man he'd brought from Popanji, set out to look for the grader. We crawled across country in the direction Alex had pointed. Whenever we came to higher ground, Red would stop and reach for his binoculars.

'Not a sign of the bugger!' he said.

We then drove through a gap between two low-lying hills: on the far side we shouted simultaneously, 'Grader tracks!'

They *had* been having fun! For miles ahead the landscape was churned up into circles, loops and figures of eight. But no matter how many times we drove round this ridiculous maze, there was still no sign of the grader.

'I think I'm going crazy,' said Red.

At that moment I glanced at a conical hillock to our right. Perched on top of it was the huge yellow thing.

'Look!' I shouted.

'Christ!' said Red. 'How the hell did they get it up there?'

We climbed the hill and found the grader, rusty, paint peeling in slabs, a bush growing up through the engine, poised with one wheel in the air, above a very steep bank. Incredibly, the tyres were hard.

Red checked the tank, which was half-full. He checked the self-starter, which was out. He then checked the slope to make sure there were no hidden dangers, and reckoned we could probably jump-start her.

'Clever so-and-sos,' he grinned. 'Knew exactly what they were doing!'

The metal of the machine was infernally hot. Red presented me with a pair of heat-resistant gloves and a spray-can. My role in this operation was, without etherising myself, to spray ether into the carburettor.

I wrapped a handkerchief round my nose. Red climbed into the driver's seat.

'Ready?' he called.

'Ready!' I answered.

He released the brake and the grader eased forward with a swish of breaking branches. I pressed the nozzle of the spray-can and hung on for dear life as, suddenly, we hurtled down the slope and the engine came alive with a roar. Red skilfully steered the machine on to level ground, and braked. He turned to me and gave the thumbs up sign.

He ordered the man from Popanji to take the wheel of the police vehicle. I rode behind on the cab of the grader. Within a mile or so of Cullen, I shouted above the din, 'Could you do me a big favour? Could I drive her?'

'Sure!' said Red.

I drove the grader into the settlement. There was no one about. I parked on a slope behind Rolf's caravan.

Now, if I saw the 'other' Bruce in Alice, I'd be able to say, 'I didn't drive a dozer, Bru. But I drove a grader.'

No COUNTRY ABOUNDS *in a greater degree with dangerous beasts than Southern Africa.*
                    Charles Darwin, The Descent of Man

◆

But where there is danger there grows also what saves.
                    Friedrich Hölderlin, Patmos

◆

Koestler's rant about the original 'bloodbath' made me realise he must have read, at first- or second-hand, the work of Raymond Dart. Dart was the young Professor of Anatomy of Witwatersrand University in Johannesburg who, in 1924, had recognised the significance of the Taung Child – a spectacular fossil skull from Cape Province – and had gone on to give it the tongue-twisting name Australopithecus africanus, *the 'African Southern Ape'.*

He deduced, correctly, that the creature had stood about four foot high; that it had walked erect, more or less like a man; and though the brain of a fully grown specimen could hardly have been larger than a chimpanzee's, it had human characteristics none the less.

The discovery of this 'missing link', he insisted (to the sneers of 'experts' in England), bore out Darwin's prediction that man had descended from the higher apes in Africa.

He also believed the 'child' had been bashed to death with a blow over the head.

Dart, a Queenslander of bush-farming stock, belongs to the generation of the First World War; and though he only witnessed mopping-up operations in 1918, he seems to have held the disillusioned view: that men enjoy killing other men, and will go on killing indefinitely.

Certainly, by 1953, with fresh evidence from a cave on the fringe of the Kalahari, he felt compelled – in a paper entitled 'The Predatory Transition from Ape to Man' – to share his belief that our species had emerged from its simian back-ground because we were killers and cannibals; that the Weapon had fathered the Man; that all subsequent history revolved around the possession and development of superior weapons; and that, by implication, men must adjust their

(235)

society to its weapons rather than weapons to the needs of society.

Dart's disciple, Robert Ardrey, was moved to rank the paper alongside The Communist Manifesto *in its long-term effects on ideology.*

In 1947–8, while excavating the Makapansgat Limeworks Cave – itself an eerie place where the Voortrekkers once massacred a tribe of Bantus – Dart had uncovered what he took to be the 'kitchen midden' of a band of Australopithecines, who, 'like Nimrod long after them', had been mighty hunters.

Although they had eaten eggs, crabs, lizards, rodents and birds, they had also butchered antelopes in quantity, to say nothing of far larger mammals: a giraffe, a cave bear, the hippo, the rhino, the elephant, the lion, two kinds of hyena – in addition to which, mixed up among the 7,000-odd bones, were a lot of baboon skulls minus *the skeletons, and the remains of a cannibal feast.*

From the fossils Dart selected one particular specimen: 'the fractured lower jaw of a 12-year-old son of a man-like ape':

> *The lad had been killed by a violent blow delivered with great accuracy on the point of the chin. The bludgeon blow was so vicious that it had shattered the jaw on both sides of the face and knocked out all the front teeth. That dramatic specimen impelled me in 1948 and the seven years following to study further their murderous and cannibalistic way of life.*

Which he did. He began by comparing the bone assemblage from Makapansgat with those of Taung and Sterkfontein (the latter, a cave site near Pretoria); and between 1949 and 1965 he published a total of thirty-nine papers elaborating his theory of an Osteodontokeratic (bone-tooth-horn) tool culture for Australopithecus.

The picture he drew of our immediate ancestors revealed them to have been right-handed; that their favourite weapon had been a bludgeon made from the distal end of an antelope humerus; that for daggers they had used horns or slivers of sharpened bone, for saws jawbones, for picks the canine teeth of carnivores; and that a mass of other bones had been smashed for the extraction of marrow.

Noticing, too, that the tail vertebrae were almost invariably missing, Dart suggested these had been waved about as flails or whips or signalling flags. Also, because the skulls of both baboon and Australopithecus *appeared to have been deliberately mutilated, he suggested the occupants of the cave had been 'professional head-hunters'. He concluded:*

The blood-bespattered, slaughter-gutted archives of human history, from the earliest Egyptian or Sumerian records to the most recent atrocities of the Second World War, accord with early universal cannibalism, with animal and human sacrificial practices or their substitutes in formalised religion and worldwide scalping, head hunting, body mutilating and necrophilic practices in proclaiming this common bloodlust differentiator, this predaceous habit, this mark of Cain that separates man dietetically from his anthropoidal relatives and allies him rather with the deadliest carnivora.

The style alone suggests that something is seriously wrong.

◆

Berkeley, California, 1969

In the People's Park, I was buttonholed by a hippie, prematurely aged.

'Stop the killing!' he said. 'Stop the killing!'

'You wouldn't by any chance', I said, 'think of telling a tiger to chew cud?'

I got up, ready to run for it.

'Shit!' he shouted.

'Think of Hitler!' I shouted back. 'Think of Rudolph Hess! Always snooping in each other's vegie picnic-baskets.'

◆

The number of murders committed during Lent is greater, I am told, than at any other time of the year. A man under the influence of a bean dietary (for this is the principal food of the Greeks during their fasts) will be in an apt humour for

enriching the shrine of his Saint, and passing a knife through
his next-door neighbour.

A. W. *Kinglake,* Eothen

◆

Witwatersrand University, Johannesburg, 1983

Professor Raymond Dart's ninetieth birthday party in the
Department of Anatomy. The old man was swinging about a
haematite dumb-bell with which he hoped to keep his frontal
lobes in shape. In a clangorous voice, he explained how to be
right-handed was to be left-brained: yet if you exercised both
hands equally, you exercised both halves of the brain.

Two black students dipped their biscuits delicately in their tea
cups, and giggled.

After the party, two of Dart's junior colleagues took me along
the passage to see the Taung Child. What an object! You had the
impression of a very wise little person staring at you down the
ages through a pair of binoculars.

The damage to the skull, they said, had nothing to do with
violence. Before fossilisation, it had simply been squashed by
the compacting layers of breccia.

They also allowed me to handle the boy's 'broken jaw' from
Makapansgat. It was greyish-black, not from being cooked but
from magnesium staining. Again, they said, the damage can
only have been caused by 'shearing', as a result of subsidence in
the strata.

So much for the barrage of nonsense raised on the evidence of
these two specimens.

◆

Swartkrans, Transvaal

With 'Bob' Brain for a day's excavation at the Swartkrans
Cave: he has been working here for nineteen seasons. Standing
above the cave shaft, I looked in one direction across a sweep of
grassy hills towards the High Veldt, in the other at the glinting
roofs of the Sterkfontein site and, beyond, the mountainous
spoil-heap of the Krugersdorp Mine.

The surface of the ground was broken by small jagged boulders, which made walking very difficult. There was a scarlet aloe in flower but there were no trees or, rather, no trees on the plain. Yet, inside the cave mouth, a stinkwood reared its spotted trunk, its leaves giving shade to the excavation. Only in protected places can seedlings survive the bushfires and frost.

Brain showed me the breccia which has yielded so many fossils of the muscular, 'King-Kong-like' form of Australopithecus, A. robustus: a creature known to have co-existed in this valley with the first man, Homo habilis, more than two million years ago.

The foreman, George, was a seasoned excavator. He would dig out one cubic foot at a time, and pass the contents through a griddle. Brain would take each fragment of bone, and scrutinise it under a glass.

In the heat of the day, we rested inside his hut. On the bookshelf was a copy of Sir Thomas Browne's Religio Medici. It was here that Brain wrote the greater part of his book, The Hunters or the Hunted? – the most compelling detective story I have ever read.

Brain, the Director of the Transvaal Museum in Pretoria, is a quiet, meditative, self-effacing man of ascetic convictions and limitless patience. His father was an English entomologist who went out to Rhodesia to work in pest control. His mother was Afrikaans. He is the great-great nephew of Eugène Marais, the poet, naturalist and recluse, whose Soul of the White Ant was plagiarised by Maeterlinck.

Brain has defined the true naturalist as 'a man who is in love with the world', and believes the only way of approaching nature is to try and see things the way they are 'without filters'. He is haunted by the fragility of human life, and always looking for ways of preserving it.

He hates being locked into any one discipline and has, at one time or another – with a kind of 'Taoist' abnegation – immersed himself in zoology, geology, prehistory and climatology. He has written on the behaviour of monkeys; on geckoes; on chameleons; and on the side-winding adder of the Namib Desert. Once he has finished with Swartkrans, he intends to go back to protozoa – 'those single-celled bundles of vitality', to be found in the most brackish desert wells, and which eat, reproduce and die within the space of a few hours.

As a young man, in 1955, Brain attended the Third Panafrican Congress of Prehistory and heard Raymond Dart expounding his views on the Bloodbath. He felt that man, as a species, was being libelled – and he was perhaps the only person present who knew why.

He had, it happened, been working as a soil geologist on the breccias of Makapansgat and doubted that Dart was justified in interpreting every scrap of bone in the cave as a tool or weapon. Besides, although murder and cannibalism did occur, sporadically, throughout the animal kingdom – usually as a response to overcrowding or stress – the idea that murder made man made no evolutionary sense.

For ten years, Brain mulled over Dart's thesis; and, on becoming Director of the Museum, he decided to take the matter in hand.

In the Sterkfontein valley there are three dolomitic limestone caves where hominid fossils have been found: Sterkfontein itself, Swartkrans and Kromdraai. Once he had satisfied himself that conditions here were essentially the same as at Makapansgat, he set to work.

Each of the caves is filled with a breccia of bone and sediment which has squashed down in layers over a period of two to three million years. The bones vary in size from those of an elephant to those of a mouse. Among them are several species of extinct baboon and two forms of Australopithecus: at Sterkfontein, the earlier, 'gracile' A. africanus; at Swartkrans and Kromdraai, its descendant, the muscular A. robustus.

There are also the bones, not many, of man.

Some of these hominid bones do show unmistakable signs of a violent end. If it could be shown that other hominids had brought them into the cave, they would have to face the charges of murder and cannibalism. If not, not.

Brain subjected about 20,000 bones to a meticulous 'forensic' examination: to decide how each one found its way into the cave and how it came to be in its present condition. Some bones were perhaps washed in by floodwaters. Some were brought there by porcupines, which are known to hoard bones and sharpen their teeth on them. The smaller rodents will have arrived in owl pellets. The bones of the larger mammals – elephant, hippo, lion – will probably have been the work of scavenging hyenas.

But none of this alters the general picture: that all three caves were the lairs of carnivores, and that the overwhelming majority of bones had belonged to animals which had been killed outside the cave, and dragged 'home' to be eaten in the darkness. The fossils represented the discarded food remains.

It is unnecessary to go over the ingenuity of Brain's method: except to point out that all those antelope bones which Dart claimed were bludgeons and daggers and so forth were precisely those parts of the skeleton which a big cat would leave after its meal.

As for the scarcity of hominid fossils – other than the skull and jawbones – Brain observed how, while eating a baboon, a cheetah will crunch up most of the skeleton, except the extremities and the skull. The slight 'mutilation' sometimes found at the base of the skull was explained by the animal's habit of breaking the braincase at its weakest point (the foramen magnum) and then licking out the contents.

A primate skeleton is that much more fragile and digestible than that of an antelope.

◆

All big cats kill with a neck bite – in common with the executioner's axe, the guillotine and the garrotte. In his Reflections on the Guillotine, Camus records how his father, a solid petit bourgeois of Oran, was so outraged by a gruesome murder that he went to the man's public guillotining – and came away vomiting helplessly.

◆

The sensation of being mauled by a big cat may, as we know from Dr Livingstone's experience with a lion, be slightly less horrific than one imagined, 'It causes', he wrote, 'a kind of dreaminess, in which there was no sense of pain nor feeling of terror. It was like what patients under chloroform describe who

(241)

see all the operation but feel not the knife . . . This peculiar state is probably produced in all animals killed by the carnivores; and, if so, is a merciful provision by our benevolent creator for lessening the pain of death.'

Missionary Travels

◆

Transvaal Museum, Pretoria

An afternoon with Dr Elizabeth Vrba, a palaeontologist, Brain's chief assistant – and a spellbinding talker! We sat on the floor of the so-called Red Room and handled, with white gloves, such famous fossils as 'Mrs Ples': an almost complete skull of A. africanus *found by the late Robert Broom in the 1930s.*

To have in one hand the delicate jawbone of africanus *and in the other the huge grinding molars of* robustus *was like handling the horseshoe of a Shetland pony and that of a Shire horse.*

The Sterkfontein Valley fossils are all late compared to those of Kenya and Ethiopia, where the archaic, midget form of Australopithecus, A. afarensis *(the type specimen is 'Lucy'), is now believed to have been walking upright around six million years ago. The earliest 'South Africans' are, on present showing, about half that age.*

Elizabeth Vrba showed me how the three forms of Australopithecus *represent three stages in an evolutionary chain, becoming bigger and more muscular in answer to progressively drier and more open conditions.*

At what point the first man splits off from this line is a question the experts are going to argue ad infinitum. *Every fieldworker wants to find* HIM. *But, as Brain warned, 'To find a beautiful fossil, and then hitch your reputation to it, is no longer to see the fossil.'*

The fact is that, at a date some time after 2·5 million, there appears in eastern Africa a small, agile creature with a very startling development to his frontal lobes. In all three stages of Australopithecus, *the proportion of body to brain stays constant. In man, there is a sudden explosion.*

Elizabeth Vrba has written a series of internationally acclaimed papers on the rates of evolutionary change. It was she who sharpened my awareness of the debate between the 'gradualists' and the 'jumpers'.

Orthodox Darwinians believe that evolution proceeds in a stately continuum. Each generation will differ imperceptibly from its parents; and when the differences are compounded, the species crosses a genetic 'watershed' and a new creature, worthy of a new Linnaean name, comes into being.

The 'jumpers', on the other hand – in keeping with the brutal transitions of the twentieth century – insist that each species is an entity with an abrupt origin and an abrupt end; and that evolution proceeds in short bursts of turmoil followed by long periods of idleness.

Most evolutionists believe that climate is a motor of evolutionary change.

Species, on the whole, are conservative and resistant to change. They will go on and on, like partners in a shaky marriage, making minor adjustments here and there, until they reach a bursting point beyond which they cannot cope.

In a climatic catastrophe, with its habitat fragmenting all around, a small *breeding community may get hived off from its fellows and stranded in an isolated pocket, usually at the far end of its ancestral range, where it must transform itself or die out.*

The 'jump' from one species to the next, when it does come, comes quickly and cleanly. Suddenly, the new arrivals no longer reply to old mating calls. In fact, once these 'isolating mechanisms' take hold, there can be no genetic backsliding, no loss of new features, no going back.

Sometimes the new species, invigorated by the change, may re-colonise its former haunts, and replace its predecessors.

The process of 'jumping' in isolation has been called 'allopatric speciation' ('in another country') and will explain why, whereas biologists find countless variations within a species – in body size or pigmentation – no one has ever found an intermediate form between one species and the next.

The search for the origin of man may thus turn out to be a hunt for a chimera.

The necessary isolation required for 'jumping' can, it seems, equally well exist along a migration path or track – which is, after all, an area of territory spun out into a continuous line, as one would spin a fleece into yarn.

Reflecting on the above, I was struck by the similarity between 'allopatry' and the Aboriginal myths of creation: in which each totemic species is born, in isolation, at one particular point on the map, and then spreads out in lines across the country.

All species must 'jump' eventually, but some jump more readily than others. Elizabeth Vrba showed me graphs on which she had plotted the lineage of two sister clades of antelopes, the Alcephalini *and* Aepycerotini, *both of which shared a common ancestor in the Miocene.*

The Alcephalini, *the family to which the wildebeeste and hartebeeste belong, have 'specialised' teeth and stomachs for feeding in arid conditions, and have thrown up about forty species over the past six and a half million years. The impala, a member of the* Aepycerotini, *being a generalist with a capacity to thrive in a variety of climates has remained the same to this day.*

Evolutionary change, she said, was once hailed as the hallmark of success. We now know better: the successful are the ones that last.

◆

The really important news is that we belong to a most stable lineage.

The ancestors of man were 'generalists': resilient and resourceful creatures who, over the same period as the impala, will have had to wriggle out of many a tight corner without having to speciate at every turn. It follows that when you do find a major architectural change in the hominid line, there must be some ferocious external pressure to account for it. Also, that we may have a far more rigid moral, instinctive backbone than we hitherto suspected.

Since the close of the Miocene, there have, in fact, been only two such major 'leaps forward', separated one from the other by an interval of roughly four million years: the first associated with Australopithecus, *the second with man:*

1 *The restructuring of the pelvis and foot from those of a brachiating forest ape to those of a walker on the plain; from a four-limb to a two-limb plan; from a creature that moved with its hands to one whose hands were free for other things.*
2 *The rapid expansion of the brain.*

Both 'leaps', it turns out, coincide with sudden shifts towards a colder and drier climate.

Around ten million years ago, our hypothetical ancestor, the Miocene ape, will have spent his days in the high-canopy rain forest which covered most of Africa at the time.

Like the chimpanzee and gorilla, he will probably have spent each night in a different spot, yet confined his wanderings to a few unadventurous square miles of territory, where food was always available, where the rain fell in runnels down the tree-trunks and sunlight then spattered the leaves; and where he could swing to safety from the 'horrors' on the forest floor.

(From Lake Térnéfine in Chad I have seen the fossil skull of a Miocene hyenid: an animal the size of a bull with jaws to slice off the leg of an elephant.)

At the close of the Miocene, however, the trees began to dwindle in size. For reasons as yet unclear, the Mediterranean seems to have absorbed about 6 per cent of the world's oceanic salt. Because of the decrease in salinity, the seas around Antarctica began to ice up. The size of the ice cap doubled. The sea level fell; and the Mediterranean, cut off by a land-bridge at Gibraltar, became one vast evaporating salt-pan.

In Africa, the rain forest shrank to small pockets – where the arboreal apes are at present to be found – while over the eastern side of the continent, the vegetation became a 'mosaic savannah': of open woodland and grass country, with alternating seasons of wet and dry, plenty and want, floodwater and lakes of cracked mud. This was the 'home' of Australopithecus.

(245)

He was an animal that walked and probably carried loads: upright walking, with its development of the deltoid muscle, seems to presuppose the bearing of weights, probably food and children, from one place to another. Yet his broad shoulders, long arms, and marginally prehensile toes suggest that, in his 'archaic' form at least, he still lived partly or took refuge in the trees.

◆

In the 1830s Wilhelm von Humboldt, the father of modern linguistics, suggested that man walked upright because of discourse which would not then 'be muffled or made dumb by the ground'.

Yet four million years of upright walking had no effect whatever on the development of speech.

◆

All the same, the 'graciles' and the 'robusts' had, it seems, the ability to fashion simple tools, of bone and even stone. The wear on these tools, when examined under a microscope, suggests they were used, not for butchery, but for rooting up bulbs and tubers. Australopithecus may have snaffled a young gazelle if one came within his grasp. He may even have hunted, systematically, like a chimpanzee. But he was still more or less vegetarian.

As for the first man, he was an omnivore. His teeth are those of an omnivore. From the stone tools strewn around his campsites, he seems to have dismembered carcasses and eaten them. He was, however, probably more scavenger than hunter. His appearance coincides with the second climatic upheaval.

Climatologists have learnt that, between 3·2 and 2·6 million years ago, there occurred a sharp plunge in world temperature known as the First Northern Glaciation, in that the North Polar Ice Cap for the first time froze. In Africa, the results were catastrophic.

Up and down the Great Rift Valley, the woodlands were swept away and replaced by open steppe: a wilderness of sand and gravel, patchy grass and thorn bushes, with taller trees lingering in the watercourse.

Thornscrub was the country into which the brain of the first man expanded: the Crown of Thorns was not an accidental crown.

◆

'Man', said Elizabeth Vrba, 'was born in adversity. Adversity, in this case, is aridity.'
  'You mean that man was born in the desert?'
  'Yes,' she said. 'The desert. Or at least the semi-desert.'
  'Where the sources of water were always undependable?'
  'Yes.'
  'But there were plenty of beasts about?'
  'A carnivore doesn't care where he lives so long as he gets his meat. It must have been terrible!'

The evolutionary record is full of 'arms races' between predator and prey, since Natural Selection will favour prey with the best defences and predators with the best killing equipment.
  A tortoise retires into its shell. A hedgehog raises its spines. A moth will camouflage itself against the bark of a tree, and a rabbit will bolt down a burrow too small for the fox to follow; but man was defenceless on a treeless plain. The response of robustus *was to put on more muscle. We used our brains.*

◆

It was nonsense, Dr Vrba continued, to study the emergence of man in a vacuum, without pondering the fate of other species over the same time-scale. The fact was that around 2·5 million, just as man took his spectacular 'jump', there was a 'tremendous churning over of species'.
  'All hell', she said, 'broke loose among the antelopes.'
  Everywhere in eastern Africa, the more sedentary browsers gave way to 'brainier' migratory grazers. The basis for a sedentary existence was simply no longer there.
  'And sedentary species,' she said, 'like sedentary genes, are terribly successful for a while, but in the end they are self-destructive.'

In arid country, resources are never stable from one year to the next. A stray thunderstorm may make a temporary oasis of

(247)

green, while only a few miles off the land remains parched and bare. To survive in drought, therefore, any species must adopt one of two stratagems: to allow for the worst and dig in; to open itself to the world and move.

Some desert seeds lie dormant for decades. Some desert rodents only stir from their burrows at night. The weltwitchia, a spectacular, strap-leaved plant of the Namib Desert, lives for thousands of years on its daily diet of morning mist. But migratory animals must move – or be ready to move.

Elizabeth Vrba said, at some point in the conversation, that antelopes are stimulated to migrate by lightning.

'So', I said, 'are the Kalahari Bushmen. They also "follow" the lightning. For where the lightning has been, there will be water, greenery and game.'

—

When I rest my feet my mind also ceases to function.
J. G. Hamann

The linguistic ability of Homo habilis may have been limited to grunts and howls and hisses: we shall never know. A brain does not survive the process of fossilisation. Yet its contours and lineaments do leave their imprint inside the skull. Casts can be taken; and these 'endocasts' be set beside one another, and compared.

Paris, Musée de l'Homme, 1984

In his meticulous office, Professor Yves Coppens – one of the most lucid minds in the fossil man business – had lined up a series of such endocasts; the moment he passed from Australopithecus to man, I had a sense of something startling and new.

Not only does the brain increase in size (by almost half), but also in shape. The parietal and temporal regions – the seats of sensory intelligence and learning – are transformed and become far more complex. Broca's Area, a region known to be inseparable from speech co-ordination, makes its first appear-

ance. The membranes thicken. The synapses multiply: as do the veins and arteries which irrigate the brain with blood.

Inside the mouth, too, there are major architectural changes, especially in the alveolar region where the tongue hits the palate. And since man is by definition the Language Animal, it is hard to see what these changes are about unless they are for language.

The subsequent stages of human evolution – through Homo erectus *to* H. sapiens sapiens *– do not, in Coppens's view, warrant the status of a separate species. Rather, they should be seen as transformation of the original model:* Homo habilis.

'Long experience of Homo habilis', *he writes in* Le Singe, l'Afrique et l'homme, *'has led me to believe that it is to him we should address the question: Who are we? Where have we come from? Where are we going? His sudden triumph seems so brilliant, so extraordinary and so new, that I would gladly choose this species, and this part of the world, to situate the origin of memory and language.'*

◆

'I know this may sound far-fetched,' I said to Elizabeth Vrba, 'but if I were asked, "What is the big brain for"?, I would be tempted to say, "For singing our way through the wilderness."'

She looked a bit startled. Then, reaching for a drawer in her desk, she fished out a watercolour: an artist's impression of a family of the First Men, and their children, tramping in single file across an empty waste.

She smiled and said, 'I also think the hominids migrated.'

◆

Who, then, was the killer in the cave?

Leopards prefer to eat their kill in the darkest possible recesses. And at an early stage of his inquiry, Brain believed it was they who were responsible for the carnage: which, indeed, they may have been, in part.

Among the fossils in the Red Room he showed me the incomplete calvarium of a young male Homo habilis. *Towards the front of the skull there are the marks of a brain tumour: so he may have been the idiot of the band. On the base, there are two neat holes about an inch apart. Brain then took the fossil skull of a leopard found in the same stratum and showed me how the lower canines fit perfectly into the two holes. A leopard drags its kill by fastening its jaws around the skull, as a cat will carry a mouse.*

The holes were in exactly the right position.

◆

Bhimtal, Kumaon, India

One afternoon, I walked over to see the Shaivite saddhu in his hermitage on the opposite hill. He was a very saintly person, who took my offering of a few rupees and wrapped them, reverentially, in the corner of his orange robe. He sat cross-legged on his leopard-skin. His beard flowed over his knees and, while he boiled the water for tea, the cockroaches crawled up and down it. Below the hermitage there was a leopard cave. On moonlit nights the leopard would come into the garden, and he and the saddhu would look at each other.

But the older people in the village could recall with horror the time of the 'man-eaters', when no one was safe, even behind bolted doors.

At Rudraprayag, to the north of here, a man-eater ate more than 125 *people before Jim Corbett shot him. In one case, the beast battered down the door of a stable; crawled over or under the bodies of forty live goats* without touching a single one; *and finally grabbed the young goatherd, asleep, by himself, in the farthest corner of the hut.*

◆

Transvaal Museum

A leopard will turn 'man-eater' usually – though not always – as a result of an accident, such as a missing canine. But once the animal gets a taste for human flesh, it will touch no other.

When Brain came to tot up the percentages of primate fossils: that is, of baboons and hominids, both in the 'robust' level at Swartkrans and the africanus *level at Sterkfontein, he found to his astonishment that primate bones accounted for* 52·9 *per cent and* 69·8 *per cent of the total prey spectrum. Antelopes and other mammals made up the rest. Whichever beast (or beasts)* used the caves as its charnel-house, it had a taste for 'primate'.

Brain toyed with the idea that 'man-eating' leopards had been at work; but there were several snags to this hypothesis:

1   Statistics from African game-parks show that baboons account for no more than 2 per cent of a normal leopard's diet.

2   In the upper levels at Swartkrans, when the cave was definitely tenanted by leopards, they left plentiful remains of their usual prey, the springbok, while baboons are down to 3 per cent.

Was it possible that leopards had passed through an 'abnormal' man-eating phase — and then returned to their previous habits?

Besides, when Elizabeth Vrba came to analyse the bovid bones from the caves, she found a preponderance of animals, such as the giant hartebeeste, too hefty for a leopard to cope with. Some other, more powerful carnivore must have been at work. Which?

There are three principal candidates, all now extinct, all of whom have left their fossils in the Sterkfontein Valley.

a   The long-legged hunting hyenas, Hyenictis and Euryboas.

b   The macheirodonts, or sabre-tooth cats.

c   The genus Dinofelis, 'the false sabre-tooth'.

The sabre-tooths had huge neck muscles and a powerful leap; and in their upper jaws they had scythe-like canines, serrated along the cutting edge, which, with a downward thrust, they would plunge into the neck of their prey. They were especially adapted for felling large herbivores. Their carnassial teeth were more efficient as meat-slicers than those of any other carnivore. Yet their lower jaws were weak: so weak that they were unable to finish off a skeleton.

Griff Ewer once suggested that the bone-crushing molars of the hyena had evolved in answer to the plentiful supply of uneaten carcasses which sabre-tooths left behind.

Obviously, the Sterkfontein Valley caves were occupied by a variety of carnivores, over a very long stretch of time.

Brain felt that a proportion of the bones, especially those of the larger antelopes, could have been brought there by the sabre-tooths and hyenas, working in tandem. The hunting hyenas, too, might have been responsible for bringing in some hominids.

But let us pass to the third alternative.

Dinofelis *was a cat less agile than a leopard or cheetah but far more solidly built. It had straight, dagger-like killing teeth, midway in form between a sabre-tooth's and, say, the modern tiger's. Its lower jaw could slam shut; and since, with its slightly cumbersome build, it must have hunted by stealth, it must also have hunted by night. It may have been spotted. It could have been striped. It might, like a panther, have been black.*

Its bones have been unearthed from the Transvaal to Ethiopia: that is, the original range of man.

In the Red Room, I've just held in my hands a fossil skull of Dinofelis, *a perfect specimen, patinated treacly brown. I made a point of articulating the lower jaw and staring steadily into the fangs as I closed them.*

The skull comes from one of three complete Dinofelis *skeletons – a male, a female and a 'boy' – which were found fossilised along with eight baboons* and no other animals *at Bolt's Farm, a short way from Swartkrans, in* 1947–8. *Their finder, H. B. S. Cooke, suggested that the* Dinofelis *'family' had been out baboon hunting, when they had all fallen into some natural pit, and all died together.*

A strange end! But no stranger than the still unanswered questions: Why, in these caves, were there so many baboons and hominids? Why so few antelopes and other species?

Brain puzzled over the possibilities with his habitual caution, and, tentatively, in the final paragraphs of The Hunters or the Hunted? put forward two complementary hypotheses.

The hominids might not have been dragged into the cave: they might have lived there along with their destroyer. On Mount Suswa, a dormant volcano in Kenya, there are long lava tunnels, with leopards living in the depths and baboon troops sheltering in the entrance by night. The leopards have a living larder at their own front door.

In the Transvaal, the winter nights are cold: so cold that the number of baboons in the High Veldt is limited by the number of caves or shelters available for sleeping in. At the time of the First Northern Glaciation, there may have been a hundred nights of frost. And in the cold, let us now imagine robustus: migrants who will have trekked to the highlands in summer and retired to the valleys in winter, without defences but their own brute strength; without fire; without warmth but their own huddled bodies; night-blind, yet forced to share their quarters with a glitter-eyed cat, who, now and then, will have prowled out to grab a straggler.

The second hypothesis introduces an idea to set the head spinning.

Could it be, Brain asks, that Dinofelis was a specialist predator on the primates?

'A combination of robust jaws', he writes, 'and a well developed component in the dentition would have allowed Dinofelis to eat all parts of a primate skeleton except the skull. The hypothesis that Dinofelis was a specialist killer of the primates is persuasive.'

◆

Could it be, one is tempted to ask, that Dinofelis was Our Beast? A Beast set aside from all the other Avatars of Hell? The Arch-Enemy who stalked us, stealthily and cunningly, wherever we went? But whom, in the end, we got the better of?

Coleridge once jotted in a notebook, 'The Prince of Darkness is a Gentleman.' What is so beguiling about a specialist predator is the idea of an intimacy with the Beast! For if, originally, there was one particular Beast, would we not want to fascinate him as he fascinated us? Would we not want to charm him, as the angels charmed the lions in Daniel's cell?

The snakes, scorpions and other menacing creatures of the savannah – which, apart from their zoological actuality, have enjoyed a second career in the Hells of the Mystics – could never *have threatened our existence, as such; never have postulated the end of our world. A specialist killer could have – which is why, however tenuous the evidence, we must take him seriously.*

'Bob' Brain's achievement, as I see it – whether we allow for one big cat, for several cats, or for horrors like the hunting hyena – is to have reinstated a figure whose presence has grown dimmer and dimmer since the close of the Middle Ages: the Prince of Darkness in all his sinister magnificence.

Without straining the bounds of scientific rigour (as I undoubtedly have), he has laid bare the record of a tremendous victory – a victory on which we yet may build – when man, in becoming man, got the better of the powers of destruction.

For suddenly, in the upper levels of Swartkrans and Sterkfontein, man is there. He is in charge and the predators are no longer with him.

Compared to this victory, the rest of our achievements may be seen as so many frills. You could say we are a species on holiday. Yet perhaps it had to be a Pyrrhic victory: has not the whole of history been a search for false monsters? A nostalgia for the Beast we have lost? For the Gentleman who bowed out gracefully – and left us with the weapon in our hand?

34

ROLF AND I WERE having an evening drink when one of Estrella's nurses came running over to say there was a man on the radio-telephone. I hoped it was Arkady. After all my outpouring on to paper I longed for a session of his cool, appraising talk.

We both hurried over to the dispensary only to find it was not a man on the air, but a very gruff-voiced woman: Eileen Houston, of the Aboriginal Arts Bureau in Sydney.

'Has Winston finished his painting yet?' she growled.

'He has,' Rolf said.

'OK. Tell him I'll be over at nine sharp.'

The line went dead.

'Bitch,' said Rolf.

Winston Japurula, the most 'important' artist working at Cullen, had, only the week before, completed a major canvas and was waiting for Mrs Houston to come and buy it from him. Like many artists, he was generous with hand-outs, and had run up big debts at the store.

Mrs Houston, who described herself as 'the doyenne of dealers in Aboriginal Art', had the habit of driving round the settlements to check up on her artists. She brought them paint and brushes and canvas, and would pay for finished work by cheque. She was a very determined woman. She always camped in the bush, alone – and was never not in a hurry.

Next morning, Winston was waiting for her, cross-legged, naked to the waist, on a patch of level ground beside the petrol drums. He was an ageing voluptuary, with rolls of fat spilling over his paint-spattered shorts and an immense down-curving mouth. His sons and grandsons bore the stamp of his magnificent ugliness. He was doodling a monster on a scrap of card. He had acquired, by osmosis, the temperament and mannerisms of Lower West Broadway.

His 'policeman' or ritual manager, a younger man in brown slacks called Bobby, was on hand to make sure Winston didn't leak any sacred knowledge.

At nine sharp, the boys sighted Mrs Houston's red Land Cruiser coming up the airstrip. She got out, walked towards the group and set her haunches on a camping-stool.

'Morning, Winston,' she nodded.

'Morning,' he said, without moving.

She was a big woman in a beige 'battle-dress'. Her scarlet sunhat, like a topee, was rammed down over a head of greying curls. Her pale, heat-ravaged cheeks tapered off into a very pointed chin.

'What are we waiting for?' she asked. 'I thought I'd come to see a painting.'

Winston fiddled with his hairstring and, with a wave, deputed his grandsons to fetch it from the store.

Six of them came back carrying a large stretched canvas, say, seven foot by five, protected from the dust with a clear plastic sheet. They set it gingerly on the ground, and unwrapped it.

Mrs Houston blinked. I watched her holding back a smile of pleasure. She had commissioned Winston to paint a 'white' picture. But this, I think, was beyond her expectations.

So many Aboriginal artists used strident colour schemes. Here, simply, were six white to creamy-white circles, painted in meticulous 'pointillist' dots, on a background which varied from white to blueish white to the palest ochre. In the space between the circles there were a few snakelike squiggles in an equally pale lilac grey.

Mrs Houston worked her lips. You could almost hear her mental calculations: a white gallery . . . a white abstraction . . . White on White . . . Malevich . . . New York . . .

She dabbed the sweat from her brow and pulled herself together.

'Winston!' she pointed a finger at the canvas.

'Yairs.'

'Winston, you didn't use the titanium white like I said! What's the use my paying for expensive pigments if you don't even use them? You've been using *zinc* white. Haven't you? Answer me!'

Winston's reaction was to fold his arms across his face and peer through a chink, like a child playing peek-a-boo.

'Did you, or did you not, use the titanium white?'

'NO!' Winston shouted, without lowering his arms.

'I thought not,' she said, and raised her chin in satisfaction.

She then looked again at the canvas and spotted a tiny tear, less than an inch long, on the edge of one of the circles.

'And look!' she cried. 'You've torn it. Winston, you've *torn* the canvas. Do you know what that means? This painting will have to be re-lined. I shall have to send this painting to the restorers in Melbourne. And it'll cost at least three hundred dollars. It's a shame.'

Winston, who had dropped his defences, wrapped his arms around his face again and presented a blank front to the dealer.

'It's a shame,' she repeated.

The onlookers stared at the canvas as though they were staring at a corpse.

Mrs Houston's jaw began to quiver. She had gone too far, and would have to assume a more conciliatory tone.

'But it's a nice painting, Winston,' she said. 'It'll do nicely for our travelling exhibition. I told you we were making a collection, didn't I? Of all the best Pintupi artists? Didn't I? Do you hear me?'

Her voice sounded anxious. Winston said nothing.

'Do you hear me?'

'Yairs,' he drawled, and let down his arms.

'Well, that's all right, then, isn't it?' She tried to laugh.

'Yairs.'

She took a pad and pencil from her shoulder bag.

'So what's the story, Winston?'

'What story?'

'The story of the painting.'

'I painted it.'

'I know you painted it. I mean, what's the Dreaming story? I can't sell a painting without a story. You know that!'

'Do I?'

'You do.'

'Old Man,' he said.

'Thank you,' she started scribbling on the pad. 'So the painting's an Old Man Dreaming?'

'Yairs.'

'And?'

'And what?'

'The rest of the story.'

'What story?'

'The story of the Old Man,' she said, furiously. '*What* is the Old Man doing?'

'Walking,' said Winston, who doodled a double dotted line in the sand.

'Of course, he's walking,' she said. 'Where's he walking to?'

Winston bugged his eyes at the canvas, and looked up at his 'policeman'.

Bobby winked.

'I asked you,' said Mrs Houston, mouthing her syllables. '*Where* is the Old Man walking?'

Winston drew in his lips and said nothing.

'Well, what's that?' She pointed to one of the white circles.

'Salt-pan,' he said.

'And that one?'

'Salt-pan.'

'That one?'

'Salt-pan. All of 'em salt-pans.'

'So the Old Man's walking over salt-pans?'

'Yairs.'

'Not much of a story there!' Mrs Houston shrugged. 'What about those squiggles in the middle?'

'Pitjuri,' he said.

Pitjuri is a mild narcotic which Aboriginals chew to suppress hunger. Winston rolled his head and eyes from side to side, like a man 'on' pitjuri. The audience laughed. Mrs Houston did not.

'I see,' she said. Then, thinking aloud to herself, she began to jot down the outline of the story, 'The ancient white-bearded Ancestor, dying of thirst, is trudging home across a glittering salt-pan and finds, on the farther shore, a plant of pitjuri . . .'

She put her pencil between her lips and looked at me for confirmation.

I smiled sweetly.

'Yes, that's nice,' she said. 'That'll make a nice beginning.'

Winston had lifted his eyes from the canvas and fastened them on her.

'I know,' she said. 'I *know*! Now we've got to fix the price, haven't we? How much did I give you last time?'

'Five hundred dollars,' he said, sourly.

'And how much did I advance you this time?'

'Two hundred.'

'That's right, Winston. You've got it right. Well, now there's the damage to be repaired. So suppose we deduct a hundred for the damage, and I'll pay you another three hundred? That's a hundred more than before. Then we'll be quits.'

Winston didn't move.

'And I'll need to take a photo of you,' she chattered on. 'I think you'd better get some more clothes on. We need a nice new photo for the catalogue.'

'No!' Winston bellowed.

'What do you mean, no?' Mrs Houston looked very shocked. 'You don't want your photo taken?'

'NO!' he bellowed louder. 'I want more money!'

'More money? I . . . I . . . don't understand.'

'I said MORE . . . MONEY!'

She assumed an aggrieved expression, as though dealing with an ungrateful child, and then said, icily, 'How much?'

Again, Winston shielded his face with his arms.

'How much do you want?' she persisted. 'I'm not here to waste my time. I've named my price. You name yours.'

He didn't move.

'This is ridiculous,' she said.

He said nothing.

'I'm not making another offer,' she said. 'You've got to name your price.'

Nothing.

'Go on. Say it. How much?'

Winston's lower arm shot downwards, making a triangular slit through which he shouted, 'SIX THOUSAND DOLLARS!'

Mrs Houston nearly fell off her stool. 'Six thousand dollars! You have to be joking!'

'Well, why are you asking seven fuckin' thousand dollars for one of my paintings in your fuckin' exhibition in Adelaide?'

GIVEN THE LINE-UP *of real monsters confronting the First Man,* it is out of the question *to suppose that tribal fighting and warfare were a part of the original scheme of things – only the classical forms of co-operation.*

Ib'n Khaldūn writes that whereas God gave animals their natural limbs for defence, he gave man the ability to think. The power of thought allowed him to manufacture weapons – lances instead of horns, swords instead of claws, shields in place of thick skins – and to organise communities for producing them.
  Since any one individual was powerless against the wild animal, especially the predatory animal, man could protect himself only through communal defence. But, in conditions of civilisation, the war of all against all broke out with equipment designed to keep away the predators.

What was the weapon to deter a beast like Dinofelis?
  Fire, certainly. I would guess that one day, somewhere, an excavator will discover that Homo habilis *did use fire.*
  As for 'conventional' weapons, a hand-axe? Useless! A club? Worse than useless! Only a spear or lance, like the one St George rams into the jaws of the dragon, would have the required effect: a lance aimed and thrust, with split-second timing, by a young man at the height of his physical powers.

Democritus (fr. 154) said it was absurd for men to vaunt their superiority over the animals when, in matters of great importance, it was they who were our teachers: the spider for weaving and mending; the swallow for architecture; the swan and the nightingale for singing.
  To which one could go on adding indefinitely: the bat for radar, the dolphin for sonar and, as Ib'n Khaldūn said, horns for the lance.

Sasriem, Namib Desert

Herds of ostrich, zebra and gemsbok (the African oryx) moving in the early light against a backdrop of orange dunes. The valley floor was a sea of grey pebbles.

The Park Warden said of the straight lances of the oryx that they were wonderfully effective against a leopard but were, in practice, a case of over-specialisation: two males, when fighting, would sometimes run each other through.

When we got out of the car there was an oryx close by, standing behind a bush. The warden warned us to be careful: they have been known to impale a man.

◆

In one Biblical tradition, the 'mark' God set upon Cain was 'horns': to defend himself from the beasts of the wilderness, who thirsted for vengeance for the death of their master, Abel.

◆

The peculiar image, in Pope Gregory the Great's Moralia, of Christ's body as a hook for the Beast.

◆

The third invention, invisible to archaeologists, will have been the sling—fibre or leather—in which a mother carried her nursing child, leaving her hands free for gathering roots or berries.

The sling was thus the first vehicle.

As Lorna Marshall writes of the !Kung Bushmen, 'They carry their children and their belongings in leather capes. The naked babies ride next to the mother supported by a sling of soft duiker leather on the left side.'

Hunting peoples have no milk from domesticated animals; and, as Mrs Marshall says, milk is what makes a baby's legs strong. The mother cannot afford to wean the child until the age of three or four or more. And either she or the father must carry it until it can keep up a day's march on its own: journeys of sixty or a hundred miles, with two or three 'sleeps' on the way.

The married couple are a unit for carriage and defence.

◆

The late C. W. Peck recorded a myth concerning the origin of weapons from western New South Wales. I suggest that its validity is universal:

Long ago, *when men had no weapons and were defenceless against the wild beasts, there was a big mob of people camped at the confluence of the Lachlan and Murrumbidgee Rivers. The day was hot. Mirages distorted the landscape, and everyone was resting in the shade. Suddenly, a horde of Giant Kangaroos attacked, crushing their victims with their powerful arms. The people fled in panic, and few survived.*

Among the survivors, however, was the headman, who called a meeting to discuss means of defence. It was at this meeting that men invented spears, shields, clubs and boomerangs. And since many of the young women had dropped their babies in the rush, it was they who invented the ingenious bark cradle.

The tale goes on to describe how the cleverest of the men, camouflaging himself with fat and dust, stole up on the Kangaroos and drove them off with fire.

There were Giant Kangaroos in prehistoric Australia – and dangerous they must have been when cornered – but they were not carnivores, not attackers.

◆

As for the young heroes, they could only become 'fit' as a result of the most rigorous training among themselves: in wrestling, grappling and the art of wielding weapons. Adolescence is the 'sparring' phase. After that, all enmities are – or should be – channelled outward on to the Adversary.

The 'war boys' are the ones who never grow up.

◆

Niger

The manager of the Campement was a Frenchwoman called Madame Marie, whose hair was the colour of goldfish and who did not like other white people. Divorced by her husband for going to bed with black men, she had lost a villa, a Mercedes, a swimming pool en forme de rognon, but she had carried away her jewels.

On the third night of my visit, she organised a soirée musicale *with equal billing for* Anou et ses Sorciers Noirs *and herself,* Marie et son Go. *When the show was over, she took one of the sorcerers to bed with her, and at two thirty had a heart attack. The sorcerer rushed from the bedroom, gibbering, 'I did not touch Madame.'*

Next day she defied the attempts of her doctor to send her to hospital and lay on her bed, stripped of make-up, gazing out across the thornscrub and sighing, 'La lumière . . . Oh! la belle lumière . . .'

Around eleven two Bororo boys arrived. They were skittishly dressed in short women's skirts and straw bonnets.

The Bororos are nomads who wander up and down the Sahel with total disdain for material possessions, concentrating all their energy and emotion into the breeding of their lovely lyre-horned cattle, and on cultivating beauty in themselves.

The boys – one with 'weight-lifter' biceps, the other slender and beautiful – had come to ask Marie if she had any spare cosmetics.

'Mais sûrement . . .' she called from the bedroom, and we all went in.

Reaching for her vanity case, she showered the contents over the bedspread, occasionally saying, 'Non, pas ça!' All the same, the boys picked up every shade of lipstick, nail varnish, eye shadow and eyebrow pencil. They wrapped their loot in a headscarf. She gave them a few back numbers of Elle *magazine. Then, dragging their sandals across the terrace, they ran off laughing.*

'It is for their ceremony,' Marie told me. 'Tonight they will both become men. You must see it! Un vrai spectacle.'

'I must!' I said.

'An hour before sunset,' she said. 'Outside the Emir's palace.'

From the roof of the Emir's palace I had a grandstand view of the courtyard, where three musicians were playing: a piper, a drummer and a man who twanged at a three-stringed instrument with a calabash for a sound-box.

The man sitting next to me, an ancien combattant, *spoke good French.*

A 'master of ceremonies' appeared and ordered two young assistants to scatter a circle of white powder, like a circus-ring, in the dust. When this was done, the young men stood guard over the space and flew at trespassers with swatches of palm fibre.

Among the audience were a lot of middle-aged Bororo ladies and their daughters. The daughters wore a kind of white wimple. The mothers were wrapped in indigo and had brass hoops jangling in their ears. They cast their eyes over prospective sons-in-law with the expertise of ladies at a bloodstock sale.

In the inner court were the young men, who for the past four years had been obliged to parade about in female dress. We heard a volley of whooping cries: then, to the rattle of drums, in walked the two boys plastered with Marie's make-up.

The 'tough' one had a pink cupid's bow around his lips; his fingernails were scarlet and his eyelids green. His strapless bouffant dress had lavender panels over a rose-coloured underskirt. The effect was ruined by a pair of fluorescent green socks and gym-shoes.

His friend, the 'beauty', wore a tight mauve turban, a sheath of green and white stripes, and had a more modern sense of fashion. He had been very careful with the lipstick, and on either cheek he had painted two neat rectangles in bands of pink and white. He had on a pair of reflecting sunglasses, and was admiring himself in a hand-mirror.

The crowd cheered.

Another young Bororo came out carrying a choice of three 'Herculean' clubs, each freshly cut from the bole of an acacia. He offered the beauty his choice of weapon.

Removing his sunglasses, the beauty pointed languidly to the biggest, popped something into his mouth, and waved to his friends on the rooftop. They howled their approval and raised their plastic boaters at spearpoint.

The master of ceremonies picked up the beauty's choice and, with the solemnity of a waiter serving a Château Lafite, presented it to the tough one.

The beauty then took up his position at the centre of the circle and, holding his sunglasses above his head, started warbling a chant in falsetto. The friend, meanwhile, swinging the club with both hands, pirouetted around the rim of the circle.

The drummer stepped up the tempo. The beauty sang as though his lungs would burst; and the tough one, whirling faster and faster, closed in. At last, with a bone-crushing thud, he whammed the club on to his friend's ribcage and the friend let out a triumphant 'Yaou . . .o . . .o . . .o . . .o . . . !' – but did not flinch.

'What was he singing?' I asked the ancien combattant.

'I can kill a lion,' he said, ' . . . I have got the biggest cock . . . I can satisfy a thousand women . . .'

'Of course,' I said.

Having repeated the same performance twice more, it was the beauty's turn to club the tough one. When that was over, the two of them – best friends and blood-brothers for life – went sauntering around the spectators, who reached their hands forward and stuck banknotes on to their face-paint.

Hand in hand, the boys went back to the palace. Two more pairs went through the same business: but they were both less 'chic'. Then they, too, retired.

The assistants erased the white circle and everyone thronged into the courtyard, waiting for something to happen.

It was almost dark when, from the inner court, there came more blood-curdling cries. Another rattle of drums, and all six boys marched in, hard and glistening, in black leather kilts, their hats stuck with ostrich feathers, swaying their shoulders, swinging their swords – as they moved in to mix with the girls.

'They are men,' said the ancien combattant.

I looked down, in the half-light, at the mass of blue and black figures, like the waves at night with a whitecap or two, and silver jewellery glinting like flecks of phosphorescence.

35

ROLF AND WENDY, TO give each other space, had set up separate establishments. Rolf and the books had the caravan. Wendy, on nights when she wanted to be alone, would sleep in a concrete lock-up. It had been the school store in the days when all lessons were in the open air.

She asked me to come and watch her at work on the dictionary. It was drizzling. A fine light rain was moving in from the west, and everyone had taken to their humpies.

I found Wendy with Old Alex, both squatting over a tray of botanical specimens: seed-pods, dried flowers, leaves and roots. He was wearing the plum velvet coat. When Wendy handed him a specimen, he would turn it over, hold it to the light, whisper to himself and then call out its name in Pintupi. She made him repeat the name a number of times: to be assured of its phonetic pronunciation. She would then tag the specimen with a label.

There was only one plant Alex didn't know: the dried-up head of a thistle. 'Come with white man,' he frowned.

'And he's right too,' Wendy turned to me. 'It's a European introduction.'

She thanked him and he walked away, his spears slung over his shoulder.

'He's the real thing,' she said, smiling after him. 'But you can't ask too much in a day – his attention wanders.'

Wendy's room was as austere as Rolf's was chaotic. She kept a few clothes in a suitcase. There was a grey metal bedstead, a wash-stand, and a telescope on a tripod. 'It's an old family thing,' she said. 'It belonged to my grandfather.'

Some nights, she would drag the bed outside and go to sleep gazing at the stars.

She picked up Alex's tray and took me to a smaller tin shed, where, laid out on trestles, were many more specimens: not only of plants, but of eggs, insects, reptiles, birds, snakes and lumps of rock.

'I'm supposed to be an ethnobotanist,' she laughed. 'But it's all got a bit out of hand.'

Alex was her best informant. You couldn't exhaust his knowledge of plants. He would reel off the names of species, when and where they would be coming into flower. He used them as a kind of calendar.

'Working out here alone,' she said, 'your head fills up with such mad ideas, and there's no one to test them out on.' She threw back her head and laughed.

'Lucky I've got Rolf,' she said. 'No idea's too mad for him.'

'Such as?'

She had never had a training in linguistics. Yet her work on the dictionary had given her an interest in the myth of Babel. Why, when Aboriginal life had been so uniform, had there been 200 languages in Australia? Could you really explain this in terms of tribalism or isolation? Surely not! She was beginning to wonder whether language itself might not relate to the distribution of the human species over the land.

'Sometimes,' she said, 'I'll ask Old Alex to name a plant and he'll answer "No name", meaning, "The plant doesn't grow in my country."'

She'd then look for an informant who *had*, as a child, lived where the plant grew – and find it did have a name after all.

The 'dry heart' of Australia, she said, was a jigsaw of microclimates, of different minerals in the soil and different plants and animals. A man raised in one part of the desert would know its flora and fauna backwards. He knew which plant attracted game. He knew his water. He knew where there were tubers underground. In other words, by *naming* all the 'things' in his territory, he could always count on survival.

'But if you took him blindfold to another country,' she said, 'he might end up lost and starving.'

'Because he'd lost his bearings?'

'Yes.'

'You're saying that man "makes" his territory by naming the "things" in it?'

'Yes, I am!' Her face lit up.

'So the basis for a universal language can never have existed?'

'Yes. Yes.'

Wendy said that, even today, when an Aboriginal mother notices the first stirrings of speech in her child, she lets it handle the 'things' of that particular country: leaves, fruit, insects and so forth.

The child, at its mother's breast, will toy with the 'thing', talk to it, test its teeth on it, learn its name, repeat its name – and finally chuck it aside.

'We give our children guns and computer games,' Wendy said. '*They* gave their children the land.'

THE MOST SUBLIME *labour of poetry is to give sense and passion to insensate things; and it is characteristic of children to take inanimate things in their hands and talk to them in play as if they were living persons . . . This philological-philosophical axiom proves to us that in the world's childhood men were by nature sublime poets . . .*
Giambattista Vico, The New Science, XXXVII

Men vent great passions by breaking into song, as we observe in the most grief-stricken and the most joyful.
Vico, The New Science, LIX

◆

The Ancient Egyptians believed the seat of the soul was in the tongue: the tongue was a rudder or steering-oar with which a man steered his course through the world.

◆

'Primitive' languages consist of very long words, full of difficult sounds and sung rather than spoken . . . The early words must have been to present ones what the plesiosaurus and gigantosaurus are to present-day reptiles.
O. Jespersen, Language

◆

Poetry is the mother tongue of the human race as the garden is older than the field, painting than writing, singing than declaiming, parables than inferences, bartering than commerce . . .
J. G. Hamann, Aesthetica in Nuce

◆

All passionate language does of itself become musical – with a finer music than the mere accent; the speech of a man even in zealous anger becomes a chant, a song.
Thomas Carlyle, quoted in Jespersen, Language

◆

Words well voluntarily from the breast without need or intent, and there has probably not been in any desert waste a migratory horde that did not possess its own songs. As an

animal species, the human being is a singing creature, but he combines ideals with the musical sounds involved.
          Wilhelm von Humboldt, Linguistic Variability and
                                    Intellectual Development

◆

According to Strehlow, the Aranda word tnakama *means 'to call by name' and also 'to trust' and 'to believe'.*

◆

Poetry proper is never merely a higher mode (melos) *of everyday language. It is rather the reverse: everyday language is a forgotten and therefore used-up poem, from which there hardly resounds a call any longer.*
                    Martin Heidegger, 'Language'

◆

Richard Lee calculated that a Bushman child will be carried a distance of 4,900 miles before he begins to walk on his own. Since, during this rhythmic phase, he will be forever naming the contents of his territory, it is impossible he will not become a poet.

◆

Proust, more perspicaciously than any other writer, reminds us that the 'walks' of childhood form the raw material of our intelligence:

The flowers that people show me nowadays for the first time never seem to me to be true flowers. The Méséglise Way with its lilacs, its hawthorns, its cornflowers, its poppies, the Guermantes Way with its river full of tadpoles, its water-lilies, and its buttercups have constituted for me for all time the picture of the land in which I would fain pass my life . . . the cornflowers, the hawthorns, the apple-trees, which I happen, when I go out walking, to encounter in the fields, because at the same depth, on the level of my past life, at once established contact with my heart.

◆

(270)

As a general rule of biology, migratory species are less 'aggressive' than sedentary ones.

There is one obvious reason why this should be so. The migration itself, like the pilgrimage, is the hard journey: a 'leveller' on which the 'fit' survive and stragglers fall by the wayside.

The journey thus pre-empts the need for hierarchies and shows of dominance. The 'dictators' of the animal kingdom are those who live in an ambience of plenty. The anarchists, as always, are the 'gentlemen of the road'.

◆

What can we do? We were born with the Great Unrest. Our father taught us that life is one long journey on which only the unfit are left behind.
    Caribou Eskimo to Dr Knud Rassmussen

◆

The above reminds me of the two undeniable fossils of Homo habilis which had been dragged into the Swartkrans Cave and eaten: one, the boy with a brain tumour; the other, an old and arthritic woman.

◆

Among the papers Elizabeth Vrba recommended was one entitled 'Competition or Peaceful Coexistence?' by John Wiens.

Wiens, an ornithologist who works in New Mexico, has been studying the behaviour of the migratory songbirds – the dirkcissels, sage sparrows, sage thrashers – that return each summer to nest in the arid brush of the Western Plains.

Here, where years of famine may be followed by a sudden onrush of plenty, the birds show no signs of increasing their numbers to match the abundance of food: nor of stepping up competition with their neighbours. Rather, he concluded, the migrants must have some internal mechanism which favours co-operation and co-existence.

He goes on to claim that the great Darwinian 'struggle for life' may, paradoxically, be more relevant to stable climates than volatile ones. In regions of assured abundance, animals will stake out and defend their lot with shows of aggressive

(271)

display. In the badlands, where nature is rarely kind — yet there is usually room to move — they make their meagre resources serve them and so find their way without fighting.

❧

In Aranda Traditions *Strehlow contrasts two Central Australian peoples: one sedentary, one mobile.*

The Aranda, living in a country of safe waterholes and plentiful game, were arch-conservatives whose ceremonies were unchangeable, initiations brutal, and whose penalty for sacrilege was death. They looked on themselves as a 'pure' race, and rarely thought of leaving their land.

The Western Desert People, on the other hand, were as open-minded as the Aranda were closed. They borrowed songs and dances freely, loving their land no less and yet forever on the move. 'The most striking thing about these people', Strehlow writes, 'was their ready laughter. They were a cheerful laughing people, who bore themselves as though they had never known a care in the world. Aranda men, civilised on sheep stations, used to say, "They are always laughing. They can't help it."'

❧

A late summer evening in Manhattan, the crowds out of town, cycling down lower Park Avenue with the light slanting in from the cross-streets and a stream of monarch butterflies, alternately brown in the shadow and golden in the sun, coming round the Pan Am Building, descending from the statue of Mercury on Grand Central Station and continuing downtown towards the Caribbean.

❧

In the course of my reading on animal migration, I learned about the journeys of the cod, the eel, the herring, the sardine and the suicidal exodus of lemmings.

I weighed up the pros and cons for the existence of a 'sixth sense' — a magnetic sense of direction — within the human central nervous system. I saw the march of wildebeeste across the Serengeti. I read of birds that 'learn' their journeys from their parents; and of the fledgling cuckoo that never knew its parents and so must have had the journey in its genes.

(272)

All animal migrations have been conditioned by shifting zones of climate, and, in the case of the green turtle, by the shift of the continents themselves.

There were theories of how birds fix their position by the height of the sun, the phases of the moon, and the rising and setting of stars; and of how they make navigational adjustments if blown off course by a storm. Certain ducks and geese can 'record' the choruses of frogs beneath them, and 'know' that they are flying over marsh. Other night-fliers bounce their calls on to the ground below, and, catching the echo, fix their altitude and the nature of the terrain.

The howls of migrating fish can pass through the sides of a ship, and wake up sailors from their bunks. A salmon knows the taste of its ancestral river. Dolphins flash echo-locating clicks on to submarine reefs, in order to steer a safe passage through . . . It has even occurred to me that, when a dolphin 'triangulates' to determine its position, its behaviour is analogous to our own, as we name and compare the 'things' encountered in our daily lives, and so establish our place in the world.

Every book I consulted had, as a matter of course, an account of the most spectacular of bird migrations: the flight of the Arctic tern, a bird which nests in the tundra; winters in Antarctic waters, and then flies back to the north.

◆

I slammed the book shut. The leather armchairs in the London Library made me feel drowsy. The man sitting next to me was snoring with a literary journal spread over his stomach. To hell with migration! I said to myself. I put the stack of books on the table. I was hungry.

Outside, it was a cold, sunny December day. I was hoping to cadge lunch from a friend. On St James's Street, I was walking abreast of White's Club when a cab drew up and a man in a velvet-collared coat got out. He flourished a pair of pound notes at the cabbie and advanced towards the steps. He had thick grey hair and a mesh of burst blood-vessels, as though a transparent red stocking had been pulled over his cheeks. He was – I knew him from photographs – a Duke.

(273)

At the same moment, a second man, in an ex-army greatcoat, sockless, and in boots tied up with twine, pressed forward with an ingratiating smile.

'Er . . . Forgive me for troubling you, Sir,' he said, in a thick Irish accent. 'I was wondering if by any chance . . .'

The Duke pressed on through the door.

I looked at the tramp, who gave me a knowing wink. Some wisps of reddish hair floated above a blotchy scalp. He had watery willing-you-to-believe eyes, focused a short way in front of his nose. He must have been in his late sixties. From my appearance, he did not think it worthwhile to urge a claim on my pocket.

'I've got an idea,' I said to him.

'Yes, guv'nor.'

'You're a travelling man, right?'

'All over the world, guv'nor.'

'Well, if you'd like to tell me about your travels, I'd like to buy you lunch.'

'And I'd be pleased to accept.'

We went round the corner into Jermyn Street to a crowded, inexpensive Italian restaurant. There was one small table left.

I didn't suggest he take off his coat for fear of what lay underneath. The smell was incredible. Two smart secretaries edged away from us, tucking in their skirts as though expecting an invasion of fleas.

'What'll you have?' I asked.

'Er . . . and what'll you be having?'

'Go on,' I said. 'Order anything you like.'

He scanned the menu, holding it upside down with the assurance of a regular customer who feels duty-bound to check the plat du jour.

'Steak and chips!' he said.

The waitress stopped chewing the butt of her pencil and aimed a long-suffering glance at the secretaries.

'Rump or sirloin?' she asked.

'As you like,' he said.

'Two sirloins,' I said. 'One medium. One medium-rare.'

He slaked his thirst with a beer, but his mind was mesmerised by the thought of food and dribbles of saliva appeared at the corner of his mouth.

I knew that tramps are systematic in their methods of scavenging, and will return again and again to a favourite set of dustbins. What, I asked him, was his method with the London clubs?

He thought for a moment and said the best bet was always the Athenaeum. There were still religious gentlemen among its members.

'Yes,' he ruminated. 'You can usually bum a bob off a Bishop.'

The next best, in the old days, used to be the Travellers'. Those gentlemen, like himself, had seen the world.

'A meeting of minds, you might say,' he said. 'But nowadays . . . no . . . no.'

The Travellers' was not what it was. Taken over by another class of persons.

'Advertising people,' he said grimly. 'Very tight, I can assure you.'

He added that Brooks's, Boodle's and White's all fell into the same category. High risk! Generosity . . . or nothing!

His steak, when it came, completely inhibited his powers of conversation. He attacked it with dull ferocity, raised the plate to his face, licked off the juices, and then, remembering where he was, set it back on the table.

'Have another?' I said.

'I wouldn't say no, guv'nor,' he said. 'Very civil of you!'

I ordered a second steak, and he launched into his life story. It was worth it. The tale, as it expanded, was exactly what I wanted to hear: the croft in County Galway, the mother's death, Liverpool, the Atlantic, the meat-yards in Chicago, Australia, the Depression, the South Sea Islands . . .

'Oooh! That's the place for you, my boy! Ta-hiti! Va-hines!'

He laid his tongue along his lower lip.

'Vahines!' he repeated. 'That's the word for women . . . Oooh! Love-ely! Did it standing up under a waterfall!'

The secretaries called for the bill and left. I looked up and saw the thick jowls of the head waiter, who eyed us with a hostile stare. I was afraid we were going to get kicked out.

'Now,' I said, 'I'd like to know something else.'

'Yes, guv'nor,' he said. 'All ears.'

'Would you ever go back to Ireland?'

'No,' he closed his eyes. 'No, I wouldn't care to. Too many bad memories.'

'Well, do you think of anywhere as "home"?'

'I most certainly do,' he jerked his head back and grinned. 'The Promenade des Anglais in Nice. Ever heard o' that?'

'I have,' I said.

One summer night on the Promenade, he had engaged a well-spoken French gentleman in conversation. For an hour they had discussed the world situation, in English. The gentleman had then unfolded from his wallet a 10,000 franc note – 'The old francs, mind you!' – and, after handing him his card, had wished him a pleasant stay.

'Bloody Hell!' he shouted. 'He was the Chief of Police!'

He had tried, whenever possible, to revisit the scene of this, the most moving moment of his career.

'Yes,' he chuckled. 'I bummed the Chief of Police . . . in Nice!'

The restaurant was now less crowded. I ordered him a double helping of apple pie. He declined a cup of coffee which, he said, made his tummy feel poorly. He belched. I paid.

'Thank you, Sir,' he said, with the air of an interviewee who has a string of afternoon engagements. 'I hope I have been of assistance.'

'You certainly have,' I thanked him.

He got to his feet, but sat down again and stared at me intently. Having described the externals of his life, he was not going to go without some comment on its inner motivation.

He then said, slowly and with great seriousness:

'It's like the tides was pulling you along the highway. I'm like the Arctic tern, guv'nor. That's a bird. A beautiful white bird what flies from the North Pole to the South Pole and back again.'

36

IT RAINED AGAIN in the night and in the morning, when I looked out of the window, the sun was up and clouds of purple vapour appeared to be peeling off the flank of Mount Liebler.

At ten, Rolf and I went over to look for Limpy. A message had come from Arkady, three weeks overdue, to expect him on the mail-plane. It was important . . . repeat, 'very important' that Limpy and Titus were available.

The medicinal smell from eucalyptus fires drifted across the valley. The dog howled at our approach. People were drying their blankets.

'Limpy?' Rolf called, and a faint voice echoed from a ramshackle caravan some way uphill.

'So that's where they are!' he said.

The caravan had been optimistically painted with the words 'Recreation Centre'. It contained a wobbly ping-pong table, minus the net, which was covered with a film of red dust.

The three grand old men were sitting on the floor: Limpy, Alex and Joshua – in hats. Limpy had on a stetson, Joshua, a Yankee baseball cap, and Alex wore a magnificent frayed-out bushwhacker.

'Is Titus out at the bore?' Rolf asked.

'Sure he's there!' said Limpy.

'He's not going anywhere?'

'Nah!' he shook his head. 'Stay right there.'

'How d'you know?' Rolf asked.

'I know,' said Limpy, and brought the conversation to an end.

Rolf told me earlier that Alex owned one of the pearl oyster-shell pendants from the Timor Sea, which had been traded across Australia from time immemorial. They were used in rain-making ceremonies: Alex's had plainly done its work for this year. He then surprised us by plunging his hand between the buttons of the velvet coat and pulled out the pendant on the end of a string.

It was engraved with a zigzag meander pattern, rubbed with red ochre: it must have been dangling between his legs.

Superficially, these pendants resemble a tjuringa; but, as far as strangers are concerned, they are *not* necessarily secret.

'So where does he come from?' I asked, pointing at the shell.

'Broome,' said Alex, definitely.

He drew his forefinger across the dusty ping-pong table and rattled off all the 'stops' across the Gibson Desert, between Cullen and Broome.

'OK,' I said. 'You get the pearl shells from Broome? What do you send back?'

He hesitated, and then drew in the dust an elongated oval.

'Board,' he said.

'Tjuringa?' I asked.

He nodded.

'Sacred business? Songs and all?'

He nodded again.

'That', I said to Rolf as we walked away, 'is very interesting.'

THE SONG STILL *remains which names the land over which it sings.*

Martin Heidegger, What Are Poets For?

◆

BEFORE COMING TO *Australia I'd often talk about the Songlines, and people would inevitably be reminded of something else.*

'Like the "ley-lines"?' *they'd say: referring to ancient stone circles, menhirs and graveyards, which are laid out in lines across Britain. They are of great antiquity but are visible only to those with eyes to see.*

Sinologists were reminded of the 'dragon-lines' of feng-shui, or traditional Chinese geomancy: and when I spoke to a Finnish journalist, he said the Lapps had 'singing stones', which were also arranged in lines.

To some, the Songlines were like the Art of Memory in reverse. In Frances Yates's wonderful book, one learned how classical orators, from Cicero and earlier, would construct memory palaces; fastening sections of their speech on to imaginary architectural features and then, after working their way round every architrave and pillar, could memorise colossal lengths of speech. The features were known as loci *or 'places'. But in Australia the* loci *were not a mental construction, but had existed for ever, as events of the Dreamtime.*

Other friends were reminded of the Nazca 'lines', which are etched into the meringue-like surface of the central Peruvian Desert and are, indeed, some kind of totemic map.

We once spent a hilarious week with their self-appointed guardian, Maria Reich. One morning, I went with her to see the most spectacular of all the lines, which was only visible at sunrise. I carried her photographic equipment up a steep hill of dust and stones while Maria, in her seventies, strode ahead. I was horrified to watch her roll straight past me to the bottom.

I expected broken bones, but she laughed, 'My father used to say that once you start to roll, you must keep on rolling.'

◆

No. These were not the comparisons I was looking for. Not at this stage. I was beyond that.

Trade means friendship and co-operation; and for the Aboriginal the principal object of trade was song. Song, therefore, brought peace. Yet I felt the Songlines were not necessarily an Australian phenomenon, but universal: that they were the means by which man marked out his territory, and so organised his social life. All other successive systems were variants – or perversions – of this original model.

The main Songlines in Australia appear to enter the country from the north or the north-west – from across the Timor Sea or the Torres Strait – and from there weave their way southwards across the continent. One has the impression that they represent the routes of the first Australians – and that they have come from somewhere else.

How long ago? Fifty thousand years? Eighty or a hundred thousand years? The dates are insignificant compared to those from African prehistory.

And here I must take a leap into faith: into regions I would not expect anyone to follow.

I have a vision of the Songlines stretching across the continents and ages; that wherever men have trodden they have left a trail of song (of which we may, now and then, catch an echo); and that these trails must reach back, in time and space, to an isolated pocket in the African savannah, where the First Man opening his mouth in defiance of the terrors that surrounded him, shouted the opening stanza of the World Song, 'I AM!'

37

I HEARD THE NOISE of the plane coming in to land. I ran across the airstrip and was in time to watch Arkady get out carrying an 'Eski'. The golden mop of Marian's hair followed. She looked deliriously happy. She was in another flowered cotton dress, no less ragged than the others.

'Hey!' I shouted. 'This *is* wonderful.'

'Hello, old mate!' Arkady smiled. He dropped the 'Eski' to the ground and drew us both into one of his Russian hugs.

'Let me introduce you to the memsahib,' he said.

'The what?'

'The memsahib.'

'Married?'

'Yes.'

'When?'

'Three days ago,' said Marian. 'And we missed you and missed you!'

'That *is* a piece of news!'

'Isn't it?' she giggled. 'It *was* a bit sudden.'

'I thought you were married,' I said severely to Arkady.

'Was married,' said Arkady. 'But the day I left, I went home to change and there was this fat envelope on the doormat. I thought it looked oppressively official. "Leave it!" I said to myself. Then it occurred to me my divorce might have come through – and that was it.

'I showered,' he went on. 'I changed. I mixed myself a drink, and relaxed into the sensation of being a free man. A fly had got into the studio and I kept looking at this bloody fly and saying to myself, "Now I'm free, there's something I've got to do." But I couldn't think what it was . . .'

Marian stuck out her tongue.

'Honestly, I couldn't!' he grinned. 'Then I jumped up, spilled the drink and shouted, "I KNOW! MARRY MARIAN!"'

The three of us were walking towards Rolf's caravan. The pilot had gone to fetch the mail-bag from the store; and when he left Rolf ran after us.

'Rolf,' I called once he was in earshot. 'These two are married.'

'It had to happen one day,' he said.

He had to stand on tiptoe when he kissed them both.

I had scarcely noticed the clean-shaven, middle-aged Aboriginal who had also come on the plane and was tagging along behind Arkady.

'Who's he?' I asked.

'Tell it not in Gath,' Arkady whispered. 'He's the spokesman for the Amadeus Mob. He's got Titus's tjuringas in his briefcase. I think I may have fixed it.'

When we reached the caravan, Rolf went into a whirlwind of activity, arranged five camping chairs in a circle, and set about making coffee.

The man from Amadeus stood watching: but within a couple of minutes Limpy appeared out of nowhere and, with a very friendly gesture, escorted him to the camp.

'Now,' said Rolf, pouring the coffee. 'More about the wedding!'

'Well, I got my divorce papers . . .'

'And?'

'I went over to this lady's house, and found two of her unworthy admirers in the kitchen. Very ratty looking, and more so when they saw me! So I called her out into the passage, and whispered in her ear. She nearly knocked me sideways with the force of her acceptance.'

'Very romantic story,' said Rolf. 'A credit to you both!'

'The lady', Arkady went on, 'then strode into the kitchen and with a positively beatific smile said, "Out! Sorry! We're busy. Out!"'

'So they went,' Marian giggled. 'There's not much more to say. He went off to Darwin. I fixed up the house. I moped. He came back. There was a ceremony. A party. And now we're here!'

'All the news is good,' said Arkady. 'It's good news . . . fingers crossed . . . on the Titus front. It's good for Hanlon . . . non-malignant blockage. It's good about the railway. They've looked again at the budget and can't see a way to build the bugger. Work's at a standstill. I'm out of a job, but who cares?'

'And you know who hexed it?' I said.

'Old Alan,' said Arkady.

'Perhaps he sang it away?'

'How's the writing?' he asked?

'The usual mess,' I said.

'Don't be so gloomy,' said Marian. 'We've got a lovely fish for supper.'

In the 'Eski' there was a 4 lb barramunda and herbs to grill it with. They had also slipped in two bottles of white, from the Wynne Vineyard in South Australia.

'Hey!' I said. 'That *is* special. Where did you get it?'

'Influence,' said Arkady.

'Where's Wendy?' Marian turned to Rolf.

'Off with the kids, getting bush-tucker,' he said.

About five minutes later Wendy drove up at the wheel of her old Land-Rover. The back was crammed with grinning children, some of whom were dangling goannas by the tail.

'These two', said Rolf, 'are married.'

'Oh, but how wonderful!' She jumped down and threw herself into Marian's arms, and Arkady then joined in.

Counting Estrella, we were a party of six at supper. We ate and laughed and drank and told ridiculous stories. Estrella was a fund of the absurd. Her favourite character was the Catholic Bishop of the Kimberleys, who had once been a U-Boat commander and now fancied himself as an air ace.

'This man', she said, 'is a *fenomeno . . . una maravilla . . .* He flies his *aeroplano* into middle of cumulo-nimbus to see which way up-or-downside he come out.'

After coffee, I went to clear up the caravan for the newly weds. Arkady started up the Land Cruiser.

He wanted to leave for Titus at eight.

'Can I come this time?' I asked.

He winked at Marian.

'Sure you can come,' she said.

We watched them go off to bed. They were two people made in heaven for each other. They had been hopelessly in love since the day they met, yet had gradually crept into their shells, glancing away, deliberately, in despair, as if it were too good, never to be, until suddenly the reticence and the anguish had melted and what should have been, long ago, now was.

The night was clear and warm. Wendy and I dragged her bedstead outside the lock-up. She showed me how to focus the telescope and, before dropping off, I travelled around the Southern Cross.

38

By EIGHT WE WERE on the move. The morning was clear and fresh but was bound to heat up later. The man from Amadeus sat between Arkady and Marian, clinging to the briefcase. Limpy, spruced up for the occasion, sat with me in the back.

We headed out towards the scene of my abortive kangaroo hunt, but then turned left along the back road to Alice. After about ten miles, the country changed from the yellow-flowering scrub to a rolling, open parkland of bleached grass and rounded eucalyptus trees – blue-green, the colour of olives with their leaves turning white in the wind; and if you soft-focused your eyes, you'd think you were in the lit-up Provençal landscape of Van Gogh's *Cornfield near Arles*.

We crossed a creek and took another left along a sandy track. There was a neat corrugated shack set in a spinney of trees, and also Titus's Ford. A woman jumped to her feet and ran off. The dogs, as usual, howled.

Titus, in shorts and a pork-pie hat, sat in front of a boiling billy on a pink foam-rubber mat. His father – a handsome, leggy old man with a covering of inch-long grey bristles – was stretched out in the dust, smiling.

'You're early,' said Titus gravely. 'I wasn't expecting you before nine.'

He amazed me by his ugliness: the spread of his nose, the wens that covered his forehead; the fleshy, down-hanging lip, and eyes that were hooded by the folds of his eyelids.

But what a face! You never saw a face of such mobility and character. Every scrap of it was in a state of perpetual animation. One second, he was an unbending Aboriginal law-man; the next, an outrageous comic.

'Titus,' said Arkady. 'This is a friend of mine from England, Bruce.'

'How the Thatcher?' he drawled.

'Still there,' I said.

'Can't say I care for the woman.'

He looked up at Marian, and said, 'I know you, don't I?'

'But what you didn't know', Arkady chipped in, 'is that she's been my wife for four days.'

'Nights, you mean,' said Titus.

'I do.'

'Very pleased to hear it,' he said. 'Lad like you needs a sensible wife.'

'I do,' repeated Arkady, and hugged her.

Arkady felt the time had come to introduce the man from Amadeus; but Titus raised his hand, and said, 'Wait!'

He unpadlocked the door of the shack, leaving it half ajar, and got out a blue enamel mug for the extra visitor.

The tea was ready.

'Sugar?' he asked me.

'No thanks.'

'No,' he winked. 'I didn't think you looked the type.'

Once we had finished tea, he jumped up and said, 'Right! To business!'

He beckoned Limpy and the man from Amadeus to go on ahead. He then swivelled round to face us.

'You mob,' he said, 'you'd be doing me a favour if you'd stay right here for half an hour.'

The dead twigs crackled underfoot and the men were swallowed up among the trees.

The old father lay there beaming, and dozed off to sleep.

A tjuringa – it is worthwhile repeating – is an oval plaque made of stone or mulga wood. It is both musical score and mythological guide to the Ancestor's travels. It is the actual body of the Ancestor (*pars pro toto*). It is a man's *alter ego*; his soul; his obol to Charon; his title-deed to country; his passport and his ticket 'back in'.

Strehlow gives a harrowing account of some Elders who discover their tjuringa storehouse has been raided by white men – and for whom this is the end of the world. He gives a joyful description of some other old men who have lent their tjuringas to their neighbours for a number of years and who, when they unwrap them on their return, break into a peal of happy song.

I have also read an account of how, when a song cycle was sung in its entirety, the 'owners' would lay out their tjuringas end to end, in order, like the order of sleeping-cars on the *Train Bleu*.

On the other hand, if you smashed or lost your tjuringa, you were beyond the human pale, and had lost all hope of 'returning'. Of one young layabout in Alice, I heard it said, 'He hasn't seen his tjuringa. He don't know who he is.'

In the Gilgamesh Epic, by way of extra comment, there is a strange passage in which Gilgamesh the King, weary of life, wishes to visit the Underworld to see his dead friend, the 'wild man' Enkidu. But the ferryman, Utnapishtim, says, 'No! You may not enter these regions. You have broken the tablets of stone.'

Arkady was peering through the door of Titus's shack.

'Don't whatever you do go in,' he spoke through his teeth, 'but if you take a look in here, you may see something that'll surprise you.'

I eased back on my haunches and peered in. It took time for my eyes to get used to the dark. On a chest beside Titus's bed was a stack of books, in English and German. On top of the pile was Nietzsche's *Thus Spake Zarathustra*.

'Yes,' I nodded. 'I am *very* surprised.'

In less than half an hour, we heard a whistle through the trees and watched the three men stepping towards us in single file.

'Business settled!' said Titus, firmly, and sat down on his mat. 'Tjuringas returned to their rightful owners.'

The man from Amadeus looked relieved. The conversation turned to other things.

Titus was the terror of the Land Rights Movement because whatever he had to say was bound to be original and uncalled for. He explained how, to the people of his grandparents' generation, the outlook had been infinitely bleaker than it was today. Watching their sons go to pieces, the Elders had frequently handed their tjuringas to the missionaries to prevent them being broken, lost or sold. One man worthy of their trust

(287)

was the pastor of the Horn River Mission, Klaus-Peter Auricht. 'My grandfather', Titus said, 'gave several tjuringas to old Auricht when this one' – he jerked his head at his snoring father – 'got taken with the booze.'

Before dying in the late 1960s, Pastor Auricht had taken the 'collection' to the Mission's headquarters in Alice, where it was kept under lock and key. When the 'activists' got wind of the fact that Germans were sitting on sacred property 'worth millions', they raised the usual ballyhoo and lobbied for their return to the people.

'What the fuckers don't understand', drawled Titus, 'is there is no such person as an Aboriginal or an Aborigine. There are Tjakamarras and Jaburullas and Duburungas like me, and so on all over the country.

'But if Leslie Watson', he went on, 'and that Canberra Mob so much as took *one* peep at my family's tjuringas, and if we're applying *law* to this situation, I'd be obliged to spear 'em, wouldn't I?'

Titus shook with laughter, and we all did.

'I have to tell you', he wheezed with a wicked grin, 'that since I saw you last, I've had some very funny visitors.'

The first were some young architects who wanted – in the name of the Pintupi Council and in the hope of shutting his mouth – to build him a house.

Titus snorted, 'They had in mind some kind of flat-roofed humpy. Fuckers! I told 'em if I was going to have a house, I wanted a house with a gable roof. I needed a library for my books. Living-room. Spare bedroom. Outside kitchen and shower. Otherwise I'd stay right here.'

The next one had been even funnier: a glib-talking individual from the mining corporation, which wanted to run seismic lines through Titus's country.

'Bastard!' he said. 'Shows me his geological survey map – which, I might add, he's obliged to by the Law of the Crown – and spouts a bunch of *total* garbage. "Here," I say, "give that to me!" I take a look at his synclines, and I have to say there's a fair chance of oil or natural gas over by Hunter's Bluff. "But look here!" I say, "We have different ways of looking at this. We've got a lot of important Dreamings in the area. We've got Native Cat. We've got Emu, Black Cockatoo, Budgerigar, two kinds of

Lizard; and we've got an 'eternal home' for Big Kangaroo. At a guess I'd say he was your oilfield or whatever. But he's been sleeping there since the Dreamtime and, if I have a say in the matter, he's going to go on sleeping for ever." '

Titus really enjoyed our visit. We had a lot more laughs. Even the po-faced man from Amadeus laughed. Then we piled into the Land Cruiser and hurried back to Cullen.

I spent the afternoon clearing up my papers. We were starting for Alice in the morning.

39

THE MAN FROM AMADEUS wanted to be dropped at the Horn River Settlement, so Arkady volunteered to drive him by the back road. It was far less frequented than the other, but everything was drying out and the mining-company man had made it in a car.

We had stocked up with food and water and were saying goodbye to Rolf and Wendy, saying how we'd write and send books and always keep in touch, when Limpy strolled up and cupped his hands round Arkady's ear.

'Sure, we'll take you,' he said.

Limpy was in his best. He had a clean white shirt and a brown tweed jacket, and his hair and face were dripping with oil, making him look like a wet grey seal.

What he wanted was to visit Cycad Valley: a place of immense importance on his Songline, to which he had never been.

Cycad Valley is a National Park – though well protected from the public – where there are a unique species of cabbage-palm and ancient stands of Native Pine. The Horn River runs through its gorge; Limpy's Dreaming, the Native Cat, ran straight down the middle of the stream-bed. The Native Cat, or Tjilpa, is not a real cat but a small marsupial (*Dasyurus geoffreyi*) with outsize whiskers and a banded tail held vertically above its back. It may, sadly, be extinct.

There is a story that a young Tjilpa Ancestor, somewhere north of the MacDonnell Ranges, watched two eagle feathers fall from the sky and wanted to know where they came from. Following the Milky Way over the sandhills, he gradually attracted other Tjilpa Men, who joined the troop. On and on they went. Their fur was ruffled in the winter wind and their paws were cracked by the cold.

At last they reached the sea at Port Augusta and there, standing in the sea, was a pole so tall it touched the sky (like Dante's Mountain of Purgatory). Its top was white with sky-feathers and its lower half white with sea-feathers. The Tjilpa Men laid the pole on its side and carried it to Central Australia.

Limpy had never come here because of some long-standing feud. But he had recently heard over the bush telegraph that three of his distant relatives were living there – or, rather, dying there, alongside their tjuringa storehouse. He wanted to see them before they went.

We drove for seven hours, from seven until two. Limpy sat in front between the driver and Marian, motionless but for a quick dart of the eyes to right or to left.

About ten miles short of the Valley, the Land Cruiser bumped across a creek flowing south.

Limpy suddenly bounced up like a jack-in-the-box, muttered things under his breath, rammed his head out of the driver's window (causing Arkady to swerve), repeated this on the other side, and then folded his arms and went silent.

'What's going on?' asked Arkady.

'Tjilpa Man go that way,' said Limpy, pointing south.

At the road sign for Cycad Valley, we took a right hairpin bend and plunged down a steep track along the bed of the Horn. Pale-green water rushed over the white stones. We forded the river several times. There were river red-gums growing out of it.

Limpy kept his arms folded, and said nothing.

We came to the confluence of two streams: that is, we met the stream we had crossed higher up on the main road. This lesser stream was the route of the Tjilpa Men, and we were joining it at right angles.

As Arkady turned the wheel to the left, Limpy bounced back into action. Again he shoved his head through both windows. His eyes rolled wildly over the rocks, the cliffs, the palms, the water. His lips moved at the speed of a ventriloquist's and, through them, came a rustle: the sound of wind through branches.

Arkady knew at once what was happening. Limpy had learnt his Native Cat couplets for walking pace, at four miles an hour, and we were travelling at twenty-five.

Arkady shifted into bottom gear, and we crawled along no

faster than a walker. Instantly, Limpy matched his tempo to the new speed. He was smiling. His head swayed to and fro. The sound became a lovely melodious swishing; and you knew that, as far as he was concerned, he *was* the Native Cat.

We drove for almost an hour; the road twisted through the purple cliffs. There were gigantic boulders smeared with black streaks, and the cycads, like magnified tree ferns, sprang up between them. The day was stifling.

Then the river vanished underground, leaving on the surface a stagnant pool with reedy margins. A purple heron flew off and settled in a tree. The road had come to an end.

We got out and followed Limpy along a well-worn footpath which threaded round the rocks and the water and came out into a basin of dark-red rock with receding layers of strata, reminding one of the seats in a Greek theatre. There was the usual tin shack under a tree.

A middle-aged woman, her breasts ballooning inside her purple jumper, was dragging a branch of firewood to the hearth. Limpy introduced himself. She flashed a smile, and beckoned us all to follow.

As I wrote in my notebooks, the mystics believe the ideal man shall walk himself to a 'right death'. He who has arrived 'goes back'.

In Aboriginal Australia, there are specific rules for 'going back' or, rather, for singing your way to where you belong: to your 'conception site', to the place where your tjuringa is stored. Only then can you become – or re-become – the Ancestor. The concept is quite similar to Heraclitus's mysterious dictum, 'Mortals and immortals, alive in their death, dead in each other's life.'

Limpy hobbled ahead. We followed on tiptoe. The sky was incandescent, and sharp shadows fell across the path. A trickle of water dribbled down the cliff.

'Tjuringa place up there!' said Limpy, softly, pointing to a dark cleft high above our heads.

In a clearing there were three 'hospital' bedsteads, with mesh springs and no mattresses, and on them lay the three dying men. They were almost skeletons. Their beards and hair had gone.

One was strong enough to lift an arm, another to say something. When they heard who Limpy was, all three smiled, spontaneously, the same toothless grin.

Arkady folded his arms, and watched.

'Aren't they wonderful?' Marian whispered, putting her hand in mine and giving it a squeeze.

Yes. They were all right. They knew where they were going, smiling at death in the shade of a ghost-gum.